UNDERSTANDING AND
EVALUATING METHODOLOGIES

UNDERSTANDING AND EVALUATING METHODOLOGIES

NIMSAD: A Systemic Framework

Nimal Jayaratna

McGRAW-HILL BOOK COMPANY

London · New York · St Louis · San Francisco · Auckland · Bogotá
Caracas · Lisbon · Madrid · Mexico · Milan · Montreal
New Delhi · Panama · Paris · San Juan · São Paulo
Singapore · Sydney · Tokyo · Toronto

Published by
McGRAW-HILL Book Company Europe
Shoppenhangers Road, Maidenhead, Berkshire, SL6 2QL, England
Telephone 01628 23432
Fax 01628 770224

British Library Cataloguing in Publication Data
Jayaratna, Nimal
Understanding and Evaluating Methodologies:
NIMSAD – A Systemic Framework. – (McGraw-Hill Information Systems,
Management & Strategy Series)
I. Title II. Series
005.7
ISBN 0–07–707882–9

Library of Congress Cataloging-in-Publication Data
Jayaratna, Nimal
Understanding and evaluating methodologies : NIMSAD, a systemic
framework / Nimal Jayaratna.
p.   cm. – (The McGraw-Hill information systems, management
and strategy series)
Includes bibliographical references and index.
ISBN 0-07-707882-9
1. Management information systems.   2. System design.   3. Problem
solving.   I. Title.   II. Series.
T58.6.J39 1994
658.4′038 – dc20
94-10969
CIP

Reprinted 1997

Typeset by Datix International Limited, Bungay, Suffolk
and printed and bound in Great Britain at the University Press, Cambridge

Printed on permanent paper in compliance with the ISO Standard 9706

DEDICATION

This book is dedicated to:

- the millions of organizational members whose lives, remuneration, career paths, job satisfaction, job security, psychological well-being and quality of life may have been adversely affected by 'systems' we design using a range of methodologies;
- the Amnesty International, which fights to preserve every human being's right to exercise his or her freedom of expression, and other voluntary organizations which continue to fight to save millions of lives from starvation and malnutrition;
- the United Kingdom university educational system which enabled me to develop the conceptual thoughts and models discussed in this book;
- my late father, my mother, brothers, sisters, and my beloved son.

CONTENTS

PREFACE   vii

ACKNOWLEDGEMENTS   xv

INTRODUCTION   xvii

PART 1
1   DOMAIN OF INFORMATION SYSTEMS   3
      Introduction   3
      Historical development   3
      Current definitions of information systems   5
      Information systems functions   8
      Information systems discipline   21
      Summary   27

2   INFORMATION SYSTEMS DEVELOPMENT AND
    METHODOLOGIES   29
      Introduction   29
      Information systems development   29
      Systems development life cycle vs systems life cycle   32
      Systems development vs software development   33
      Systems development vs methodologies   34
      Definitions of 'methodology'   35
      Methodology vs framework   42
      Summary   42

3   RATIONALE FOR THE NIMSAD FRAMEWORK   44
      Introduction   44
      Reasons for a framework   44
      Aims of the NIMSAD framework   45
      Approaches to methodolgy evaluation   46
      Approach to the development of the NIMSAD framework   47
      The NIMSAD rationale   49
      Summary   53

PART 2

4   NIMSAD FRAMEWORK (The 'problem situation' and the
    intended problem solver)   57
        Introduction   57
        Element 1: the 'problem situation' (methodology context)   57
        Element 2: the intended problem solver (methodology user)   63
        The 'mental construct'   70
        Summary   73

5   NIMSAD FRAMEWORK (The problem-solving process)   74
        Introduction   74
        Element 3: the problem-solving process   74
        Stage 1: understanding of the 'situation of concern'   75
        Stage 2: performing the diagnosis (where are we now?)   79
        Stage 3: defining the prognosis outline (where do we want to be and why?) 84
        Stage 4: defining 'problems'   86
        Stage 5: deriving notional systems   88
        Systemic analysis   90
        Summary   91

6   NIMSAD FRAMEWORK (The problem-solving process:
    contd.)   93
        Introduction   93
        Systems design or systemic design   93
        Systemic analysis vs systemic design   95
        Stage 6: performing the conceptual/logical design   96
        Stage 7: performing the physical design   100
        Stage 8: implementing the design   102
        The completed NIMSAD framework   106
        Summary   107

7   NIMSAD FRAMEWORK (The evaluation)   108
        Introduction   108
        Evaluation of the 'problem situation'   110
        Evaluation of the methodology user (intended problem solver) 113
        Evaluation of the methodology (problem-solving process)   114
        Conditions of use   116
        Specific questions about the 'problem situation'   117
        Specific questions about the methodology user   119
        Specific questions about the methodology   121
        Summary   127

PART 3

8   CRITICAL EVALUATION OF STRUCTURED ANALYSIS
    AND SYSTEMS SPECIFICATION   131
        Introduction   131
        Element 1: the 'problem situation'   131
        Element 2: the methodology user (intended problem solver) 134

Element 3, stage 1: understanding of the 'situation of concern'   136
Element 3, stage 2: performing the diagnosis   139
Element 3, stage 3: defining the prognosis outline   144
Element 3, stage 4: defining 'problems'   144
Element 3, stage 5: deriving the notional system   144
Element 3, stage 6: performing conceptual/logical design   146
Element 3, stage 7: performing the physical design   148
Element 3, stage 8: implementing the design   149
Element 4: evaluation   149
Summary   150

9   CRITICAL EVALUATION OF 'ETHICS' METHODOLOGY   151
Introduction   151
Element 1: the 'problem situation'   151
Element 2: the methodology user (intended problem solver)   154
Element 3, stage 1: understanding of the 'situation of concern'   159
Element 3, stage 2: performing the diagnosis   162
Element 3, stage 3: defining the prognosis outline   165
Element 3, stage 4: defining 'problems'   166
Element 3, stage 5: deriving the notional system   166
Element 3, stage 6: performing the conceptual/logical design   168
Element 3, stage 7: performing the physical design   172
Element 3, stage 8: implementing the design   173
Element 4: evaluation   173
Summary   174

10   CRITICAL EVALUATION OF 'SOFT' SYSTEMS
METHODOLOGY   175
Introduction   175
Element 1: the 'problem situation'   175
Element 2: methodology users (intended problem solvers)   181
Element 3, stage 1: understanding of the 'situation of concern'   183
Element 3, stage 2: performing the diagnosis   185
Element 3, stage 5: deriving the notional systems   189
Element 3, stage 6: performing the conceptual/logical design   199
Element 3, stage 7: performing the physical design   201
Element 3, stage 3: defining the prognosis outline   201
Element 3, stage 4: defining 'problems'   203
Element 3, stage 8: implementing the design   204
Further analysis   208
Element 4: evaluation   215
Summary   218

PART 4

11   CONCLUSIONS ON METHODOLOGIES AND
     FRAMEWORKS   221
     Introduction   221
     Conclusion 1: learning phase of a methodology   221
     Conclusion 2: methodology philosophy   222
     Conclusion 3: methodology steps   223
     Conclusion 4: methodology emphasis   224
     Conclusion 5: methodology focus   225
     Conclusion 6: methodology success   227
     Conclusion 7: methodology context   228
     Conclusion 8: the 'context' environment of methodologies   231
     Conclusion 9: framework use as a methodology   231
     Conclusion 10: framework on problem formulation   232
     Conclusion 11: framework on the role of methodology users   233
     Conclusion 12: framework as an instrument of learning   234
     Summary   235

APPENDICES   237

GLOSSARY OF TERMS   240

BIBLIOGRAPHY   245

INDEX   256

PREFACE

Methodologies are explicit ways of structuring (rationalizing) our thinking and action, involving both critical and creative thinking. Their application in practice has serious implications for others in organizations. Through these rational processes, the changes that we bring about in organizations affect the lives, psychological well-being, remuneration, job satisfaction and quality of life of other people. Methodology users' reasoning processes have to display consciousness to these wider issues. Therefore, a book of this nature has a major contribution to make in alerting its readers to the effects of methodologies on their reasoning.

This book is the result of my attempts to externalize the methodological conceptual issues that create internal conflicts in human reasoning and to separate 'what is intellectually desirable' from 'what is politically expedient'. Raising questions based on the former inevitably leads to problems with the latter.

I was born into a family of eight children. My mother considered me at an early stage to be a 'problem' child because I always wanted to know the reasons for doing things, and the desire to know why has continued to cause problems. Early difficulties with this questioning attitude occurred in school, and I can vividly recollect one of these occasions. Facing a group of inattentive children, the priest was explaining the omnipresence of the Almighty God in the catechism class.

'He is here and everywhere. He can see and hear everything. In fact, this very minute he is listening to your thoughts and conversations.'

Suddenly, there was complete silence in the classroom. I was terrified that God could listen to our private conversations, but as usual my hand went up all the same.

'Yes Nimal, what is it this time?'

'Father, if God is everywhere and he can see and listen to our thoughts and conversations, why do we have to go to confession every Sunday?'

'Out'.

So there it was. I was considered a troublemaker to have in the class, thus reinforcing my mother's opinion of me. I suppose that if his reasoning had been dominated by intellectual thought processes then he could have used the occasion to encourage discussion, debate and participation. For instance, he could have said, 'Let us discuss the notion of God. What are the things that can help us to reason whether such a being exists?' If his reasoning had been dominated by political thought processes then he would have said, 'God still wants you to go to confession so that he can check whether in addition to your impure thoughts you are prepared to lie about them as well!' He did not try to do either, and my role of questioning has continued to cause severe political difficulties. (By the way, there are very good intellectual reasons as to why God exists.)

The attitude of questioning things critically has continued, at great cost to me. But it has also won me friends and opened up industrial opportunities among those who are not constrained by politics. In one 'industrial project' case study which is to be published later, the analysis led to the identification of the client as the problem. To my surprise, the client responded by offering me an industrial relations management position after the project was completed! Most importantly, this project enabled me to understand some of the underlying concepts of human decision making and action. In the context of methodologies, these concepts have enabled me to abstract their roles; what they attempt to do, why they attempt to do it, how they help to transform situations and, particularly, their influence on human reasoning processes. Above all, they helped me to understand my role as a methodology user.

Methodologies exist to help us in our reasoning. They attempt to raise our conscious thinking, to make us question the rationale of our planned action and to guide us in the transformation of situations. The aim of this book is to explain the concepts underpinning methodologies and to show their use in human reasoning processes. These concepts and lessons are useful for understanding *any* problem-solving situation. The role of this book is:

- to help its readers and those using methodologies to break free from political constraints
- to raise their consciousness to consider the desirability of their actions *before* their feasibility

- to consider the effect of their actions on others as well as on themselves
- to enable more open and facilitating debate and discussion
- to minimize the desire to achieve self-needs sat the expense of others. Instead, such achievements can be accomplished in the context of others without destroying their hopes and opportunities.

This book is aimed at methodology selectors, users and their clients, for they have an important role to play in organizations, being uniquely placed to bring about the transformation of the working lives of members of the organizations as well as the healthy growth of those organizations. The book attempts to make them question many of their actions and intentions. It is also geared towards final-year students and postgraduates who are considering careers in information systems, computing, business or management. The objective here is to encourage them to question the underlying concepts and notions in problem solving. We examine a general framework that was built based on the concepts derived from critical evaluation of problem solving; it focuses on the effects of methodologies on the intellectual thought processes of their users. It has absolutely *nothing* to contribute to the political thought processes of the methodology users. However, when evaluating specific methodologies, the book will question how these methodologies address the political processes.

In keeping with the intellectual nature of methodologies, I make three requests to the reader:
- to read the whole book and to consider the discussions and arguments put forward and not simply their conclusions (unless he or she is in agreement with these). It is disagreement with the arguments that will contribute to the development of new ideas;
- to consider the choice and the use of methodologies as much an ethical consideration as a rational one. Readers have a unique opportunity to improve the conditions of others, especially those with less power;
- not to hand over his or her thought processes to be directed by any external person, model, methodology or framework, including the one advocated in this book. Methodology users must become responsible and accountable for their thinking and actions.

It has not been an easy experience writing this book. In fact, I suffered many hours and days of agonizing over how to present the issues that I consider to be fundamentally important for a problem solver. The raising of issues and questions are critical for the intellectual well being of problem solvers, clients and members of organizations. They are also very important to students who are tomorrow's problem solvers and practitioners. As an academic, it is my role to raise my students' intellectual reasoning abilities. This means that most often I need to ask my students to explain their reasoning for arriving at their conclusions especially, if their conclusions happen to coincide with my own. Though difficult most students have appreciated this questioning. I have used the same philosophy in raising issues for discussion in this book.

I hope you enjoy the book.

Nimal Jayaratna
Edinburgh
United Kingdom

__ ACKNOWLEDGEMENTS __

A book of this kind is never the result of a single individual's thought processes. Countless discussions, debates, agreements, disagreements, challenges, reinforcements and arguments with my friends, critics and colleagues have contributed to the development of the ideas, concepts, models and discussions in this book. Most have been disagreements. At times they have been very demoralizing and frustrating, but those people mentioned below have given me hope and encouragement to continue.

I would like to thank Trevor Wood-Harper, who originally introduced me to the ideas of 'systems' and has continued to support my work; Brian D'Arcy, who introduced me to the epistemological notions of 'systems' and who has subjected me to many hours of critical questioning; Frank Land, who as my PhD supervisor urged me to consider the plight of the users (other than the clients) in my research; David Tranfield, who exercised considerable influence in opening my mind to the psychological and behavioural dimensions of organizations; Ian Draffan, who provided support for my initial research; John Jones, who gave me the first opportunity to pursue an academic direction; Patrik Holt, who has acted as a mentor; and Bela Banathy, for encouraging the publication of my original research findings.

My thanks are also due to D. Theotokis, L. Chan, J. Fong, K. Gibson, C. Wilson, B. Ash, B. Nilsen, J. Collier, C. Thomas, C. Skelsey, N. Dexter, S. Roberts, C. Leask, S. Woods, K. Ateueyi, M. Farmer, W. Caravajal, H. Compain, J. and N. Pilokyprou, K. Hodson, S. Tyrrell-Lewis, M. Reyes and C. Ford, and numerous others who as students carried out some of the practical research activities and assignments as well as endured intense critical discussion sessions with me.

I wish to thank J. Gordon, T. Liddle, M. Connolly, V. Holt, A. Stevenson, D. McKenna and many others for permitting their organizations to be used for consultancy and industrial activities.

I would also like to thank Jean McKerral, Gwen Draffan, Sigga Holt, Ron and Renata Parkin, Susan Dunigan, Diana Lilley, Marilyn Wilson, Sharon

Hanson, Tom Rodrigo, Gordon Sutherland and countless others for their moral support. Some with whom I have exchanged constructive viewpoints are Ray Miles, Chris Hall, Jack Hanson, Bob Galliers, Richard Bertram, Ian Thomson, Yasmin Merali, Ricardo Rodriguez-Ulloa, Frank Gregory, Bela A. Banathy, Jacques Meyranx, Bob Dunigan, Don Atkinson, Bengt Lundberg, Ces Weatherlake and Philip Hills. Special thanks to Jean McKerral who proof read the earlier versions of the manuscript. I would also like to thank Hans-Erik, Ingmar and the late Gertrud Nissen and Jean-Michel Larrasquet with whom I have had ongoing dialogues. To all these friends and colleagues I offer my gratitude.

I must take this opportunity to make special mention of a unique Masters programme at Sheffied City Polytechnic with which I have had close involvement for a number of years. Since its first intake in 1975, the programme has always retained a philosophy of encouraging its students to choose or construct a methodology of their choice for intervention; justify and rationalise their choice and critically evaluate the methodology and their actions in the 'action research' part of their programme. It is the supervision of these 'action research' projects that prompted me to conceptualise the problem-solving issues and encouraged me to develop the framework discussed in this book. I am indebted to my former colleagues and friends Brian D'Arcy, David Tranfield, Tony Wood, Ian Draffan, David Walker, Graham Carr and Stuart Smith who collectively helped to instill *critical* and *independent* thinking abilities of the students.

Special words of thanks are due to the creators of the methodologies chosen in this book for critical evaluation: to Peter Checkland, who has been an intellectual inspiration both through his book on 'Systems Thinking, Systems Practice' and through his encouragement of critical research discussions and debate; to Enid Mumford, who has carried on a personal crusade for over two decades of encouraging the rights of ordinary people in organizations to benefit from our designed systems; and to Tom De Marco, who through his structured techniques helped to bring about a fundamental step change in the design of better functional information systems.

Last, but not least, I would like to thank my critics, without whom there would have been very little inspiration to persevere and undertake critical research.

_____ INTRODUCTION _____

Methodologies are explicit mechanisms for helping to solve 'problems'. However, as soon as we have more than one methodology for solving problems, we have an additional problem of choice, i.e. 'Which one should I choose?' The field of information systems is fortunate to have a wide range of methodologies: it is estimated that there are over 1000 brand-named methodologies in use all over the world. This is not surprising given the number of consultancy companies engaged in commercial and business activities. Moreover, these numbers do not take into account organizational-specific unpublicized methodologies.

Most methodologies originate from academic, industrial, business and consultancy companies. Understandably, some of the creators or owners of methodologies try to promote their wide use. However, the 'choice' problem is not resolved as they are reluctant to divulge the weaknesses, shortcomings or inappropriateness of their methodologies, and are not open about the difficulties or situations that are not covered. Therefore, potential methodology users need some independent support to help them evaluate and select a relevant methodology for the 'problem situation' that they face.

This book describes a methodology-independent framework that was developed from experiences gained in industrial practice, consultancy, theoretical research and 'action research'. The framework discussed and used here is a _general_ framework that can be used for understanding and evaluating _any_ methodology, not simply those relating to information systems.

The framework is called NIMSAD. It is an acronym for **N**ormative **I**nformation **M**odel-based **S**ystems **A**nalysis and **D**esign and aims to serve three purposes: first, it helps us to understand problem-solving processes in general and of any nature; secondly, it helps us to evaluate methodologies before, during and after use; and thirdly, it assists us in evaluating industrial/business practice.

The book is organized into four parts.

Part 1 examines the context of methodologies. Chapter 1 clarifies information systems from an organizational and an educational perspective. Information systems have evolved in the last two decades to embrace many important functions; these developments are discussed here. The chapter concludes with a comprehensive definition of information systems. Chapter 2 discusses systems development and the role of methodologies and frameworks in this process. Chapter 3 explores the need for a framework and explains the approach taken to the development of the NIMSAD framework. All three chapters attempt to clarify terminology used in the field.

Part 2 deals with the development of the framework, which has been abstracted from practical problem-solving experiences and is constructed in this book to show the reasons for the inclusion of its component elements. Four essential elements of the framework are identified, namely: the 'problem situation', the problem solver, the problem-solving process and the evaluation. Chapter 4 discusses the first two elements; Chapters 5 and 6 examine the third element and the stages involved in *any* problem-solving process. Chapter 7 explores the use of evaluation. Readers are requested not to skip this section as it explains the reasons for the elements and stages of the framework and also shows how problems are conceived and solved in any situation.

Part 3 discusses the application of the framework. Chapters 8, 9 and 10 show its use in evaluating three well-known methodologies, namely: Structured Analysis and Design Specification (De Marco, 1979), 'ETHICS' (Mumford, 1983a, 1983b), and 'Soft' Systems Methodology (Checkland, 1981; Checkland and Scholes, 1990). These methodologies were chosen as they perform different transformations and have different structures, steps and rationale; there is no attempt to compare them directly with one another. In this way, the reader is able to observe the use of the framework in methodology evaluation at first hand and, using the framework, should be able to perform evaluation of *any* methodology. The evaluation presented in this section is based on the author's viewpoint; however, it is important that readers carry out their own evaluations of the same methodologies and come to their own conclusions.

Readers please note that the evaluation of the methodologies in this section is based on the *published* (public domain) descriptions, statements and case studies of the methodologies. Therefore, any critical evaluation is based on the published material and, in that context, the failure of the methodology creators to make their assumptions explicit. For example, if the published methodology proposes a particular step, but does not show how to perform it, then we critically examine the implications of this gap for the methodology user.

Part 4 discusses the conclusions reached from the use of the framework in methodology evaluation and practice.

Readers are reminded once again that methodology evaluation is as much an intellectual as a practical activity. Therefore, they should not accept any of the evaluation conclusions or lessons derived in this book unless they have examined them from their own knowledge and experience. As much as this book attempts to contribute to the methodology debate, the richness of human reasoning processes cannot be advanced if readers do not question the arguments, discussions and debates advocated in the book. Without operating at a conscious level of concern, we will be in no position to help others.

NIMSAD FRAMEWORK IN PRACTICE

Case studies of action research projects using the NIMSAD framework are available via e-mail. You need access to World Wide Web (i.e. using Mosaic or XMosaic).

Please type the following instructions:

http://www.cee.hw.ac.uk/~nimal/case.html

Ask your computer officer for details on accessing the World Wide Web.

PART 1

DOMAIN OF INFORMATION SYSTEMS

INTRODUCTION

'Information systems' is one of the most widely interpreted terms in use today. It means many things to many people. For the purpose of understanding the role of methodologies discussed in this book, it is important that we clarify the meaning of information systems. The role of this chapter is to show that information systems has a more comprehensive meaning than is simply implied under the traditional definitions. It will also show that information systems can be considered as having five distinctive functions when viewed from an organizational context, which collectively form the domain of *organizational* information systems. Finally, the chapter will discuss the subject areas that constitute the discipline of information systems. This involves a much broader study than that of the five functions of information systems. By clarifying these areas, we hope to assist two groups of readers, namely: practitioners who need to direct their attention to the information systems functions of their own organizations that may require immediate and considered action, and students/researchers who need to focus on areas for study.

HISTORICAL DEVELOPMENT

The subject of information systems grew out of computer science to fill a gap created by the failures of machine-code programmers to understand and solve user problems. Historically, the users had no concept of *how* the technology operated or *what* the technology could offer them. On the other hand, the knowledgeable machine-code/assembler programmer had considerable under-standing of the machine operations and of what instruction sets could make the machine perform, but had very little comprehension of the user application needs or the user environment. This gap was recognized by both researchers and manufacturers, resulting in the development of high-level languages (Algol, Fortran, COBOL). Those who learned to operate the new languages did not have to be so machine-dependent as the previous machine-code programmers; therefore they were able to concentrate on user requirements and attempt to meet them with machine solutions. Their role was one of bridging technology solutions with user requirements. Thus, the term 'information systems' came into being. Since then, the term 'information systems' is used to encompass many activities: essentially, it covers the use of techniques for defining user requirements, designing and implementing solutions to satisfy those requirements, and even today, the success of information systems is measured by how well the solutions satisfy user requirements.

Historically, there were no generic methods or techniques for bridging the gap between user needs and technology capabilities. Therefore, methods from Work Study and Organization & Methods (O&M) disciplines were adopted for information systems development (Daniel and Yates, 1969). However, rapid developments in hardware and software soon rendered these techniques outdated. These new developments were not only in speed and volume handling, but also in languages, programming techniques, software tools and new concepts which help to solve new classes of problems. Today, the field of information systems spans many activities, ranging from information technology on the one side to organizational activities on the other.

This expansion and the development of the *use* of technology within many disciplines, professions and application environments have made the subject of 'information systems' mean many things to many people. For instance, in many universities 'information systems' is still a subject theme within their undergraduate programmes in computer science/studies. In some institutions it is considered as a sub-discipline within the departments of electrical and electronic engineering. The British Computer Society considers information systems to mean both an engineering and a business application discipline (*The Computer Journal*: Special Issue on Information Systems, April 1991). Historically, the term has also been used within the disciplines of economics and statistics to mean organized collections of survey or source data as well as the orderly cataloguing and retrieval of information within the discipline of library studies. In others, it is the name of a department which covers topics that fall between computer science and management/organization science.

What is information systems?

One of the best ways of answering this question is to examine what current literature defines as 'information systems'. Let us examine some of the definitions and then clarify their meaning within an organizational context. This is essential for examining the methodological contributions discussed and examined in the later chapters of this book.

CURRENT DEFINITIONS OF INFORMATION SYSTEMS

One way to understand the domain of information systems is to examine some of the current definitions. Listed below are definitions given by some authors in the field.

> An information system exists only to serve the business system of which it is a component. It keeps records and maintains the various facts and figures needed to run the business.
> (Kendall, 1992)

> An information system (IS) is a formalized computer information system that can collect, store, process and report data from various sources to provide the information necessary for managerial decision making   (Hicks, 1993)

> . . . may be defined as a system that serves to provide information within an organisation when and where it is needed at any managerial level. Such a system must take the information received and store, retrieve, transform, process and communicate it using a computer system or other means. (Aktas, 1987)

> One of the components (or sub-systems) of an organisation is the 'information systems'. The components of this system are people, hardware, software, data and procedures. The organisational information system thus collects, transmits, processes, and stores data, and retrieves and distributes information to various users in an organisation. (Ahituv and Neumann, 1990)

If we examine these definitions we find that all of them concentrate exclusively on the *processing* role of information systems in order to meet some user need. Most definitions also recognize the fundamental role of computers in the processing of this information.

Today it is not easy to think of information systems without computers. In effect, information systems would not exist as a distinctive field of study without the role of computers. Nevertheless, it is essential for a definition to recognize information systems as a concept and to define it at a logical level (what it is) free of its physical form (how it is to be performed using or not using computers). The latter is not easy to ignore because many information notions such as 'real-time access' have become meaningful only because of computers. Despite these and many developments taking place in information technology, general definitions help people to think conceptually and to consider their relevance to many situations. Therefore, in its widest sense, information systems could be thought of as having both computer- and non-computer based activities within an organizational context.

Later in this chapter we will provide a comprehensive definition of information systems which will assume the use of information technology to process and store information. But before we undertake that, we need to clarify two terms which seem to be used in the field in an interchangeable way, i.e. 'computer technology' and 'information technology'.

In essence, the terms 'information technology' and 'computer technology' refer to the same technology. However, the term 'information technology' is used to emphasize the *use* of computers for information processing, storage, transmission and presentation with a clear need for satisfying user needs. The term 'computer technology', on the other hand, is used to emphasize the experimentation and exploration of the computational power of the technology, whether or not that achieves any given end. In the former it is considered to be only a *means to an end* while in the latter it is considered as *an end in itself*. This distinction will be examined later in the context of information technology being considered as 'data manipulation' machines. In many instances, what becomes a research issue in computer technology today, if successful, may end up as an application issue for tomorrow's information technology. For instance, relational databases were a research issue at one time, but are now well established as usable database application software. Similarly, what emerges as a well defined problem issue in information technology may lead to a hypothesis for exploration within computer technology. For instance, the notion of self-management is now a research issue in Artificial Intelligence. Therefore, as a discipline, computer science can be considered as being concerned with the exploration of computer technology while information systems can be seen as dealing (*as part of its domain interest*) with the application of information technology. We should note, however,

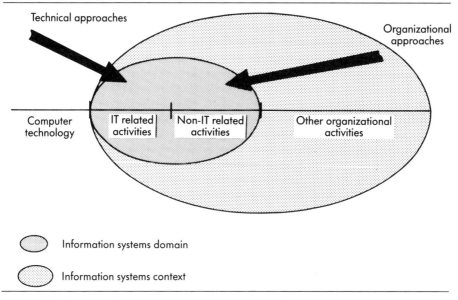

Figure 1.1   Information systems content and context

that information systems are concerned with a much wider domain than the mere application of information technology. Information systems can be defined as an organizational function that embraces information technology (considered as a powerful component), information activities (role, tasks and functions), and organizational activities (context). Figure 1.1 shows a continuum in which the functional domain of information systems can be illustrated.

If we examine Figure 1.1 we notice that information systems is set within the context of organizations. This shows that information systems has to demonstrate its application potential within an organizational context.

Those who try to develop information systems from a technical perspective tend to see them as a set of activities that are very much related to what is possible with the use of current information technology—see the left arrow in Figure 1.1. Structured methodologies (e.g. data flow description/design, database design, structured programming) have attempted to draw designers' attention away from the pure technical approach to the design of information task activities, but they still carry technical notions, i.e. technologically possible activities are abstracted from the situation. On the other hand, those who try to develop information systems from a purely organizational perspective tend to address only the meaningful aspects of human activities and tend to ignore the capabilities of the technology—see the right arrow in Figure 1.1. However, information systems is an *interdisciplinary* subject containing both technical and organizational dimensions. Whatever the background of information systems specialists, they need to have both technical and organizational knowledge/skills in order to address the IT and non-IT related activities (see the shaded area in Figure 1.1) if they are to design, develop or manage effective information systems.

INFORMATION SYSTEMS FUNCTIONS

So, what is the role of information systems?

The role of information systems cannot simply be about collecting, storing, processing and distributing information, as described in many definitions, although this may be its main function. There are four other important functions of information systems; including the processing function described in the definitions listed earlier, these are:

(1) Information processing and usability function
(2) Educating and learning function
(3) Information systems development function
(4) Management and control function
(5) Strategy and planning function.

These five functions collectively form the domain of information systems. Figure 1.2 illustrates the interconnections between them. Many practitioners may readily recognize some or all of these functions in their organizations. It is, however, important not to look for people or departments with the above or similar labels—these are functions which may be undertaken by one or several distinctively organized physical units or persons. The paramount consideration is to recognize the different but logically connected nature of the functions. We will describe these functions below.

INFORMATION PROCESSING AND USABILITY FUNCTION

Most definitions of information systems concentrate exclusively on this function. This is not surprising—as an applied field of science, information systems has to demonstrate its usability in practice. Taking into consideration the

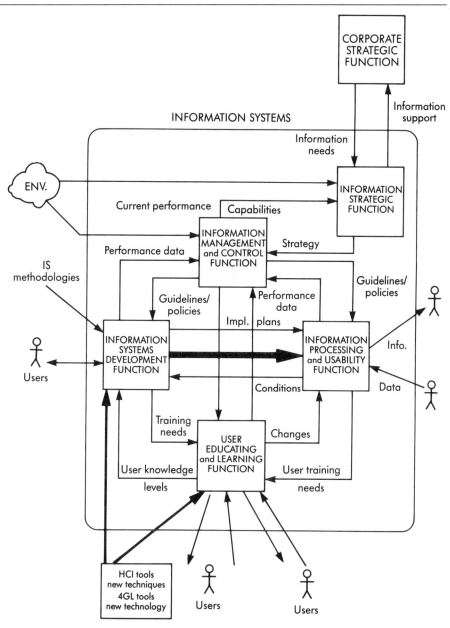

Figure 1.2   Information systems functional model

processing function discussed in the earlier definitions, we can state that an information system is:

. . . a system whose main function is to provide information to support user decision making and action at whatever level within the organisation. The role of this function is to ensure that most efficiently organised technical, manual, formal and informal means are employed for the acquisition, storage, processing, dissemination and presentation of information for supporting user decisions and actions on a continuing basis.

What is the difference between this definition and others found in the literature?

First, there is a need for examining the most *efficient* means of providing information. Efficiency can be defined as the value of the cost/benefit ratio of providing information. For example, if a given information-processing task can be carried out at a lower cost in terms of resources while still producing the same usable information, then we can define it as an improvement in efficiency. Most organizations continue to look for improvements in efficiency as this function has become extremely expensive. Questions of outsourcing and facilities management are of importance within this functional context.

Secondly, the information must match user needs on a *continuing* basis. The matching of user needs is the measure of its *effectiveness*. Effectiveness is the measure of the usefulness of the output when measured against some objective. For example, if a manager needs to take a decision on market expansion and the processed information is considered useful for taking that decision, then we can say that the information is effective.

The role of those who are engaged in this function is to monitor and evaluate techniques, methods, concepts and, technology that can help to improve the continuous acquisition, processing, storing and presenting of information. Figure 1.3 shows a schematic model of the information processing and usability function. Data are captured according to predetermined criteria and processed for producing usable (not just meaningful) information.

The word usability is very important. In many organizations, information is processed at considerable costs to the organization but is never used. We explain briefly below an industrial project example that discusses this very point.

Many examples of achieving improvements in the efficiency and effectiveness of information processing and usability have come from information technology, i.e. software packages, hardware updates, etc. Rhodes (1987) explains

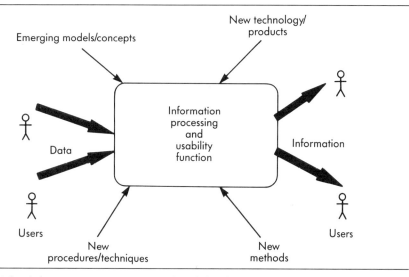

Figure 1.3   Information processing and usability function

how the performance of Security Pacific National Bank in Los Angeles was increased by the acquisition of a software package which improved the efficiency of its memory management. The result was a 40 per cent reduction in time to complete a transaction, with a drop in total elapsed time from two and a half hours to fifteen minutes. It was estimated that Security Pacific saved millions of dollars as a result.

EDUCATING AND LEARNING FUNCTION

This is an area which has received very little attention from the information systems community. However, the function of information systems is not simply to provide information for users' decision making and action. They should also provide learning opportunities. Learning is not just about learning how to use information, but also to help users evaluate the effectiveness of their own decision making, actions and modelling activities. This function provides advice to users and facilities to improve the decision and information models used within the information processing and usability function. Continuous examination and modification of models and decisions is necessary where the users have to operate in a dynamic environment.

The role of those performing this function is therefore not only to examine the methods of meeting user needs, but also to work with users to help them examine the relevance of the information to decision making. The lack of such support and its implications became apparent in an industrial-based study briefly explained below.

> In an action research project conducted at a distribution company, the action researcher examined the rationale for a management information system and the subsequent realisation of the objectives in the newly installed information system. The group controller who was responsible for policies on stock purchasing, issues and levels had confided in the researcher that he had no knowledge of the models that formed the basis of the new computerised stock control system. He was going to continue to base his decisions on familiar models derived from experience and on informal information from the network of depot managers.
>
> (Jayaratna, 1986)

The facilities of this package, particularly its models on optimization, efficiency, effectiveness, and its ability to manipulate objectives and constraints, could have given the company considerable scope for reducing its stock levels, pilferage/shrinkage, insurance costs and opportunity costs while increasing its sales, cash flow, customer service and market share. However, because there were no explanations, discussions, training, demonstrations or consultations on this new package for processing information, the stock controller was not able to consider the relevance or usefulness of the information. Instead of the package contributing to the service goals, to the performance of the company or to the quality of decision making, it added considerable costs to the company capital and running costs.

We should not realistically expect users to abandon their 'secure' models (however crude we may consider them to be) and embrace sophisticated models whose logic is not made explicit for their understanding and critical examination. Since it is the users, *not* the information specialists, who are responsible for the outcome of the decisions, it is not a realistic strategy to impose designer-driven models on the users. Clearly, this case study illustrates the need for information systems specialists to work closely with the users, demonstrating as well as *learning* the difficulties of user decision-making environments. In this case it would have been a useful strategy to have involved the users *before* any decisions were made to acquire the software package. Comparison of package outcomes, and users' experience-based decisions over a trial period, could have helped to determine the effectiveness of the package.

This role of learning is critical for improving user decision making, whether it is performed by the information systems specialist, or whether it is an inbuilt feature of the technology for self-learning. The reason why there is such reluctance to get involved with users is the lack of experience on the part of information systems specialists in the user areas of decision making, weak interpersonal skills or lack of abstraction skills. These shortcomings have to be overcome.

The role of the **educating and learning function** is an evolving, continuous and joint one for both the users and the information systems specialists. In the light of this function, the previous information system definition could be extended to include:

> . . . a system that provides information to its users not only for taking effective decisions and actions but also to help the users and information systems specialists measure and, if necessary, improve the effectiveness of their decision models, thus providing an educating and learning function.

Figure 1.4 illustrates this function of information systems and its relationship to the processing and usability function.

INFORMATION SYSTEMS DEVELOPMENT FUNCTION

This area is the main concern of the methodology issues discussed in this book. The role of the information systems development function is to:
- identify current and potential user needs
- identify current and potential problems
- formulate and evaluate user expectations
- develop usable information processing systems

using appropriate methodologies, techniques, models, tools and technology.

There are many methodologies for developing information processing systems. Among the best known structured methodologies are those of De Marco (1979), Gane and Sarson (1979), Page-Jones (1988), Jackson (Ingevaldsson, 1990; Sutcliffe, 1988), Yourdon and Constantine (1979), Yourdon (1990), SSADM (Downs *et al.*, 1988; Ashworth and Goodland, 1990) and Merise (Quang and Chartier-Kastler, 1991). The De Marco methodology will be selected for critical evaluation in Chapter 8.

The function of information systems development and its relationship to the

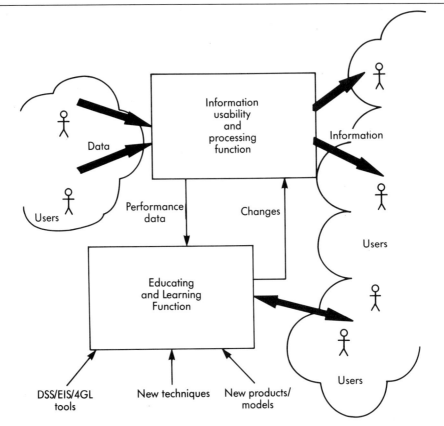

Figure 1.4   Educating and learning function

information processing and usablility function can be illustrated as in Figure 1.5.

This model shows the output of the development process as a 'product'—an information processing system. This information processing system which is to meet user requirements becomes part of the **information processing and usability function** when its operations begin.

Sprague and McNurlin (1986) discuss the trends in the information systems development process. They have identified a new role for designers—that of 'information specialist'. This new role is closer to the organizational/user end than to the computer technology end of the continuum of Figure 1.1, thus reflecting both the problems and potential areas for growth in the field of information systems. Their model is consistent with the distinctions made earlier between computer technology and information technology. However, their discussions show the growing use of sophisticated products by customers,

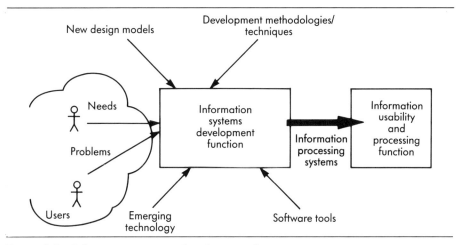

New design models

Development methodologies/
techniques

Needs

Problems

Users

Emerging
technology

Information
systems
development
function

Information
processing
systems

Software tools

Information
usability
and
processing
function

Figure 1.5   Information systems development function

indicating that the systems development function is not the only means by which users can acquire information technology products for processing information; for example, the attempts by manufacturers to reach users direct in order to expand their market share gave rise to the development of 4GL software (Jayaratna, 1988).

The role of information systems specialists is being further challenged by the growing range of user-centred technology products (software packages that can be used directly by end-users) and the acquisition of information technology knowledge by the end-users. However, the notion of a 'product push' approach to information systems development is being challenged by those (including the author) who feel that placing a high priority on technical aspects alone does not necessarily help to realize the effectiveness of information processing systems because the development process excludes the complex multi-dimensional nature of organizations.

Many researchers, such as Mumford (1981, 1983a, 1983b), Land (1987), Land and Hirschheim (1983) and Newman (1989), have highlighted the effects of ignoring the psychological needs of people. They stress the need for addressing the 'people' dimension in the development of information processing systems, and advocate user participation in the systems development process as the way of ensuring that genuine user needs are satisfied. The ETHICS methodology (Mumford, 1983a, 1983b) will be critically examined in this book.

Beer (1979, 1988) and Espejo and Watt (1988) advocate the use of the Viable

Systems Model (VSM) as the basis for designing information processing systems. They argue that if organizational structures and their internal and external relationships are not understood in a different conceptual way, the application of information technology and the design of information processing systems will only reinforce the outdated organizational structures, resulting in marginal improvements to organizational effectiveness.

Checkland's (1981) methodology, widely known as 'Soft' Systems Methodology (SSM), has been adopted for addressing many critical organizational issues. Miles (1988) discusses the problems of integrating SSM in information processing systems development. SSM has subsequently been modified (Checkland and Scholes, 1990) to show links to incorporate information systems design. The contribution of Soft Systems Methodology will be examined critically in Chapter 10.

Wood-Harper (1989) and Avison and Wood-Harper (1990) have incorporated components of SSM, participative and structured methodologies as a way of addressing the multiple dimensions of organizations and have developed the Multiview methodology. In addition, there are a large number of methodologies, all claiming they are the best means of developing information processing systems. This has caused considerable confusion in the field of information systems as to what methodology to adopt, standardize, select, combine and/or use.

The main focus of the book is to explain the steps of a conceptual framework derived from industrial work and its use in providing a clearer understanding of *what* methodologies attempt to do and *how* they are used in practice. The framework was developed and used by the author and others for comparing and evaluating methodologies. Chapters 4, 5, 6 and 7 will discuss the framework in the context of systems development, while the subsequent chapters will discuss the use of the framework in the evaluation of methodologies and their practice.

MANAGEMENT AND CONTROL FUNCTION

The central focus of the book will be on the role of methodologies in the **systems development function**. However, it is important to understand the wider domain of information systems, so that the implications of methodologies for other functional areas and for the organizational context can be understood.

An examination of the functions previously discussed reveals that they are primarily concerned with the operational aspects of information systems development, use and evaluation within the organization. Each function is complex enough to warrant some form of management action. Furthermore, if we are to consider the number of development projects proceeding at any one time within the **information systems development function**; the number of new products and techniques that are considered for use within the **information processing and usability function**; the training and retraining that needs to take place to support organizational performance within the **education and learning function**, and the number of changes required to ensure the performance of the current **information processing and usability function** within acceptable levels of efficiency and effectiveness, then we can imagine the degree of complexity that needs to be managed. If the high degree of human effort and costs involved are to be added to this, then it is apparent that some formalized management function is necessary to coordinate these efforts and control the activities organized and described under the three functions previously defined. According to Palvia and Nosek (1989), investments in information processing systems, their asset values and recurrent expenditure exceeded over US$1 million in 30 per cent of the companies surveyed. In many organizations, budgetary provision for information processing and development activities exceeds that of many other user functions such as accounting, sales, distribution and so on. Given the significance and increasing vulnerability of organizational failure owing to the poor performance of information processing systems, it is not surprising that information is now regarded as a corporate resource to be managed in the same way as people, finance, equipment and products (Galliers 1991; Ward *et al.*,1990).

In the context of the previously defined functions, the role of the **management and control function** can be defined as one of maintaining the efficient and effective performance of the other three functions.

The first management task is to ensure that investments in the **information usability and processing function** are fully utilized by the organization. The acquisition of new hardware and software, skilled personnel or the replacement of existing equipment, procedures, techniques or methods of data capture, processing, storage and retrieval need to be justified in the same way as other acquisitions and assets of the organization. According to Zelkowitz (1978), the biggest proportion of costs in information systems expenditure (67 per cent) arises in systems maintenance activities, i.e. to improve the efficiency and effectiveness of the **information usability and processing function.**

This area consumes a large amount of human effort, i.e. human activities to ensure the continuous high utilization of information processing systems. An additional cost of this function comes from expenditure on replacement of hardware and software. Unlike other user functional areas (e.g. production), the old technology has virtually no resale value, thus requiring high depreciation allowances to be made. This makes the **management and control** even more difficult to perform, as it has to strive for even higher levels of effectiveness from the use of information technology because of its short life-span.

From a management perspective, there are a number of critical decisions that need to be taken to ensure the efficiency and effectiveness of current information processing systems. They include guidelines and policies covering supplier and service contracts, criteria for determining priorities, policies for ensuring service level performance, communication and procedural aspects governing request handling, complaints, revisions and amendments, establishing performance targets for hardware, as well as monitoring and control to ensure that these targets are achieved. For example, in some industries such as banking and airlines, where continuous systems availability is required, measures such as MTBF (mean time between failures) are used to indicate service level performance. Failure to provide continuous uninterrupted service levels of information processing can have catastrophic implications for these types of organizations.

As far as the **education and learning function** is concerned, management needs to ensure that there is provision for training and retraining of users both in the competent use of existing information processing systems output as well as in new methods, procedures, and decision models. Training should also extend to information systems specialists. Some organizations locate their information systems specialists in the users' working environment to enable them to gain a realistic appreciation of the types of user problems as well as the users' real information wants and needs. The working experience gained within the user environment helps information specialists to increase the efficiency and effectiveness of information processing systems. From a management perspective, there is a need for bringing together users and information systems specialists in order to develop effectiveness of performance.

The third area that requires management attention is that of the **information systems development function**. Since development processes require considerable human effort and costs, and their effectiveness can be measured only *within* the **information usability and processing function**, management has to ensure that the development efforts are also effective. According to a US survey (US General Accounting Office FMGSD-80–4), 47 per cent of systems delivered were never used. Later chapters will examine some of the reasons for this type of failures; however, it is highlighted here to demonstrate the need for a management focus.

Among many other issues that require management attention are decisions on the standardization of methodologies, techniques, tools, hardware and software, and policy issues on performance and delivery targets. At a project progress level they involve project management techniques for ensuring that projects are completed within agreed time scales and within budget constraints, as well as for ensuring that information processing systems being developed meet users' needs. On the latter point, it is interesting to note that many methodologies are weak in identifying the real needs of the user. From an organizational perspective, this level of expenditure cannot be sustained by any organization which has to derive its income by selling products and/or services in a competitive marketplace. Figure 1.2 illustrates the links between the management and control function and the other functions.

STRATEGY AND PLANNING FUNCTION

This has become one of the most significant functions in organizations. The role of information systems in decision making has been recognized for many years (see, for instance, the predictions and discussions of Ackoff, 1976; Davis, 1974; Murdick, 1975; Beer, 1978; 1981; Leavitt and Whistler, 1958; Sprague and McNurlin, 1986). Leavitt and Whistler (1958) are also credited with the anticipation of the impact of information technology at the strategic level of management as well as on the rationalization of middle management. However, the recognition of the importance of the role of strategic information systems to corporate planning is a recent development.

The role of strategic information systems can be considered at two levels.

First, the role of information systems' *support* for corporate strategies of the organization. Executive Information Systems (EIS) are expected to fulfil this role. Houdshel and Watson (1987) discuss the use of EIS at Lockheed-Georgia Company and how they helped the company's strategic moves into different marketplaces.

Secondly, is the role of information systems to help *derive* the corporate strategies of the organization by providing a proactive role. For example, strategic information systems have helped to devise new concepts in banking transactions, giving rise to new banking strategies, e.g. the concept of logical banking (bank without a building). Some of the leap-frogging opportunities provided by new information systems have been discussed by McFarlan (1984) and Porter and Millar (1985). These authors discuss how information technology can help organizations to change their balance of power with current and potential competitors, suppliers and customers, i.e. stronger links with customers and suppliers, and altering the basis of competition in price, image, customer services and product features.

The distinction between strategic information systems and other types of information systems is explained by Wainwright *et al.*:

> An information system is strategic if it changes an organisa-
> tion's products or service or the way it competes in its
> industry   (Wainwright *et al.*, 1991)

Strategic information systems cannot be left to chance, nor developed in a random way. Because they require significant investments and affect organizational culture, the development needs to be carefully planned, and their impact along economic, social, cultural and technical dimensions explored in a systematic way. Most companies do not consider the importance of strategic information systems planning as a coherent organized activity, nor the significance of their links to corporate strategies. In this context, Galliers (1991) identifies several critical success factors that need to be considered, among which senior management commitment is considered to be a key element. To this list must be added the creative skills and commitment of information systems specialists who need to step beyond their expert domain to gain experience in the organization, and its customer and competitor environments—see also Ward *et al.* (1990), Galliers (1991) and Galliers *et al.* (1994).

Any information systems definition should cover more than information processing to include the functions discussed in this chapter and illustrated in Figure 1.2. Therefore, a definition covering the five functions is given below.

An information system can be defined as:

> a system for the most efficient and effective means of identify-
> ing the 'real' needs of users, and developing information
> processing systems for satisfying these needs; ensuring that the
> resulting information processing systems continue to satisfy
> changing user needs by the most efficient means of acquiring,
> storing, processing, disseminating and presenting information;
> by providing facilities and a learning environment for users
> and information systems specialists to improve the effective-
> ness of their decision models; and by supporting operational,
> control and strategic organisational objectives.

INFORMATION SYSTEMS DISCIPLINE

What is the role of information systems as a discipline? In what way does it
differ from the role of information systems in an organization? What should
be included in an information systems curriculum? These are the questions
that will be addressed in this section.

The five different functions that were discussed earlier, and illustrated in
Figure 1.2, help us to understand the role of information systems in the
business, commercial and public sector and industrial organizations, i.e.
information systems in practice. Understanding these functions helps us to
analyse which areas of information systems within an organization need
attention, require control, have to be monitored and managed, etc.

However, information systems as a subject area for study or as a discipline
requires a different structural organization. As a discipline, it needs to
incorporate not only the study of the five functional areas discussed earlier,
but also many other subjects. The discipline is *interdisciplinary* and has an
applied theory focus. By viewing information systems from a discipline
perspective, the reasons for the inclusion of relevant subjects for study can be
considered.

Figure 1.6 illustrates the links between the domains of information systems as
a discipline and in practice.

The main areas for study can be organized under the following headings, namely:

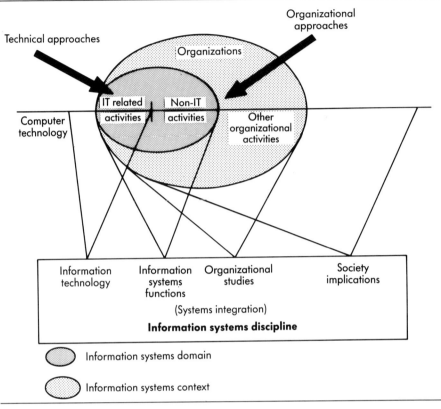

Figure 1.6   Information systems discipline

(1) Information technology
(2) Information systems functions (the five functions)
(3) Organizational studies
(4) Social implications
(5) Systems integration.

INFORMATION TECHNOLOGY
Why study technology?

The discipline of information systems should give a high priority to the study
of information technology. (The difference between information technology
and computer technology has already been discussed.) There are several
reasons for this. First, there is no aspect of life that escapes the influence of
technology directly or indirectly. Even the availability of a book is partly due
to technology, e.g. paper manufacturing, ream rolling, word processing,

typesetting, printing, distributing. Many improvements to the performance of organizational activities seem to stem from the application of technology. Even if the role of information technology in the design is to be excluded, such a decision should only be taken based on an appreciation of what technology can or cannot do, and only after considering the implications of using or not using it. The less understanding a designer has of technology, particularly of how it can be utilized, the narrower the range of design options available in a given practical situation. In this context, note that current technology is always the result of previous human effort. By engaging in design, the designer consciously or unconsciously contributes to the birth of new technology concepts.

The second reason is far more fundamental. Many believe that information technology should be considered only as a means to an end, i.e. consider *what* needs doing and then, and only then, consider *how* the technology is able to help achieve the *what*. This is a reaction against technology trained information systems specialists who have been applying technical solutions to problems without an adequate understanding of the nature of the problems they are trying to solve. However, taking an anti-technology perspective can be equally flawed. Such a stance denies users the benefits that may be gained from the *opportunities* created by modern information technology.

Thirdly, there is a misconception that information technology is a 'data manipulation' machine. This arises from the notion that 'information = data + meaning'. This is a notion that prevailed in the early 1970s when computers were mere calculating machines.

In the context of the current state of awareness, the notion of information as data with meaning unique to the person has to be further challenged. Since, in any organized information collection activity, the judgement as to what data to collect, process and use has already been made *prior to* the data collection, some of the meaning (relevance that gives rise to meaning) has already been applied in the selection. In addition to this, rules which create meaningful information are also applied to these data and determined beforehand as being relevant and useful. The late R. A. Anderton discussed the use of Dretshe's semantic theory of information and suggested that it is the semantic structures in the mind that determine what is meaningful. Accordingly, 'information is needed on the input so that appropriate transformation can be selected' (Anderton, 1987).

To treat computers as mere 'data manipulation' machines is to ignore the capabilities of information technology to process and *act upon* selected data based on externally assigned interpretations. For example, in the early information technology-based stock control systems, the machine produced information on stock levels so that humans could apply their interpretation and take action to order goods. Today, humans assign the functional (and sometimes behavioural) decision criteria to information technology-based systems, so that instead of producing information for human decisions the technology can automatically decide and generate orders. In this case, the action of the majority of humans is reduced to physical tasks, i.e. posting of orders. Mumford (1983a, 1983b) criticizes this kind of systems design which reduces the role of humans to the performance of uninteresting tasks. The latest applications are based on the ability of technology based systems not only to take decisions based on the human assigned criteria, but also to evaluate and change the priorities of these criteria. This has led some scientists to apply human notions such as 'intelligence', 'expert' and 'machine learning' to technologies, as if the latter have any understanding and feelings about what it is that they are dealing with! Equally, we must be cautious not to think that technology is concerned with mere data manipulation. The technology which drives the operations of chemical stations, medical systems and aircraft had better be machines which operate consistently according to well considered and 'taken-as-assigned' interpretations.

The separation of technology and humans based purely on *physical* criteria is not very useful for information systems design activities. As discussed earlier in this chapter, there is a clear need to recognize the role of technology as a *means* as well as generating *ends*. Technology will never learn to love, care, feel, cry or become intelligent in the same way as humans do. In essence people who treat information technology as 'intelligent' human-like machines are no different in conclusions to those who treat their fellow humans as if they are mere 'data manipulation' biological machines (i.e. without emotions).

In information systems design, one needs to have a knowledge of the capabilities, application potential, role, functions and possible implications of using information technology. Any experience in the use of technology (use of languages, 4GL software, emerging tools, etc.) can provide a greater number of options and confidence and help to expand the number of design options. In Figure 1.6, the domain knowledge can be extended to cover some elements of potential technology in order to understand the implications of future technology. Equally, the information systems practitioner must know that any skills acquired in technology can also unduly influence his or her problem analysis. Therefore, the choice of which approach to take is crucial for information systems development, hence the interest of this book in addressing methodology evaluation. Students should consider both the capabilities and the implications of using information technology in their study of information systems.

INFORMATION SYSTEMS FUNCTIONS

The focus here is mainly the study of the five functional areas discussed earlier within an organizational context (Figure 1.2). Given the emphasis of particular educational programmes, studies may be focused on different functional areas. For instance, information systems programmes which place emphasis on the **information systems development function** may focus heavily on methodologies but less so on information strategies. In the same way, a programme in Library Science may place greater emphasis on information retrieval, Human Computer Interactions (HCI) and database design (data organization). A 'good' information systems programme will attempt to provide an appreciation of all five functional areas before developing specialist skills in a chosen function. Whichever area is selected, potential practitioners need to develop skills in the analysis, design and implementation of information processing systems.

ORGANIZATIONAL STUDIES

All the functions of information systems previously discussed operate within the context of organizations (Figures 1.1, 1.2 and 1.6). Information systems have to serve their organizations, whether to help their members achieve their purposes efficiently and effectively, or whether to help them decide what strategies to adopt for survival and growth. There are two reasons why organizational studies are important for information systems programmes.

First, the subjects that come under organizational studies help students to understand and appreciate the organizational dimension. A study of organizational activities and performances are bound to assist the students in gaining a much richer appreciation of situations in which they will eventually become effective practitioners. Depending on the nature and the emphasis of the academic programme, it may include subjects such as organizational structures, psychology, social and cultural studies, politics, economics, accountancy, communication studies, philosophy and so on. These subjects enable students to develop an awareness of the context issues which are critical for developing, using and evaluating the effectiveness of information systems.

Secondly, information systems specialists themselves have to operate as members of the organization, and the greater the insight they can gain into the understanding of organizations and how they operate, the better the position they will be in to perform as effective practitioners. In the context of Checkland's (1981) solution options, an in-depth understanding of organizations helps one to generate feasible solutions.

SOCIAL IMPLICATIONS

This is an important subject area, and one which is neglected by many educational programmes. As employees, information specialists have a responsibility to the members of the organization in which they practise, but as citizens, they also have a responsibility to society at large, which expects its professionals to not only consider the welfare of the organization but also, through their actions, to look after the welfare of society. This orientation helps potential practitioners to widen their problem and solution domain in order to consider explicitly the implications of their design actions. Information systems specialists have to consider explicitly the ethical and moral issues that arise from their designs (e.g. redundancies, effect on quality of life, redistribution of power, freedom of expression, rights to privacy, etc.) no matter what the eventual outcome there can be no prescribed solutions, but awareness of these issues is expected to help individuals to consider the implications of their designs in the wider context. They need to contribute to the national and international debate, policy formulation, legislation and so on. For this reason, most professional institutes require their members to be aware of their social responsibilities, and expect them to take an active part in influencing and shaping government policies and legislation in this context. If professionals take part in these activities, there will be better and more effective policies and legislation safeguards for ordinary people.

SYSTEMS INTEGRATION

Integration of subject areas is a very difficult task. This is because our educational programmes are very much compartmentalized. Subject partitioning is useful for the in-depth study and development of a particular subject area; however, this same partitioning reduces the opportunity for students to consider the knowledge interconnections, particularly when they have to develop solutions within an organizational context.

Information systems is an *interdisciplinary* subject. Simply having a range of subjects on a programme does not necessarily lead to their integration; a conscious effort needs to be made to interconnect the subjects. Some educational programmes try to achieve this by individual/group case study methods and industry-based projects while others use theory as the basis for interlinking the different subject areas. One major philosophy and theory that can provide this integration is 'Systems', which is very much focused on teasing out the integrative and 'holistic' properties of a situation. For an excellent reference to the emergence of 'Systems', see Checkland (1981). For a foundation knowledge, please see Kendall and Kendall (1992) and Burch and Grudnitski (1989).

SUMMARY

Information systems is not just about collecting, storing, processing and supplying information for decision makers in an organization. It has at least four other functions. These five areas collectively form the function of 'information systems'. The functional areas that were identified and discussed in this chapter were:

(1) Information processing and usability function
(2) Educating and learning function
(3) Information systems development function
(4) Management and control function
(5) Strategy and planning function

An information systems definition should therefore consist of at least the above five functions. This chapter provided a more comprehensive definition than those found in the current literature.

Information systems have no independent existence of their own unless taken in the context of the organizations in which they serve.

Information systems as an applied theory discipline has to offer theory which is relevant to the understanding, analysis, design, implementation and evaluation of information systems in organizations. Therefore, as a discipline it has to cover a much wider knowledge set. In this chapter we discussed the relevance of five subject areas, namely:
- Information technology
- Information systems functions

- Organizational studies
- Social implications
- Systems integration

The unique nature of information systems is that it is *interdisciplinary* both in practice and as an academic discipline.

2

INFORMATION SYSTEMS DEVELOPMENT AND METHODOLOGIES

INTRODUCTION

Chapter 1 discussed five functional areas which together constitute the domain of information systems when taken in the context of an organization. It clarified the meaning of computer technology and information technology and also proposed a comprehensive definition of information systems.

This chapter deals with information systems development. The **information systems development function** is concerned with the identification and formulation of user needs, with the design and implementation of information processing systems in accordance with those needs. The operations of the resulting systems and their maintenance to satisfy user needs on a continuing basis (i.e. continuous adaptability) is the responsibility of the **information processing and usability function** and the **education and learning function** as illustrated in Figure 1.2. Here we discuss methodologies for the development of information processing systems within the **information systems development function**, the rationale of these methodologies and the clarification of concepts related to them. The latter issue is very important for the understanding of evaluation issues discussed later in this book.

INFORMATION SYSTEMS DEVELOPMENT

The main role of the **information systems development function** is to develop effective information processing systems in the most efficient way. There could be many such developments taking place in parallel within this function, the number and the scale of which depend on the resources, urgency and needs of the organization. The activity set that goes towards the development of information processing systems is variously called the 'systems development cycle' or the 'systems life cycle'.

INFORMATION SYSTEMS DEVELOPMENT CYCLE

Wainwright *et al.* (1991) identifies several steps in an information systems development cycle. They are:

- Definition phase
  - Feasibility analysis
  - Requirements definition
- Construction phase
  - Systems design
  - Systems building
  - Systems testing
- Implementation phase
  - Installation
  - Operations and maintenance

Another list is offered by Kendall (1992). She defines seven steps in a systems development cycle, namely:

- Problem definition
- Feasibility studies
- Analysis
- Design
- Construction
- Conversion
- Maintenance

While the lists of steps of these two cycles are similar, Kendall's definition implies that for the cycle to begin it should be realized that some form of information system is necessary or at least desirable. She describes problem definition as a step in the development cycle:

> when managers or users realise that an information system is needed for a new business or that the information system for an existing business is no longer reflective of the organisation's functions.   (Kendall, 1992)

A third well known systems development cycle is called the Waterfall model—see Figure 2.1 (Boehm *et al.*, 1977).

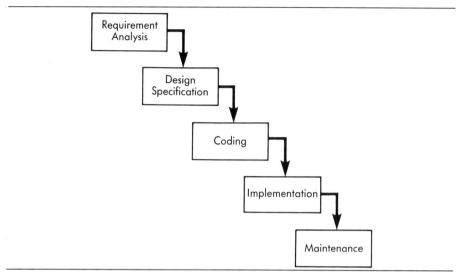

Figure 2.1   Waterfall method

When examining the steps of these systems development cycles, we note that what steps are included or excluded depends very much on the author. Therefore, it is not advisable to consider a systems development cycle as containing a fixed number or similar steps.

In a sense, the inclusion of requirement/problem definition as a step also highlights a general problem within the information systems field, i.e. how terminology is used. For example, many authors include requirement/design specification as one of the steps in the systems development cycle. This is clearly a description of an event, i.e. a particular state that is reached as a result of a set of activities, but not the activity set itself. The step is the formulation of a design definition.

An event is an outcome or a 'state' following or preceding a set of activities. The design specification is clearly an event. Since the author does not discuss what activities need to be performed for arriving at such an event, design specification cannot be considered as a *step* within the development life cycle. The arguments are similar to those distinguishing a decision–making process (a set of activities) and the decision outcome (an event).

While the design specification itself cannot be included as a step because of the reasons outlined above, the activity set that contributes to the production of the specification should be incorporated. The design specification is a

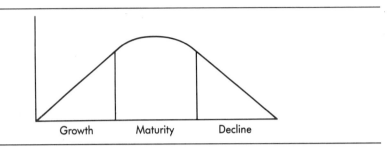

Figure 2.2   Product life cycle or systems life cycle

document which outlines what a systems design activity set has to achieve. The difference between activities and the outcome of the activities (i.e. an event) is an important distinction for understanding some of the concepts of methodologies discussed in Chapters 5, 6, 7, 8, 9 and 10 of this book.

Collectively, the steps outlined in the definitions and many similar models are described as 'systems development life cycles' or 'systems life cycles', as mentioned above. These two terms require clarification.

SYSTEMS DEVELOPMENT LIFE CYCLE vs SYSTEMS LIFE CYCLE

There is a clear distinction between a systems development life cycle and a systems life cycle. For a systems life cycle to be considered as a system it has to exist first i.e. have a life. The concept of a systems life cycle originated in marketing with the notion of a product life cycle.

A product life cycle or a systems life cycle can be considered as having three stages, as illustrated in Figure 2.2.

Whereas a systems development life cycle outlines the steps that are taken to 'give birth' (creation) to a system and terminates when that system begins to perform, a systems life cycle comes into being only when the system begins to *operate*. Clearly, the two concepts of life cycle are distinctively different, with an overlap in the systems implementation step and the growth step of the two life cycles respectively, as illustrated in Figure 2.3. If you examine the information systems model in Figure 1.2, the systems development life cycle falls within the **information systems development function** while the systems life cycle falls within the **information processing and usability function**.

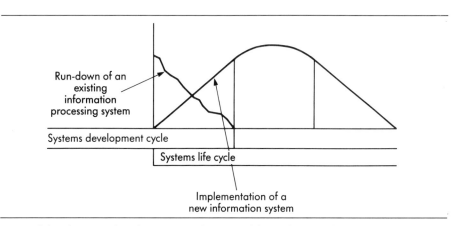

Figure 2.3   Systems development and systems life cycles overlap

SYSTEMS DEVELOPMENT vs SOFTWARE DEVELOPMENT

These two terms are used interchangeably and also need clarification.

'Software development' or 'software engineering' are terms used within the information systems field by computer scientists and engineers whose interests lie in software construction. Peters (1988) describes a number of interpretations among which the following make clear reference to the software construction aspects:

> A Software Life Cycle is a step-by-step breakdown of the software development process ... A Software Life Cycle is both a management and a technical tool for organising, planning, scheduling and controlling the activities associated with a software development and maintenance effort.
>
> (Peters, 1988)

Pressman (1982) defines software engineering as:

> ... a set of techniques to deal with software as an engineered product that requires planning, analysis, design, implementation, testing and maintenance.   (Pressman, 1982)

The two definitions also confuse the differences between the development and life cycles. They consider maintenance as a stage of a software life cycle which, in the light of the distinctions presented in this chapter, should clearly belong to the 'maturity' stage of a systems life cycle, as illustrated in

Figure 2.2. In effect, maintenance should be seen as a set of activities which attempts to extend the useful life and functions of an existing information processing system before a decision is made to replace or terminate its life. Therefore, it is an activity set that should be considered as being within the **information processing and usability function**. Similarly, feasibility studies should be considered as being within the **management and control function**. As we can see, the clarification of the functions of an information system in Chapter 1 helps us to locate the functions within which these activities are undertaken.

The terms 'software engineering' or 'software development' are not comprehensive enough to cover information systems development because they are concerned with activities that are solely to do with software construction and quality assurance. While these are of critical importance to computer-based information systems development, the role of software engineering does not cover many important organizational issues that are critical for information systems development. Land (1987) makes this distinction between software engineering and information systems engineering:

> Software Engineering is primarily a technical task. Its problems—quality of the product, the productivity of those producing software products—are being tackled by the development of formal methods and tools. Information Systems Engineering relies on social processes. Its tasks—the decision and implementation of information systems which contribute to the effective operations of an organisation—have to be carried out under conditions of uncertainty.
>
> (Land, 1987)

The latter, information systems engineering, is consistent with the role of information systems development, and is concerned with the effectiveness of information for organizational performance. The task of software engineering is to produce software to match the quality and needs of a particular *software specification*, while that of systems development is to match the quality and information needs of a particular *user(s)*.

SYSTEMS DEVELOPMENT vs METHODOLOGIES

What then is the connection between systems development and methodologies?

As we have discussed so far, systems development is concerned with the development of information processing systems. Systems development may define the *general* set of activities that need to be performed in order to produce information processing systems, but by no means is there agreement even at a general level as to what these sets of activities should be. A comparison of definitions of Wainwright *et al.* (1991), Kendall (1982), Peters (1988) and Pressman (1982) reveals these differences. The difference between systems development and methodologies is that the former may define what steps and activity sets constitute the development of information processing systems, while the latter is more specific as to *what* steps may be selected as essential, in *what* order they should be performed, and *how* they are to be carried out. The reasons for choosing a set of activities and structuring these into some coherent form is a question that has to be addressed by methodologies.

DEFINITIONS OF 'METHODOLOGY'

What is a methodology? For the purpose of evaluation, discussed later in this book, a clear definition of methodologies is essential.

'Methodology' is a Greek term meaning the 'study of methods'. The Oxford Dictionary defines a methodology as the 'study of systematic methods of scientific research'. However, the term 'methodology' in the information systems field has come to mean the same as a 'method'. Stamper (1988) has expressed his dissatisfaction of the use of the term as follows:

> I use the term 'methodology' under protest bowing only to customary usage. It would be better, as in the philosophy of science, to speak of 'methods' when referring to specific ways of approaching and solving problems, and to reserve 'method-ology' for comparative and critical study of methods in general; otherwise this vital field of study is nameless.
>
> (Stamper, 1988)

We agree with Stamper's concerns over the gap that has been created by the new use of the word 'methodology'. This gap is now being filled by long descriptions, i.e. 'approaches to appreciate information systems methodologies' (Nielsen, 1990). However, the term 'methodology' is pragmatically well established within the field of information systems to mean the same as method'.

Given that the reasons for using the term 'methodology' have been clarified, the question that should still be addressed is, what is a methodology?

For Checkland (1981), a methodology is intermediate in status between a philosophy, using that word in a general rather than a professional sense, and a technique or method.

> A methodology will lack the precision of a technique but will be a firmer guide to action than a philosophy. Where a technique tells you 'how' and a philosophy tells you 'what', a methodology will contain elements of both 'what' and 'how'.
> (Checkland, 1981)

We wish to disagree with this role of philosophy. Philosophy attempts to answer the question 'why'. Philosophies help to make sense of 'reality' by providing a set of paradigms (a consistent set of beliefs for underpinning understanding and action) about that 'reality'. For example, the positivistic philosophy helps us to believe that by continuous engagement of enquiry we will be able to uncover the facts and rules on which 'reality' is based. Phenomenology helps us to believe that 'reality' does not exist independent of the perceiver. 'Reality' is constructed by each individual from observable phenomena; therefore, it depends very much on the perceiver. Meaning construction in social interactions, is sometimes referred to as 'negotiated reality'. Hermeneutics helps us to believe that 'reality' is constructed not only from observable phenomena, but that the meanings attributed to observable phenomena are very much constructed from our own historicity. Thus, a philosophy provides a set of paradigms to make sense of why 'reality' exists as it is. No one philosophy by itself can explain all the complexity of 'reality'.

If we examine Checkland's definition, we find that it provides more of a *context* than a *content* (i.e. what is included) meaning of the term 'methodology'. This is because Checkland uses his 'Soft' Systems Methodology (SSM) to illustrate the 'content' meaning. However, this general definition provides a useful basis for developing a content oriented general methodology definition.

Avison and Wood-Harper (1990) have used Checkland (1981) as the basis for deriving a methodology definition. They define a methodology as:

> a coherent collection of concepts, beliefs, values and principles

> supported by resources to help problem-solving groups to
> perceive, generate, assess and carry out, in a non-random
> way, changes to an information situation.
>
> (Avison and Wood-Harper, 1990)

This definition focuses our attention on two important issues. First, it talks about the notion of coherence. Without such coherence, the collection of the sets of beliefs, values or principles lack a reason to be together, thus implying that a methodology has to have a structure to demonstrate its coherence. Secondly, the definition focuses on the problem solving intention of methodology users, i.e. their ability to identify and solve problems.

If a methodology is perceived as a problem-solving mechanism, then it must show how it performs problem solving. A problem-solving process can be considered as consisting of three major phases, namely:
- a problem formulation phase
- a solution design phase
- a design implementation phase.

Taking these features into consideration, it is appropriate to define a methodology as a goal-directed way of solving problems. A definition should be general enough to apply to *any* problem-solving situation, not necessarily limited to the information systems domain. It should focus on the process of problem solving rather than just its outcome.

In this context we define a methodology as simply:

> an explicit way of structuring one's thinking and actions.
> Methodologies contain model(s) and reflect particular perspec-
> tives of 'reality' based on a set of philosophical paradigms. A
> methodology should tell you 'what' steps to take and 'how'
> to perform those steps but most importantly the reasons
> 'why' those steps should be taken, in that particular order.

This definition raises five important questions for consideration.

First, the focus is on *structuring* and not on a *structure*. This has more of a *verb* sense of meaning rather than a *noun* as described in the Avison and Wood-Harper definition. Structuring can be interpreted as the ordering or making sense of a situation. While methodologies may display an apparent structure

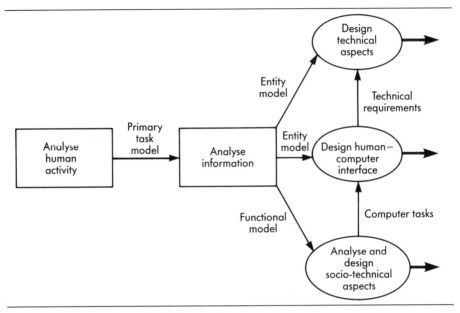

Figure 2.4   Multiview methodology outline

(see Appendix A for a structure of a methodology), when applied within a given situation, the structural properties may be changed reflecting the methodology user's interpretation, knowledge, attempts to sequence steps for intervention, and the situation characteristics. For example, the Multiview methodology described in Avison and Wood-Harper (1990) shows that the 'root' definition stage is to be followed by structured techniques and socio-technical components (see Figure 2.4).

While the structural sequence of these steps seems logical, there exists a considerable gap in the way a transition can be made from the hermeneutic philosophy-based 'soft' systems step to the scientific philosophy-based structured systems step. The problems of these philosophical paradigm shifts will be discussed later in Chapters 8, 9 and 10.

Secondly, the reason for defining 'structuring' in an explicit way is to make a methodology user consider the *reasons* for the ordering of the set of activities or steps as implied by the methodology. Just as a book, with all its apparent structure, may make only limited sense to a reader who fails to structure its content into a coherent meaning unique to him/herself (abstract its essence), so a branded methodology with its apparent structure may still fail to structure the information systems specialist's thinking process. This is the reason why

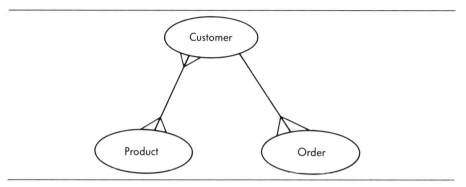

Figure 2.5   Entity-relationship model

some find it easier than others to follow the storyline of a book. Thus, according to the definition, those who follow any established methodology structure without understanding explicitly the reasons for following the suggested steps may be doing permanent damage to the operations and members of an organization. The assistance for structuring does not have to come from a brand-named, established or published methodology; any explicitly ordered set of activities (steps) with a convincing rationale and ways of performing the steps to bring about transformation can qualify as a methodology.

Thirdly, one of the most important issues that needs to be discussed is the models embedded in the methodologies. Their role and contribution needs to be understood by the methodology users. The models, their type and form help to determine what aspects of 'reality' are captured, appreciated and understood. For instance the entity–relationship models in some structured methodologies, e.g. SSADM (Ashworth and Goodland 1990; Downs *et al.*; 1988), Merise (Quang and Chartier-Kastler, 1991), focus the attention of the methodology user on the *formal* relationships of data, as illustrated in Figure 2.5. In so doing, the methodology helps its users to abstract some structural properties of data (e.g. a customer ordering goods) but closes their thinking to the importance of data which have no signs of regularity or permanency (e.g. the customers sensitivity to changes in product characteristics).

In an industrial project (to be published later) we failed to capture essential information on emotions because the formal explicit models of the methodology closed our user's mind to objects, entities and information flows which had no formal status. The use of models in the context of the proposed

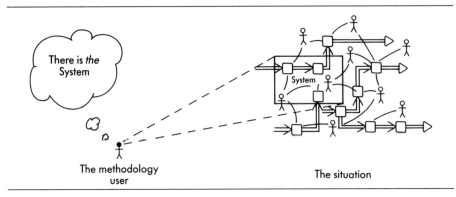

There is *the*
System

System

The methodology
user

The situation

Figure 2.6   Ontological use of the notion 'system'

framework will be discussed in Chapter 4 and their implications in Chapters 8, 9 and 10.

Fourthly, methodologies which help to structure thinking are underpinned by different philosophical assumptions of 'reality'. For instance, methodologies based on positivistic paradigms, such as structured methodologies (Gane and Sarson, 1979; De Marco, 1979; Jackson (Sutcliffe, 1988; Yourdon, 1990; Page-Jones, 1988) help to structure 'reality' by making the methodology user look for 'factual' data about a single *correct* state. Once a data flow diagram or a data model is constructed and authorized by the user as accurate, then it becomes the 'true' representation of a situation. Methodologies based on hermeneutics paradigms, such as SSM (Checkland, 1981; Checkland and Scholes, 1990), make the methodology user search for many states, any or all of which may be argued to have the same *truth* value. In SSM, many 'root' definitions and associated conceptual models are constructed, and each is considered as having the same *truth* value for debate and discussion.

In structured methodologies, the notion of 'systems' is used in an ontological sense, i.e. systems are taken as given without question. Methodology users search for *the* system and do not question its boundary. Most often, methodology users are unconsciously conditioned by powerful clients to arrive at a given system's boundary with which they agree. Figure 2.6 illustrates the ontological use of the notion of 'system'.

In SSM, the same notion is used in an epistemological sense, i.e the notion of 'systems' is used for examining and mapping situations. Methodology users employ this notion for conceptualizing many systems boundaries, any of

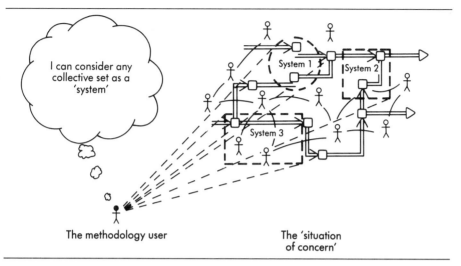

The methodology user

The 'situation of concern'

Figure 2.7   Epistemological use of the notion 'system'

which can be considered as relevant and useful for gaining an insight into the situation. This means that the methodology user has to justify why he or she considers a particular selection as a system. Figure 2.7 illustrates the epistemological use of the notion of system.

New versions of structured methodologies have now partially recognized these problems of boundary definitions (Yourdon, 1989).

Finally, there is the role of the methodology user. How individuals structure their thinking and, in that process, how they interpret the structures of the methodologies, depends very much on the way they view the world. Dilthey (1931) defines this as the *Weltanschauung* (i.e. world images) of the individual (see also Kluback and Weinbaum, 1957). Checkland (1981) defines *Weltanschauung* as:

> ... the particular non-absolute world image which we take for granted and through which we construct/attribute meaning to human activity or interpret reality ... There will never be a single (testable) account of a human activity system, only a set of possible accounts all valid according to a particular Weltanschauung.   (Checkland, 1981)

Given this most important human characteristic, the study of methodologies raises further questions.

(1) Methodologies reflect the *Weltanschauungen* of their creators. The steps of methodologies, their structure, chosen models and implied values give an indication as to how their creators perceive 'reality'. For example, ETHICS methodology reflects its creator's concerns for the welfare of the people whose lives are affected by the designs.

(2) Users of the methodology try to interpret it through their own *Weltanschauungen*. Unless the *Weltanschauung* of the methodology user is congruent with the philosophy, values, beliefs and concerns of the methodology creator as implied within the methodology, the ultimate structuring of the methodology used may be very different from the structure and steps intended by the creator. For example, Newman (1989) discusses how the notions of participation have been misinterpreted by designers with different *Weltanschauungen*.

METHODOLOGY vs FRAMEWORK

A framework also helps to structure one's thinking. However, it is a static model which provides a structure to help connect a set of models or concepts. In this context, a framework can be perceived as an integrating meta–model (a higher level of abstraction) through which concepts, models and methodologies can be structured and their interconnections or differences displayed to assist understanding or decision making.

A methodology is different from a conceptual framework in that a methodology *always* implies a time-dependent order of thinking and/or action stages.

A conceptual framework can be perceived as a form of lens through which an observer can view and understand (i.e. make sense of) a range of concepts, models, techniques and methodologies. In essence, a conceptual framework is a meta-level model through which a range of concepts, models, techniques and methodologies can be clarified, categorized, evaluated or integrated.

SUMMARY

A systems development cycle outlines the steps that may be taken when developing information processing systems. The nature and the number of steps depends very much on the perception of the author describing the development cycle. The systems development cycle includes activity sets which contribute to the development of *new* information processing systems, while the systems life cycle includes activity sets which enhance and help adapt *existing* information processing systems to changes in the environment. Systems development activity sets fall within the **information systems development function** and maintenance activity sets fall within the **information processing and usability function**. Software development is a much narrower subset of activities within information systems development. Methodologies are specific ways of performing systems development. A methodology can be defined as:

> an explicit way of structuring one's thinking and actions. Methodologies contain models and reflect particular perspectives of 'reality' based on their embedded philosophical paradigms. A methodology must show 'what' steps to take, 'how' those steps are to be performed and most importantly the reasons 'why' the methodology user must follow those steps and in the suggested order.

> A conceptual framework on the other hand is a meta-level model through which a range of concepts, models, techniques, methodologies can either be clarified, compared, categorized, evaluated and/or integrated. A methodology differs from a conceptual framework in that a methodology always implies a time-dependent order of thinking and/or action stages.

3

RATIONALE FOR THE NIMSAD FRAMEWORK

INTRODUCTION

This chapter discusses the reasons for a framework as opposed to any other mechanism for evaluating methodologies. It explores the options that are available for developing a framework and the implication of following those options, finally, it examines the rationale for the NIMSAD framework which is central to methodology evaluation and used in this book.

NIMSAD was framed as a title by our students. It became the acronym for **N**ormative **I**nformation **M**odel-based **S**ystems **A**nalysis and **D**esign. It is a *general* framework which was derived from problem solving in industry, consultancy practice and 'action research', and can be used for evaluating *any* methodology, not just information systems methodologies. The elements of the framework will be described in Chapters 4, 5, 6 and 7, and its use in the evaluation of methodologies will be demonstrated in Chapters 8, 9 and 10.

REASONS FOR A FRAMEWORK

The reasons for developing a framework (meta-model) for assisting methodology users arose because of the availability of so many methodologies, and the difficulties for problem solvers in selection and use. It is estimated that there are over 1000 brand-named methodologies in use all over the world. The arrival of Computer Aided Software/Systems Engineering (CASE) tools that support specific methodologies have added to these pressures. Things are made more difficult for methodology users because methodology creators generally do not discuss or present situations where their methodologies have been unsuccessful or have failed to bring about successful transformations. As early as the 1980s we recognized the need for a methodology-independent framework that could be used for examining the claims of methodologies.

A framework is useful for practitioners who have to select, standardize and use methodologies in practice. It is equally important for lecturers, researchers and students who wish to develop a critical awareness of methodology capabilities, and their applications and effects in practice. (Readers: please note that these are roles and not persons. For instance, consultants play all these roles in their daily lives, sometimes learning, teaching, researching or acting, although they may only emphasize their industrial action roles.)

AIMS OF THE NIMSAD FRAMEWORK

In the light of the above reasons, the aims of the NIMSAD framework are to:

(1) Serve as a way of understanding the area of problem solving, in general
(2) Help evaluate methodologies, their structure, steps, form, nature, etc.
(3) Help to draw conclusions.

These aims are addressed in this book in the following way.

The first aim will be addressed in Chapters 4, 5, 6 and 7, which will construct and discuss the reasons for each element of the framework. The elements will be constructed in an ordered way, with supporting reasons. These reasons are essential for anyone contemplating using the framework for understanding, evaluating and using methodologies.

The second aim will be addressed in Chapters 8, 9 and 10. The discussions in these chapters will be used to demonstrate the use of the framework in methodology evaluation. Chapters 8, 9 and 10 will show the use of the framework in the evaluation of three well known methodologies.

The third aim will be addressed in Chapter 11 where general lessons will be summarized.

APPROACHES TO METHODOLOGY EVALUATION

According to Bubenko (1986), there are a large number of methodologies which more or less cover the same aspects, i.e. their theory is essentially the same, but they may vary in detail, such as the shape of symbols. A comparison of methodologies has been undertaken by many people for some time. However, most have concentrated on the techniques and features of methodologies. Olle *et al.* (1982, 1983) have been responsible for organizing a number of successful conferences where different methodologies have been presented and their relative merits discussed and, unlike others, they have not attempted to rank or judge the relative strengths of methodologies. However, most methodologies selected were based on data modelling, which formed the primary interest of research at the time.

Chapin (1981) undertook a comparison of a large number of structured methodologies including graphic techniques. He used criteria such as:

- purpose
- manner of production
- ease of production
- ease of use
- ease of maintenance.

Martin and McClure (1988) also undertook a comparison of structured methodology features. They selected the following criteria:

- easy to read
- quick to draw and change
- user-friendly (easy to teach end–users)
- good stepwise refinement.

Exhaustive though these comparisons have been, the level at which they have been made are not significant enough for our purposes. Alternative criteria are needed both for evaluation and for selection of methodologies. We need to have much more useful and general criteria for evaluating *any* methodology. Therefore, it would be useful to develop a generalized framework that could be used for understanding what methodologies attempt to do and how they help to transform situations. The next section shows the rationale taken for developing the NIMSAD framework.

APPROACH TO THE DEVELOPMENT OF THE NIMSAD FRAMEWORK

Sol (1983) discusses five different but useful ways of undertaking methodology comparisons. These are essentially:

(1) Describe the 'ideal' methodology, then compare other methodologies
(2) Construct a 'generalized' measurement tool by selecting appropriate features from a number of existing methodologies
(3) Test hypothesis about the features based on the study of different methodologies
(4) Develop a common frame of reference for viewing the different methodologies (this will provide a 'meta-language' for communication)
(5) Develop a contingency framework to allow the appropriate methodology to be mapped to a particular environment.

Sol's criteria were very useful for examining the approach taken to develop the NIMSAD framework.

Developing an 'ideal' methodology was not taken as the basis for the construction of the NIMSAD framework, for the following reasons:

(1) Selecting and passing 'ideal' judgements is very subjective. Given our discussions in the previous chapters, we can conclude that there simply cannot be an ideal methodology.
(2) Even if this was possible, how are we to select an ideal methodology? If the criteria for determining an objective 'ideal' can be established, and a methodology can be found to fit this 'ideal', then there would be no further need for comparisons, or for the development of a new methodology. Besides, if the criteria were to be accepted as an objective 'ideal', then all existing methodologies would attempt to copy the 'ideal'. In fact, many methodology creators attempt to promote their methodologies as the 'ideal' methodology for all situations.
(3) Since methodologies are explicit structuring processes, there can be many possible ways of structuring our thinking and action. Therefore, we cannot hope to have one 'ideal' but will have many, depending on the situation and on what issues are to be addressed by the methodologies.

It is important to establish that a framework should not become an 'ideal', either. It should be useful insofar as to raise questions about methodologies and their practice; however the decision as to whether to adopt a methodology for use should still be a conscious and considered decision by the intended problem solver. We also feel, for that reason, that research into methodology evaluation should continue, and existing frameworks should be subjected to critical evaluation. For instance, Nielsen's (1990) criticisms of 'systems analysis' in the NIMSAD framework led to the revision of the presentation format of the problem formulation phase in order to make the conceptual aspects more understandable.

The second approach, the idea of a 'generalized' measurement tool (this should be referred to as a 'generalized framework' because of the different interpretations that could be attributed to the term 'tool'), is a useful one for constructing a framework. If such an approach is to be adopted, then there must be some *explicit* theory to assist the generalization process.

However, the idea of selecting appropriate features poses a similar set of problems to those discussed in the first approach, i.e. how are we to determine the appropriateness and which methodologies do we select for extracting the appropriate features?

The third option also presents similar problems. What features, in what methodologies, are to be selected for setting a hypothesis? Morever, the idea of 'hypothesis' testing is not useful for human activity systems of this nature. Fitzgerald (1991) discusses the problems with hypothesis testing in an organizational context:

> If we used the same people then what they learned from the
> first modelling experience could be argued to have influenced
> the second.   (Fitzgerald, 1991)

Our experience of methodology application shows that methodology success cannot be 'proved' in practice, but that only its relevance for structuring our activities can be established.

The fourth approach is consistent with that taken to develop the NIMSAD framework. In the case of the latter, generalized notions came from 'Systems' philosophy and theory (Ackoff, 1971; Churchman, 1971; Checkland, 1981), while the extraction of generalized criteria came from our industrial experience, 'action research' and consultancy practice.

The last option is prescriptive. The aim of a conceptual framework is to assist in understanding. If it goes beyond this level to suggest or recommend methodologies, then it loses its ability to generate ideas for independent thinking. Instead, the framework becomes a form of template. A contingency framework would involve finding problems (i.e. environments) to match the solutions (i.e. methodologies). Changing a conceptual framework from providing an understanding (providing clarity or generating thought) to a contingency framework (providing problem types to match given solutions) is not the intention of the NIMSAD framework. This is because we believe that the problem is not just one of selecting a methodology for a given situation, but also one of continuously changing its steps, structure and form to match the changing needs of the situation.

Sol (1983) provides a rich discussion on the problems discussed above.

We strongly believe that readers must make up their own minds about which methodology to select, adopt, adapt or even create in a given situation. The role of this book is not to provide a 'cook-book' recipe, but to sharpen the potential methodology user's thinking and decision-making processes.

The approach taken to develop the NIMSAD framework came from models such as those of Leavitt (1972), Beer (1979, 1981), Harrison (1987) and the epistemological notions of systems (Checkland, 1981; Churchman, 1968, 1971). The activity sets were abstracted to a generalized level in order to gain an understanding of the essential features of the practical situations. This abstraction helped us to move away from comparisons at the levels of technique or detail, such as whether a symbol is circular or rectangular in shape or whether diagrams are decomposable. The abstraction of activities came from reflections in industrial experience, consultancy practice and 'action research'.

THE NIMSAD RATIONALE

The NIMSAD framework has four essential elements, namely:
- the 'problem situation' (the methodology context)
- the intended problem solver (the methodology user)
- the problem-solving process (the methodology)
- the evaluation of the above three.

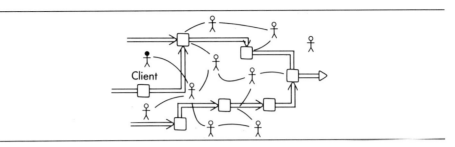

Figure 3.1   The 'problem situation'

The best way to discuss the rationale that formed the basis for NIMSAD is to start from the context in which most methodologies are applied, i.e. an organization. Organizations are the common context for many methodology practice. Figure 3.1 shows a simple illustration. (The essential features of organizations will be discussed in Chapter 4.) We would like to draw the attention of the reader to the client in Figure 3.1. Clients are those who are responsible for decisions on change. Checkland (1981) defines clients as those who are responsible for a study taking place.

Clients may be concerned with a need to understand, or to undertake changes, or to know whether a change may bring about benefits, or how they can overcome a perceived 'problem'. In essence, they are concerned with the transformation of a current situation to a new desirable situation.

The term 'real world' is used in the literature to distinguish between academia and industry or between theory and practice. This implies that the latter is complex and full of action and the former is less complex and involves only thinking. This is not a useful distinction. In order to distinguish between the two modes we would like to use the terms 'action world' and 'thinking world', both of which take place in the 'real world'. This would remove the idea that theory and thinking are the exclusive property of academics and that application and practice are the exclusive property of industrialists. Academics and industrialists both undertake thinking and action, although the environ-ments in which they operate may generally tend to emphasize one or the other. Problem solvers who do not spend sufficient time in the 'thinking world' may create the next set of problems by their actions, while those who do not spend sufficient time in the 'action world' may invent hypothetical 'problems'. We hope the adoption of these terms will help to distinguish between the modes of operations and not be based on people's working environment.

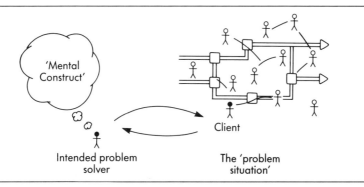

'Mental Construct'

Intended problem
solver

Client

The 'problem
situation'

Figure 3.2   Intended problem solver–client interactions

Clients' concerns for change in the 'action world' prompts them to seek the
help of an external problem solver to assist in the transformation. This gives
rise to the role of an intended problem solver (a consultant, a troubleshooter,
a systems analyst or a designer). It is also possible that the client could assume
the role of the intended problem solver. The essence here is to focus on the
role and not the person. One of the first things to note is that the client(s) and
the intended problem solver may have some initial expectations from each
other. These make them enter into a working relationship which, if successful,
will match the expectations of both groups. These relationships create considerable interactions of both a conscious and unconscious kind. The major
concern of the intended problem solver at this stage would be to find out
about the client's concerns, what the situation is and what it should be. Figure
3.2 shows the intended problem solver and client interactions.

In situations where intended problem solvers have considerable experience in
assessing and solving problems of a similar type, they may be able to
recommend solutions without much help from external mechanisms (as may
be the case with a troubleshooter). However, where the situations are of a
sufficiently new or complex nature, our intended problem solver may very
well seek the help of some external mechanism (models, concepts, techniques,
formulae, methodologies, etc.) in formulating and solving the identified
problems. The questions for the intended problem solver at this stage would
be of the kind:
  • 'What' is to be transformed?
  • 'How' am I going to:
    – identify these problems?
    – extract the essential features from the situation?
    – design solutions?

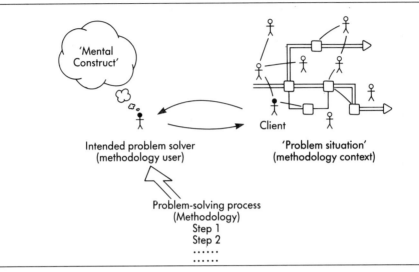

Figure 3.3   Methodology contribution

        – implement these changes?
        – and many others.

Therefore, we need to ask whether this external 'helping' mechanism should be a methodology?

We have already established in Chapter 2 that methodologies are goal-directed and that they help to structure our thinking and actions. An examination of methodology outlines (Appendix A) shows that they are concerned with the transformation of situations and offer steps for undertaking this process. This is exactly what clients seem to want, i.e. a transformation of the 'current situation' into a 'desired situation'. Therefore, we can safely establish that the external mechanism must be a methodology of some form and not simply a model, concept, formula or idea. Figure 3.3 shows the contribution of methodologies to this transformation process.

The transformation of the 'action world', of course, is far too complex for any methodology to cope with it. Methodologies do not have sufficient variety to match the diversity or complexity of the 'action world'; therefore, they alone cannot bring about 'action world' transformation. However, they can *help* in the transformation by encouraging intended problem solvers to ask relevant questions, by reducing the complexity of the elements of the situation that need to be addressed and, in general, by helping to abstract useful perceptions

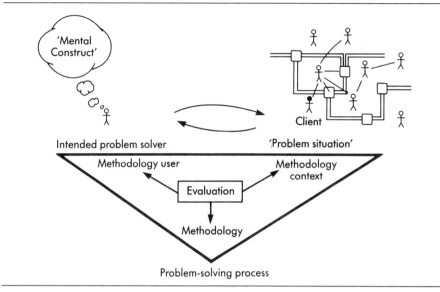

Figure 3.4   The essential elements of the NIMSAD framework

about the situation. For these reasons we have made some amendments to Figure 3.3 by renaming the intended problem solver as simply 'methodology user'. The actual transformation and, in that process, solving problems, is dependent on many issues, namely: the abilities and skills of the intended problem solver; the situation characteristics; the acceptance of and commitment to change by those in the situation; and how the intended problem solver may interact on a dynamic basis to bring about the transformation. Methodologies can only *assist* in this transformation.

If we are to examine methodology contributions, then the conceptual framework should contain an additional element, i.e. evaluation. Evaluation should be carried out on the three elements we have identified so far, namely: the 'problem situation' (methodology context); the problem-solving process (the methodology); and the intended problem solver (the methodology user). It needs to be performed at three stages: initially before intervention; then during intervention in order to help the intended problem solver to make any necessary adjustments; and after the intervention to establish whether the 'problems' have been solved and to derive important lessons. Figure 3.4 shows the four elements of the NIMSAD framework. Details of these elements will be discussed in the next four chapters.

SUMMARY

Methodology comparisons based on the features of existing methodologies is a practical but not very effective way of understanding the strengths and weaknesses of methodologies. In order to develop a useful framework, some of the current practice and 'action research' activities were abstracted using 'systems' theory. The four fundamental elements identified are the 'problem situation' (methodology context), the intended problem solver (the methodology user), the problem-solving process (the methodology), and the evaluation. The NIMSAD framework was built based on these four essential elements.

PART 2

4

NIMSAD FRAMEWORK (THE 'PROBLEM SITUATION' AND THE INTENDED PROBLEM SOLVER)

INTRODUCTION

This chapter discusses the first two elements of the NIMSAD framework highlighted in Chapter 3, namely the 'problem situation' (methodology context) and the intended problem solver (methodology user). The third element, the problem-solving process (methodology) consists of many stages and will be discussed in Chapters 5 and 6. The fourth element, the evaluation, will be considered in Chapter 7. These four elements are essential if we are to assess the problem-solving capabilities of specific methodologies.

ELEMENT 1: THE 'PROBLEM SITUATION' (METHODOLOGY CONTEXT)

In Chapter 1, we stated that organizations serve as the context for information systems. In Chapter 3 we discussed the importance of including the 'problem situation' as an element of the framework. Most problem situations are set within an organizational context, but why is the organization (the problem situation context) so important for methodologies when we are only concerned with how we develop information processing systems?

Organizations are important for methodologies for a number of reasons.

First, the effectiveness of information processing systems can be measured only to the extent of their contribution to information users in the organiza-tion. It is some of these organizational members who provide data, and it is mostly they who use the resulting information, as was illustrated in Figure 1.2. Without an understanding of what users do with the information, it is not possible either to know or to measure the effectiveness of information processing systems. This is the reason why we suggested that, as information systems specialists, we need to work with users, and hence the case for Educating and learning as a function of information systems. Some authors, such as Stage (1990) and Dahlbom and Mathiassen (1993), have recognized the need for problem solvers to become competent in the understanding of organizational activities.

Secondly, in order to develop information processing systems we need to interact with organizational members, to know what information they use now, to discover what problems they are trying to solve with this information, to understand how the information processing systems that we design are going to operate, and to know how exactly they are going to solve the identified problems and so on. Therefore, an understanding of organizations (methodology context) is very useful for comprehending usability aspects of information.

Thirdly, this is where the intended problem solvers (methodology users) are introduced to a particular section, area, unit or department of the organization in which 'problems' are perceived by clients. While this introduction may be considered explicit for an outsider (i.e. an external consultant), it is also (and should be) of considerable interest to the methodology users who are members of the organisation. In the case of the latter, it provides an opportunity for them to re-examine the situation in a much more rigorous or critical way. This examination may help them to gain different insightful perceptions of the situation about which they may have already formed unquestioned assump-tions or developed emotional attachments.

Fourthly, this is also where interpersonal relationships are formed (or renegoti-ated, in the case of methodology users working in already familiar environ-ments) with the problem perceivers, problem owners, clients, and potential beneficiaries or victims. These are members (there may be one or several) through whom, at least initially, the intended problem solvers are introduced to the situation in which problems are perceived.

One of the major weaknesses of most current information systems methodolo-

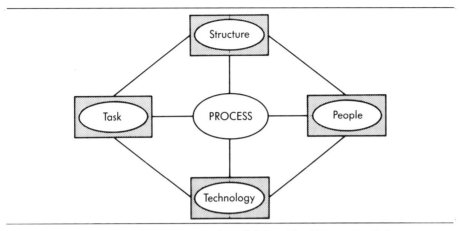

Figure 4.1   Organizational dimensional model (modified Leavitt model)

gies is that they are not concerned with what really happens in organizations. They limit their concerns to finding out the information requirements of the users, and then developing processing systems for supplying it. Once they supply this information they feel that their tasks or obligations are complete. In Chapters 8, 9 and 10, we will examine the implications with respect to specific methodologies. At this stage, however, we are concerned with the need for an intended problem solver, to acquire as much knowledge as possible about the organization as a whole and not just about those aspects that may be the concern of methodologies. For every aspect of the situation that the methodology does not offer help to comprehend or transform, the intended problem solver has to devise ways of coping with it.

One useful way of understanding organizations is to consider them as purposeful systems. Purposeful systems have to be designed or formed to achieve their purposes. This unique nature of organizations has been recognized for some time (Ackoff, 1971; Ackoff and Emery, 1972; Leavitt, 1972; Checkland, 1981). Leavitt provided a simple but very effective model for understanding organizations, and we have extended this to incorporate a 'process' element to illustrate the interactions of the four dimensions. The extended version is illustrated in Figure. 4.1.

Note that no model or modelling technique is capable of expressing the degree of complexity or dynamics of an organization. Some of these aspects are extremely difficult to capture in diagrammatic or any other form, nor can the captured aspects convey multiple meanings. For example, it is difficult to

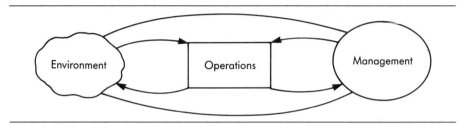

Figure 4.2   Organizational homeostasis

capture the emotional and interpersonal relationships in a model of the form as expressed in Figure 4.1 or in data flow diagrams. Nevertheless, diagrammatic expressions can be considered as an effective way of conveying or illustrating ideas, facts, opinions, concepts, etc.

Beer (1978, 1981, 1988) offers a fundamentally new model for conceptualizing organizations. According to his model, we need to understand an organization's role as a system trying to maintain a dynamically balancing (homeostatic) relationship with its environment. Figure 4.2 shows a fundamental building block used in Beer's five-stage systems model. The model proposed by Beer is very useful for understanding two fundamental concepts, i.e. stability, and change. These two concepts seem to be opposite in meaning to each other, but Beer's models help us to see their close connection which is essentially described as the notion of a 'homeostat'. In Figure 4.2, the information flows from the operations to the management are not about the operations themselves, but about how well the operations match (or not) the environment. The application of some of these concepts helped us to derive radical thinking of problem understanding in industrial activities.

Morgan (1986) uses a different approach to helping us understand organizations. He explores the subject using metaphors such as organizations as machines, organisms, rational control structures, social cultures, political systems, psychic prisons, flux and transformations, instruments of domination and so on. These insights provide an epistemological way of understanding how organizational members operate. Checkland (1981, 1988), and Checkland and Scholes (1990), on the other hand, to promote the expression of participants' 'world views' and their accounts of organizations with the use of the notion of 'human activity systems'. This concept is used as a more appropriate way of describing purposeful human activities. He states that:

> the concept of a human activity system is crucially different from the concepts of natural and designed systems. These latter, once they are manifest, 'could not be other than they are', but human activity systems can be manifest only as perceptions of human actors who are free to attribute meaning to what they perceive. There will never be a single (testable) account of a human activity system, only a set of possible accounts all valid according to a particular Weltanschauung.
>
> (Checkland, 1981)

While Beer's concept of an organization as a homeostatic system helps us to understand its relationship with the environment, Morgan's and Checkland's views help us to understand that these purposes are very much activities of human actors within an organization. There is no such thing as a taken-as-given mission statement for an organization! All mission statements and objectives are devised or changed by a powerful individual or group of individuals of the organization or parent organisation in the light of interpretations derived by them at different times and in different circumstances. While there may be publicly stated organizational mission statements, sometimes even their own creators may not act consistently with these statements.

Since the study of organizations is of interest to the fields of both science (i.e. systems engineering, operations research, control science) and social science (i.e. behavioural science, political science, management science) and covers most of purposeful human activity, this book cannot justifiably deal with the complex issues governing organizations. However, intended problem solvers need to acquire the richest possible understanding of organizations if they are to become effective problem solvers.

In the NIMSAD framework we use a general model to show some of the essential elements of a 'problem situation' and their formal and informal interconnections and relationships. Note that these elements and their interconnections are dynamic; the degree of the connections depends not only on time and space but also on the perceiver. This means that different people perceive different connections or levels of connections between the elements, whether they be human relationships, work procedures or technical interactions and so on. In order to help us focus on the information systems context, some of the significant aspects of organizations are illustrated in Figure 4.3.

Here the processes that consist of groupings of technology and people are undertaking some transformation of material to semi-finished or finished

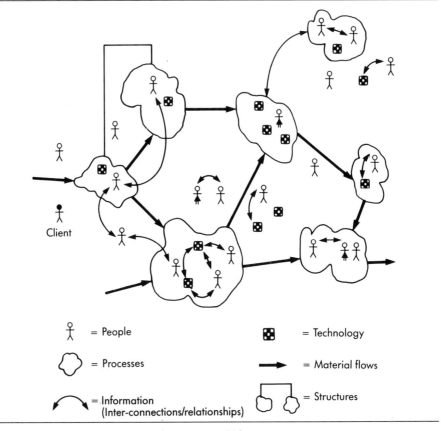

Figure 4.3 'Problem situation' ('action world')

products. In other situations, these transformations could simply be of information or services. These processes in the organization may be represented by departments, sections or units. Note also the special identification of the client(s) as an important person for particular consideration. The identification and definition of client(s) is not an easy process, particularly if the intended problem solver is to enter a complex problem situation. Checkland and Scholes (1990) discuss these difficulties.

> ... Who is in the role of client? And it is worth asking because it is wise to keep in mind (but not be dominated by) the client's reasons for causing the intervention to be made. In the role of 'would–be problem solver' (and it could be who- ever is also client) will be whoever wishes to do something about the situation in question, and the intervention had

better be defined in terms of their perceptions, knowledge
and readiness to make resources available.

(Checkland and Scholes, 1990)

Intended problem solvers need to manage their interpersonal relationships
with clients and others as an ongoing process, as being equally important as
the management of the 'problem situation' itself. These relationships have a
significant impact on the problem formulation and solutions recommendation.
However, very few methodologies alert their users to these issues.

The study of a specific organization is not a task that can ever be completed,
even by long-serving members of the organization. However, depending on
the number of years of experience and the level of observation and abstraction,
some members may be able to make very useful assessments as to the 'state' of
the organization. On the other hand, this same experience and knowledge
may hinder their ability to suggest radical solutions to the problems they face.
This is known as *conditioning*.

The richer the knowledge the intended problem solvers can obtain about the
organization, the better the position they may be in for understanding the
'real' problems of the organization. It may also help them to make better
judgements about the relevance of information to those in the 'problem
situation' and ready to raise questions.

Note that the 'problem situation' serves as the context in which methodologies
will be used. Sometimes we will use the term 'action world' to refer to the
'problem situation' because it helps us to consider the possibility that we may
not be solving any problems! For other problem solving domains this element
serves as the context.

ELEMENT 2: THE INTENDED PROBLEM SOLVER (METHODOLOGY USER)

The previous section stressed the importance of understanding the *context* of
information systems (the 'problem situation' or the 'action world'). This
section focuses the reader's attention on the role of the intended problem
solver. However powerful, useful and effective a methodology may be, the
success of effective and efficient information processing systems design and
development depends, among other things, on the personal characteristics of
the intended problem solver.

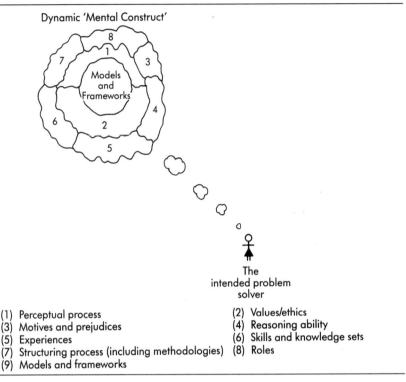

Dynamic 'Mental Construct'

The
intended problem
solver

(1) Perceptual process
(3) Motives and prejudices
(5) Experiences
(7) Structuring process (including methodologies)
(9) Models and frameworks

(2) Values/ethics
(4) Reasoning ability
(6) Skills and knowledge sets
(8) Roles

Figure 4.4   'Mental construct'

Intended problem solvers, by being human, tend to select some elements of the situation as being relevant and useful for study and transformation. Some of this selection is implicit and unconscious (i.e. based on gut feelings, hunches, assumptions), but at other times the selection is prompted by explicit concepts, models and methodologies that are employed.

What makes the intended problem solvers select some elements of the 'action world' as relevant, significant and useful while dismissing others as being irrelevant, insignificant and useless? How do they select or abstract certain features of the 'action world' for consideration? What are the implications of this selection? These are the questions that will be addressed here. (Note that these issues are of importance to *any* intended problem solver.)

We have identified, from our industrial work and consultancy practice, several characteristics that help to shape this selection process. These characteristics constitute the intended problem solver's 'mental construct'. We discuss each of these characteristics below and illustrate them in Figure 4.4.

Perceptual process is one of the most influential characteristics of the intended problem solver's 'mental construct'. It acts as a filter to information from the 'action world' and determine what information is to be significant. Each person perceives 'reality' in different ways. According to Kolasa (1969), perception is a brain-processing activity. He defines perception as:

> the interpretation of the data that are received from inputs. The system, or organism, recognises the information, assembles it, and makes comparisons with material previously stored, in the 'central information processing storage'. . . . It is a process that shapes whatever comes in from the outside; in turn, what is there is changed by what comes in.
>
> (Kolasa, 1969)

Sometimes it is not sufficient to identify and solve 'problems' in the 'action world'. We may also have to deal with the perceptions of the problem stakeholders because they may not consider our definition of 'problems' as valid or consistent with theirs. If our perceptions are incongruent, then we may have an additional problem of managing our relationships with the stakeholders. Simply aligning our perceptions with theirs will not necessarily solve the 'real' problems.

Values are beliefs that we consider to be 'good' without question. We inherit some of these from our parents, peer groups and the media, and form others from our own life experiences and observations. These values help us to pass judgement on situations or to assess the actions, behaviour, output and performance of others. For example, intended problem solvers who hold economic values as uppermost may consider a situation of interactions of a large number of employees to be highly wasteful and inefficient. This same situation may be perceived by an intended problem solver with social values to be highly effective. According to Guth and Tagiuri (1965), values provide a form of guidance system.

> Values are actually part of an individual's personality, especially if some values clearly dominate over others. . . . In effect, values comprise a guidance system used by an individual faced with a choice among alternatives.
>
> (Guth and Tagiuri, 1965)

We possess a hierarchy of values, and whichever dominates the hierarchy determines what judgements are passed on a particular situation. In most instances, the interactions and influences of others may help to shift these values; hence the chance of achieving consensus. However, when a number of stakeholders with conflicting values refuse to change their value priorities and continue to judge the same situation using their strongly held value systems, then they create for themselves an 'ill-structured' situation. Such situations are extremely difficult to resolve, and the intended problem solver may require very sensitive interpersonal relationship management skills.

Ethics, on the other hand, relates to the standards which we and others place on a person's expected behaviour. For example, most problem solvers believe that it is highly unethical to divulge sources of information. Professional institutes, stakeholders, organization culture and one's own values also dictate what ethical norms and standards must be followed in a given situation. Some consultants describe ethics as the threshold beyond which they would not be prepared to act, thus implying a minimum tolerable limit for the expected behaviour. For a comprehensive and thought provoking discussion of ethical issues see Churchman (1982) and Etzioni (1988). Also see Nissen (1987) and Banathy (1989) who call this responsible human action.

Motives are those needs that we try to satisfy in a given situation but keep private to ourselves. Most of us who enter a problem solving situation have personal motives which we try to satisfy whether we are conscious of these needs or not. Despite being old, Maslow's (1943) and Herzberg's (1959) theories provide very useful ways of understanding these personal needs. Our industrial activities demonstrate that these needs have an overwhelming influence on the designed solutions and on how methodologies are used in practice. We are not advocating the abandonment or sacrifice of one's own motives in information systems development; however, by becoming conscious of the inner needs that we may be trying to satisfy in a given problem situation, we may be in a better position to appreciate others' needs as well as our own. It may also help to reduce the tensions that may arise in our interactions with others in the 'problem situation'. See later discussions on political and intellectual thought processes.

Prejudices can be defined as persistent opinions which we form from our values, experiences or out of insecurity, i.e. fear of the unknown. They can be formed about persons, situations, objects, techniques, subjects, professions, etc. Prejudices may be useful to the extent that they help to reduce the time we spend on information gathering and for handling the complexity of the 'action world'; however, most have a harmful effect as they prevent us from searching for valid information. For example, if we are prejudiced against a particular technology because of our lack of experience then we may not explore the application potential of that technology. Similarly, many technically trained problem solvers may display prejudices against the usefulness of non-technical knowledge or skilled persons. These are simply mental blockages. If we do not open ourselves to others' viewpoints, then there is little chance of examining the validity of our prejudices. Feedback (especially of the negative kind) from others is very useful for examining our own prejudices.

Experiences are an invaluable source for developing knowledge and skills, and help to form implicit models for structuring our understanding of situations. These models dictate once again what information to seek or what action to take in a given situation. The more experience we have of a particular working environment, the easier it may be for us to assess similar situations. Experiences make us more confident and enable us to assume 'expert' status. However, while experience-based models may help to reduce time, provide a range of easy and 'obvious' solutions and help to develop confidence, the same models may prevent us from exploring new ideas or becoming effective listeners to others' ideas.

Reasoning ability is our ability to abstract the essential aspects from any situation and to understand the concepts underlying our thought processes, i.e. examine what makes us reason in a particular way. For some, these qualities come naturally (without any training or education), while others may have to work at developing their ability to think in this way through education, training and critical self-reflection. Contrary to popular belief, reasoning ability is not something that can be measured by any form of IQ test—there are many people without any formal education who demonstrate unique insights into 'problem situations'. They can provide solutions, draw analogies from their past experiences in 'current' situations and articulate their reasons, yet untrained they may fail the IQ tests and be condemned forever. We believe that every human being possesses reasoning abilities and that, given the right opportunities, everyone is capable of exercising these skills. Our interest in problem solving is to develop our abilities not only to think in many different ways, but also to explain clearly those thought processes (i.e. explain the rationale for arriving at a conclusion). Checkland (1981) illustrates how 'systems thinking' can be used in this process of reasoning.

If we consider ourselves as driven by intellectual thought processes, have belief in our own reasoning processes, and have confidence in why and how we arrive at our conclusions, then we do not need to resort to political action (manipulation of other human beings for satisfying our own needs). Contrary to popular belief, the secret manipulation of other human beings is not a sign of our problem solving ability, but visible evidence of our sense of insecurity and our lack of confidence in our own ability to pursue desirable actions. In other words, we sacrifice our intellectual reasoning in the face of pragmatic difficulties. In the context of Checkland's solution categories of desirability and feasibility, the latter overrides the former because the latter helps us to achieve our needs and motives. We will examine how political and intellectual thoughts compete to dominate our reasoning process later in this chapter.

Knowledge and skills are acquired from education, training and experience. These are essential if we are to undertake any transformation of a situation. For example, in Chapter 1 we discussed the importance of information systems specialists' technical skills in order to extend their range of design options. Similarly, interpersonal knowledge and skills enable us to handle our relationships with our clients and other organizational members in an effective way. (For example, the author is aware that he has a very good knowledge and understanding of interpersonal relationship issues, i.e. what action would be desirable or undesirable in order to maintain good interpersonal relation-ships. However, he finds it difficult to transform this knowledge into action. Many of the questions that are raised later in this book about methodologies demonstrate the author's difficulties of balancing interpersonal relationship and political skills, but this is considered a worthy sacrifice to make if it enables methodology users to become conscious to the implications of using methodologies and for increasing their sense of responsibility towards the potential victims or beneficiaries of their actions.)

As intended problem solvers, we must become very conscious of the knowledge sets and skills that are required to practise a methodology, and the methodology creators must state what knowledge sets and skills we should possess if we are to become effective users. In fact, every methodology should come with a 'health warning'.

Structuring processes are unique to each individual. We have already discussed how methodologies may be used for explicitly structuring our thinking and action, and it is these explicit structuring processes that we shall examine in this and the following chapters. Whether we have access to methodologies or not, we continue to structure our thinking and action, learning to structure our thinking in many different ways helps us to gain new insights about the same situation. In the context of methodologies this may happen only if we become aware of what they attempt to do, of what actions have been undertaken in the situation, of what results have been yielded and if we examine who has benefited or suffered in the process. The discussions in this book are about the *critical examination* of methodologies and assessment of how they help to structure our thinking and actions.

Roles can be defined as the explicit behavioural characteristic sets that can be attributed to someone responsible for performing a set of tasks. By virtue of holding a position of responsibility and authority, we assume a set of role characteristics. For example, we automatically assume that measurement of performance is a role attribute of a manager, an auditor or an accountant. Our role as an intended problem solver may be to act as an advisor, an analyst, a consultant, a designer, an implementor or a facilitator. Our role expectations may have to match the expectations others may have of that role. Differences between the two can lead to role conflicts, while the suppression of our natural behaviour and personality in order to conform to others' expectations of our roles may lead to considerable personal stress. Note that when we engage in 'organizational politics' we do not suffer from these stresses, as we see the organization as a 'game board' or a 'battleground' in which to demonstrate our fighting and winning abilities. We may be quite happy to adopt *any* role behaviour and value set as long as it helps to maximize our personal needs and motives. For those who hold or attach themselves to a particular set of ethical and moral values, however, the different role expecta-tions based on politics can create very considerable stress. The reason for raising these issues here is to make the intended problem solvers examine their own circumstances and those of others who may become the victims or beneficiaries as a result of their actions. The intended–problem solvers must examine what kind of role they are expected to perform or adopt in a given situation and take full responsibility for their role clarification and actions. It is the duty of methodology creators to explain the role expectations implied by their methodologies. The concern of this book is to raise the consciousness of the intended problem solver to these dimensions.

Models and frameworks have already been discussed in the previous chapters. Frameworks are static structures. These structures can be perceived as meta-models which show the connections of a set of models. For instance, Leavitt's model (1972) can be considered as a framework as it helps to connect some essential elements of an organization for consideration. Some models are derived from experience (e.g. models that direct our walking), others are acquired through conscious training (e.g. driving), and yet others by conscious effort of engaging in debates, discussions and reflections. Modelling helps to develop one's reasoning abilities.

THE 'MENTAL CONSTRUCT'

The above elements are those which we have discovered from our 'action research', industrial and consultancy practice as being relevant for creating a 'mental construct'. As intended problem solvers we should be free to change these or incorporate new elements in order to understand how our own 'mental constructs' are formed, which elements have strong influences on our actions and so on. In other words, we need to identify what characteristics influence our own sense-making and decision-making activities.

The identified elements interact in a dynamic way to form the 'mental construct', to help us make sense of the situations, to manage our relationships with others, to take action and to identify and solve problems. The 'mental construct' illustrated in Figure 4.4 is dynamic. This means that it can be influenced by external inputs and critical self-reflection. It can also help to derive new meaning from the same situations.

Human reasoning which results from the interactions of the elements of the 'mental construct' can be perceived as being dominated by political and intellectual thought processes.

Political thought processes are those which direct our minds to reach favour-able conclusions, i.e. those which help to extend our power and control over others, their behaviour and actions. Through these processes we are able to exploit the weaknesses in others and to make them support our viewpoints and conclusions that favour our position. Political thought processes help us to offer incentives/disincentives, influence others and change their behaviour in order to maximize our personal benefits. These intentions have to be hidden if others are to help us achieve our personal needs. The role of political thought processes is to enable us to manipulate others without divulging our hidden agendas or motives. Dominated by these thought processes, we engage in sophisticated game-playing with others. However, unlike the fairly innocent games we normally play, the stakes here can be very high, and the accrual of power which enables us to extend our control may come only at the expense of others, their careers and sometimes their organizational survival. Ironically, most often this drive for power takes place without our even being aware of it. The discussion of the issues in this book aims to alert methodology users as to the influence these processes may have on their decisions and to show how they can nullify the beneficial effects of using methodologies.

Intellectual thought processes, on the other hand, are directed at our reasoning processes themselves, and not at our conclusions. Their focus is to alert us to the possible implications of our decisions and their outcome. They help us to arrive at conclusions only after considerable efforts at reasoning; these conclusions may or may not afford us personal advantages or help to maximize our gains. They do nevertheless demand considerable investment of our conscious time and energy. Instead of manipulation, intellectual thought processes help us to persuade others by discussion, debate and reason. In turn, we are also persuaded by the reasoning processes expressed by others. Intellectual thought processes enable us to accept different conclusions provided the reasoning process of arriving at those conclusions can stand up to critical examination and scrutiny.

While political thought processes are different from intellectual thought processes, they nevertheless demonstrate the presence of intelligence. Any thought process that helps us to understand and, on the basis of that understanding, makes us manipulate others, to make them behave in ways favourable towards us (without physical threats or punishments), is an extremely intelligent activity.

While the satisfaction we derive from our intellectual thought processes comes from the *challenges* to our reasoning process from others, the satisfaction we derive from political thought processes rests with the *minimization* of challenges from others. Intellectual thought processes help us to admit to failures, while political thought processes help us to find others to blame for our failures. The former helps us to consider failure as a *challenge* to discover the causes of failure, while the latter requires us to consider failure as an admittance of a *weakness* to be avoided. Intellectual thought processes help us to find many different ways of rationalizing and arriving at conclusions, while political thought processes help us to find favourable conclusions first and then to find rationalizations to justify and support those conclusions.

There is, of course, *a very serious penalty* for allowing political thoughts to dominate our reasoning for any length of time. Without intellectual thoughts (externally or internally induced) to challenge the politically dominated reasoning processes, we have no option other than to take action to protect our intellectually weak reasoning process from challenges by others. Any individual who raises intellectual questions is considered by our politically driven reasoning process to be a threat to our credibility, position or ambitions. The desire to acquire power through organizational hierarchy—and to exercise that power—is not only our way of extending control over others, but also a way of protecting our reasoning processes from the intellectual questions of others. For this reason we resort to the removal, exclusion or avoidance of intellectually challenging individuals from our decision-making environments. The formation of committees with members who conform to the same value systems, promoting or surrounding ourselves with reinforcing individuals, are some of the actions we take to provide protection for our intellectually starved reasoning processes. This is a 'closed loop' situation. Denied of intellectual challenges, we become incapable of generating new ideas, of innovating or of grasping the fundamental issues in problem-solving situations. We then have to rely on others' ideas in order to maintain status and credibility. But if we surround ourselves with other politically reasoning individuals then we have to reach further and further away to obtain new ideas. This is the reason why we become incapable of innovation. In contrast, the intellectually dominated reasoning processes enable us to seek out individuals with ideas and thought processes which are radically different from our own. It is the challenges to existing ideas with different intellectual reasoning that help us to develop new ideas, to become innovative, and to understand the fundamental causes of failure.

People, whose reasoning processes are dominated by both intellectual and political thought processes, inevitably suffer considerable internal value conflicts. These conflicts arise because of a drive to pursue action based on intellectual reasoning while at the same time seeking to pursue action based on political reasoning. We are trapped in a value conflict which inevitably forces us into politically expedient action.

If this is so, how can we break away from this cycle?

One way is to adapt the rules of the organizational political systems, to become a member of the tribe and behave as the natives do, then, once accepted, gradually introduce more intellectually challenging ideas. The danger with this strategy is that once absorbed we begin to acquire power and soon it becomes very difficult to relinquish that power. We then fail to upset the network of political friendships that we have nurtured, to break the links that we have so painfully forged and to undermine the very system itself. In other words, we forget why we entered the network in the first place.

Another way is to ignore the rules of the political systems, and to use the opportunity to disturb the existing networks that prevent discussion of fundamental problem issues, to expose the weaknesses (poverty) of existing reasoning processes and to create a climate of open exchange of ideas. The danger with this situation is that we may not gain entry or that change may come only at the expense of personal advancement. Pettigrew (1984) defines these individuals as 'sacrificial change agents', who have to sacrifice their career development in order to bring about change. While they may be in the best position to offer solutions to the problems, this strategy may never give them that opportunity because of others' action. A failure to exercise power is seen by others as a weakness to be exploited for the extension of their control.

Both thought processes require intelligence. To be an effective practitioner we may need to be competent in both. However, the balancing between the two creates ethical and moral tensions. My role as an academic is to alert my students and colleagues to the intellectual issues but some of my colleagues feel that I am being unnecessarily difficult (they feel uncomfortable) by my discussions of these issues. Others think that I am being brave. I am neither. I suffer from considerable internal conflicts that are generated when forced to decide between intellectual and political thoughts-driven reasoning.

SUMMARY

In any problem-solving context there exist four essential elements, namely: the problem situation, the problem solver, the problem-solving process, and the evaluation. This chapter discussed two of the essential elements of the NIMSAD framework, namely the 'problem situation' in which information processing systems are designed, implemented and have to perform; and the intended problem solvers and their 'mental constructs' which influence their thinking processes and actions. We examined particularly the dilemmas we face when our reasoning processes are affected by intellectual and political thought processes.

5

NIMSAD FRAMEWORK (THE PROBLEM-SOLVING PROCESS)

INTRODUCTION

This chapter and Chapter 6 are concerned with the third element of the framework, namely the problem-solving process. This has three essential phases: problem formulation; solution design; and design implementation. Just as with the first two elements of the framework (discussed in Chapter 4), the problem-solving process phases discussed in this and the next chapter were also abstracted from industrial practice and consultancy using 'systemic' concepts.

If a methodology is to be considered as a *way* of problem solving, then it needs to show that it can help to perform the three essential phases mentioned above. These three phases have been expanded to form eight detailed stages which are applicable to *any* problem-solving process.

ELEMENT 3: THE PROBLEM-SOLVING PROCESS

PHASE 1: PROBLEM FORMULATION

(1) Stage 1: understanding of the 'situation of concern'
(2) Stage 2: peforming the diagnosis
(3) Stage 3: defining the prognosis outline
(4) Stage 4: defining problems
(5) Stage 5: deriving notional systems

SOLUTION DESIGN
(6) Stage 6: performing conceptual/logical design
(7) Stage 7: performing physical design

DESIGN IMPLEMENTATION
(8) Stage 8: implementing the designs

This chapter discusses the problem formulation phase and Chapter 6 discusses the solution design and design implementation phases. Chapter 7 discusses the last element—the evaluation. The four elements will then be applied to the study of three specific methodologies in Chapters 8, 9 and 10.

STAGE 1: UNDERSTANDING OF THE 'SITUATION OF CONCERN'

Problem solving of the organizational kind is a complex activity. Before any problem formulation can take place, we need to have a good grasp of the situation in which various people perceive 'problems'. Without this understanding, we are not in a position to formulate problems or suggest solutions. (At a political level, of course, this lack of understanding does not prevent problem solvers from suggesting solutions!) However, for rational problem solving, we need to have a 'good' understanding of the situation; hence its inclusion as a stage within the problem formulation phase.

We, who either as external or internal intended problem solvers enter a given 'problem situation', carry with us our unique 'mental constructs', discussed in Chapter 4. Figure 5.1 shows this coming together. This 'mental construct' can have several effects on our appreciation of the 'problem situation'.

First, it helps us to derive a boundary on the situation, thereby identifying possible 'areas of interest'—see Figure 5.2. Checkland (1981) has argued against the use of 'systems' notions at this stage in order to obtain the fullest range of information possible. However, by the cautious use of these notions, we have been able to form deep insights into the understanding of problem perceptions. Checkland's arguments, we believe, are against the use of 'systems' in an ontological sense of the term, i.e. locating systems in the world (see Figure 2.6). We have used it in an epistemological sense of the term, as was discussed in Chapter 2 (see Figure 2.7). The latter notion has also been successfully used by Beer (1988) and Espejo and Watt (1988) to structure their understanding of organizational behaviour. We believe that if we, as the

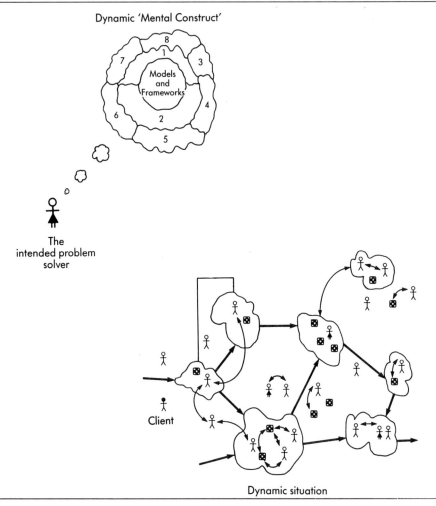

Dynamic 'Mental Construct'

The
intended problem
solver

Client

Dynamic situation

Figure 5.1   The intended problem solver and the 'problem situation'

intended problem solvers, do not subject our 'mental constructs' to self-critical examination, then we may indeed end up accepting the boundaries as defined by our clients. We may also construct implicit boundaries, thus not becoming conscious to where and why we have drawn those boundaries. Since the boundary determines the focus of the investigation and establishes the 'situation of concern', we need to examine whether we have identified relevant elements (persons, materials, activities, flows) in the situation for study. It is this conscious level of structuring support that we need from methodologies. Unless we are prepared to operate at this level of consciousness (ability to examine why and how we select relevant elements), we may not

PROBLEM FORMULATION PHASE

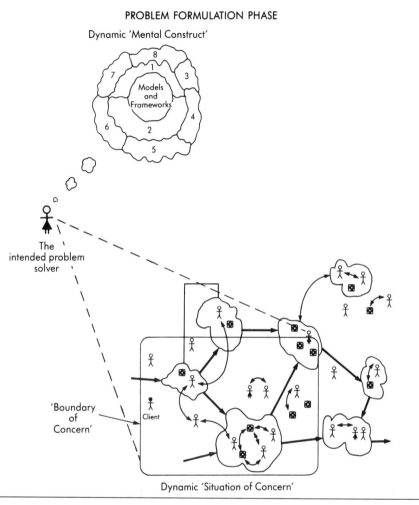

Figure 5.2   Boundary construction

recognize the effects of a chosen methodology on our boundary construction. Figure 5.2 shows how the 'mental construct' of an intended problem solver helps to build a boundary around some elements of the situation for exploration and subsequent design.

Secondly, the 'mental construct' helps to determine 'what' information to collect, as well as providing models and frameworks for determining the nature of the information to be collected. In industrial work, the use of cybernetic models of Beer (1981) and Koontz and Bradspies (1969) within the 'mental construct' helped to understand many decision-related issues such as what information to collect, and which personnel were likely to respond. The models also helped to extend the boundary of the project that was originally established by the managers. The richer the models and frameworks of the 'mental constructs', the more rigorous the examination of the situation and the more open we become to the *artificial* nature of the boundary construction around the 'situation of concern'.

Thirdly, it helps us to select the most appropriate methods of investigation. General techniques of investigation are published widely and are discussed in many information systems texts. Most texts discuss the choice of investigation methods exclusively from a practical perspective, e.g. the questionnaire method to be employed for collecting information from a geographically widespread population or for obtaining general information from a large group of people. In addition, these texts provide checklists and techniques on how to prepare the investigation activities. However, the use of sophisticated models such as Beer (1981) help to determine not only the nature of the information but also who is in the best position to respond.

We must, therefore, evaluate the steps of any methodology, our own 'mental constructs', and the dynamic interactions we have with the client(s) in the situation, as these factors collectively have a strong influence on our boundary construction.

So why should we be concerned with boundary construction in problem solving?

We should be concerned because it excludes so many elements from being considered by the subsequent steps in the problem-solving process. Our attention from this stage onwards is going to be focused on the elements within the 'boundary of concern'—see Figure 5.2. If the causes of the identified 'problems' lie with the elements *outside* the boundary, then no matter how well the *content* of the boundary is redesigned or transformed, the 'problems' will not be solved. This is why we called this selection the 'situation of concern' (D'Arcy and Jayaratna, 1985) and recommended that we examine and evaluate our own 'mental constructs' at a conscious level of concern and on a continuing basis. This reflection-in-action characteristic of the NIMSAD framework has been compared to Schon's (1983) conceptual framing of content by Nielsen (1990), who concluded that the NIMSAD framework is the only approach to methodology evaluation that has provided this feature.

STAGE 2: PERFORMING THE DIAGNOSIS (WHERE ARE WE NOW?)

What do we do with the information that we gather from the situation?

In most problem solving, we store this information in our brains, updating (or not) on a continuing basis depending on the sensitivity and the nature of our unique 'mental construct' to the 'problem situation'. However, where we have to deal with a large number of elements, or manage dynamic interactions or complex relationships, we need some external way of expressing our understanding.

'Diagnosis' is the explicit projection or expression of the understanding we gain from our investigation. Usually, this is a static expression (i.e. like a frozen image, a snapshot) of the 'situation of concern'. The form of expression depends very much on the techniques and tools at our disposal, our familiarity with the 'situation of concern', and our ability to abstract essential elements from it. However, we should note that this expression is very much a function of the interactions of two dynamic processes (i.e. the 'situation of concern' and our 'mental constructs') with respect to a particular instance of time. Figure 5.3 shows the result of the understanding expressed as the diagnosis. However, we cannot expect an expression like this to represent or reveal the true nature, complexity or behaviour of the elements in the 'situation of concern'.

In this sense, the diagnosis is more than just a mere description; it reveals that we as intended problem solvers understand the *reasons* for the state of the 'situation of concern', e.g. why such a state exists. As the diagnosis forms the basis for all subsequent problem-solving stages, we must understand that the more dynamic the nature of the situation, the more out-of-date the relevance of the diagnosis is likely to be for these subsequent stages i.e the diagnosis is no longer representative of the 'situation of concern'. Methodology users should also examine the relevance and the nature of the techniques/tools provided by methodologies for the expression of their understanding, e.g. data flow diagrams, 'rich' pictures, etc. Note that no model or technique is able to capture the complexity of a situation; however, they can help, to the extent of alerting our 'mental constructs' to the features/elements in the

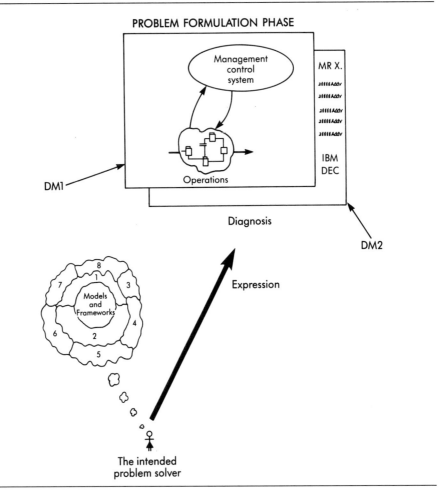

PROBLEM FORMULATION PHASE

Figure 5.3   The diagnosis

situation, or hinder, to the extent of closing our minds to those features that are not addressed by the models. For example, the use of data flow diagrams can help to focus attention on formal data, but they can also close our minds to informal and non–regular communications of the situation.

The diagnosis serves three *additional* needs.

(1) The explicit expression of our understanding of the situation helps us to identify our gaps of knowledge or misunderstandings; hence the process

is, in itself, a useful exercise for learning about a situation and for improving our ability to model a situation effectively.

(2) The expression helps us to communicate particularly with the clients and problem owners, to derive agreed understandings, to clarify differences of perceptions or indeed, as in the case of 'Soft' Systems Methodology, to explore the different 'world images' of the participants. In this context, Vickers (1983) stated that:

> Virtually all professionals are systems analysts in this sense. The Lawyer, questioning his client, needs to construct in his mind both a perception of the client's situation adequate at least for the purpose for which he is being consulted and also a perception of the way that situation appears to the client. Both activities are forms of systems analysis.   (Vickers, 1983)

(3) The expression serves as the basis for undertaking further activities in problem solving.

The expression can be in any form as long as it serves the four purposes outlined above. Of course, how rich an expression is will depend on the models used in the abstraction and the techniques used for the expression.

Two main *levels* of expression have been identified for the purpose of problem solving. The first of these is what we define as a conceptual/logical expression. We have used Beer's (1981, 1988) model in a number of 'industrial work' projects to understand and express the nature of situations. We also used this kind of model for understanding the conceptual notions underpinning 'exception reporting' in management accounting (Jayaratna and Thomson, 1993). In 'Soft' Systems Methodology, this expression is known as a 'rich' picture. Variance grids in ETHICS (Mumford, 1981), data flow diagrams (Gane and Sarson, 1979), actigram/datagram (Ross, 1977), and bubble charts (De Marco, 1979; Page-Jones, 1988) are examples of other forms of logical expressions.

The second level, as illustrated in Figure 5.3, is the expression of physical characteristics of the 'situation of concern'. These may cover the actual products, specific individuals, documents, computers and so on. In the case of the latter, they could also include speeds, capacities, performance, volume, statistics, costs, etc.

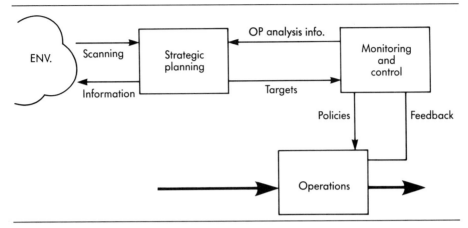

Figure 5.4   Pharmaceutical general model

'Soft' Systems Methodology does not make a distinction between these two forms. Its use of 'rich pictures' is conceptual/logical (i.e. in essence they illustrate roles, functions, 'world views', tasks) and physical (i.e. they show individuals, documents, buildings)—see Appendix C.

Structured methodologies, such as those of De Marco (1979) and SSADM (Downs *et al.*, 1988; Ashworth and Goodland, 1990) maintain the distinctions of logical and physical models, while Gane and Sarson (1979) do not make this distinction. These are techniques for expressing data. What is needed is some form of conceptual model to help derive useful information. For example, the application of a feedback conceptual model based on Davis and Olson (1985), Schoderbek *et al.* (1990) and Beer (1979) in an 'industrial project' helped us to derive a much clearer understanding of the situation—see Figure 5.4 for a generalized model.

The model contained both conceptual/logical and physical aspects of the 'situation of concern'. The separation of conceptual/logical and physical models is useful for the subsequent mapping activity in problem formulation discussed later in this chapter and implementation in Chapter 6.

We call the conceptual/logical expression Diagnosis Model 1 (DM1—see Figure 5.3). This retains both the general and the situation-specific information to make it meaningful, thus making logical sense to the participants. The details could include information flows, people's tasks, roles, functions and so on.

We call the physical expression Diagnosis Model 2 (DM2). This contains physical aspects such as who performs these tasks and what technology or products are used. These can be expressed in descriptive or tabular form. The general guideline for separating the two forms is to consider DM1 as describing the '*what*' issues (i.e. what activities, functions, roles, decisions, etc. are taking place in the 'situation of concern') and DM2 as describing '*who*' or '*how*' issues (i.e. how those activities, functions, decisions, etc. are supported or carried out). The separation of the two forms may be possible in many situations, but this is by no means an easy task. However, it is certainly very useful for later stages of the problem–solving process.

These two expressions collectively help to explain the 'current state' of the 'situation of concern'. (This is the reason why we clarified the notion of *state* in Chapter 2.) Note that these expressions stored within the mind may change incrementally (like a film strip), in line with the changes perceived in the situation without our having to make an effort to change or notice the changes taking place. For example, consider our views of the workplace, home or other familiar situations. Changes are hardly noticeable unless they are fundamental.

Changes to external expressions such as data flow diagrams, on the other hand, require conscious effort. This is the reason why software tools that help to modify expressions are so popular. It is difficult to update constantly changing features, and we believe it is for this reason that methodologies help to capture and express permanent and consistent features of the situation (for example, structured methodologies help their users to capture and express formal data or processes, e.g. invoice processing activities). In political, economic and social methodologies, this stage is concerned with expressing the *states* of the political, economic or social situation. In Figure 5.3 we indicate this perceived 'current state' as the *outline shape* of the diagram. It is important to note that the content within the boundary provides a *description* of the situation, while the outline shape of the diagram expresses an impression of the *state* of that situation. Together they form the diagnosis.

In constructing DM1 and DM2, the approach taken by structured methodologies is to express physical data flows and then to abstract the logical aspects. However, this approach does not provide many opportunities for fundamental re-examination of the 'situation of concern'. Our experiences show the reverse move from conceptual/logical to physical to be more insightful (i.e. providing fundamental new thinking), but difficult. The difficulties arise because of the nature of conceptual models. Some methodologies help to overcome these difficulties by offering simplistic rules, e.g. the use of the magic formula 7 ± 2 (Miller, 1956) to limit the number of data flows to and from any process symbol.

We must not forget that these expressions (diagrams, graphs, tables) are the output of our 'mental constructs' and that they may not really represent the 'action world'. Nor can we expect them to convey the full complexity of the 'action world'. The richness of the expressions depends on our skills and on the models and techniques employed.

STAGE 3: DEFINING THE PROGNOSIS OUTLINE (WHERE DO WE WANT TO BE AND WHY?)

The two previous stages were centred around the role of the intended problem solvers, with a view to helping them obtain the deepest possible understanding of the 'situation of concern'. While the primary focus of the diagnosis is to assist the intended problem solver, it also helps to clarify our understanding and communications with the organizational members.

However, now that an understanding has been gained and some aspects of that understanding have been expressed in a very clear, easily understood form, we could ask the question, *So what?*

The answer to this question is that the client or the problem owners would like this *state* (the outline shape as illustrated in Figure 5.3) to be changed. This leads us to the definition of 'prognosis'.

'Prognosis' is the expression of a desired situation. This stage is concerned with defining a *desired state* for the current 'situation of concern'. The 'desired state' is illustrated in Figure 5.5 by the outline shape. The shape is deliberately drawn differently from that of the diagnosis: this is to indicate that there is indeed a difference between the prognosis outline (desired state) and the diagnosis outline (current state). (Note that these are *perceived* states even though we will continue to use the terms 'current state' and 'desired state'.)

An important point for discussion is that there is a difference between the two 'states' (i.e. a problem). At a conceptual level, this allows us to define *any* problem as:

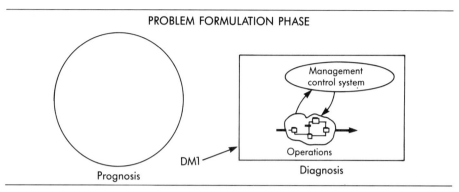

PROBLEM FORMULATION PHASE

Prognosis

DM1

Management control system

Operations

Diagnosis

Figure 5.5   The prognosis outline

> the difference between perceived 'reality' and perceived 'expectation' for that 'reality', together with a desire to make the perceived 'expectation' become 'reality'.   (Jayaratna, 1991a)

Using this definition, we can understand problems of *any* human activity.

If the two states (illustrated by the outline shapes in Figure 5.5) were to be the same, then there would be no problem, and the services of an intended problem solver would not be required. One of the most serious weaknesses of many methodologies is that they force their users to accept, particularly in an intellectual sense, the prognosis outline (desired state) of the client without critical examination or question. In fact, most methodologies do not even alert their users to the 'desired states': they remain private to the clients and problem owners. Furthermore, our personal needs and motives act as a strong influential reason for accepting or not questioning the 'desired states' of the clients.

Naturally, it is assumed that the clients and problem owners have a more thorough knowledge of the 'action world' and have good reasons for their expectations. Equally, if equipped with relevant models and skills, we as intended problem solvers should examine the validity of their expectations— the clients and problem owners may or may not have formulated their expectations in a rigorous way. In many cases this is the reason why clients change their requirements during systems development.

Clearly, the questioning of expectations is rare in many problem-solving domains. However, failure to question the validity of the 'desired states' may lead to many irrelevant solutions, expensive investments and implementations, and significant maintenance. Once a 'desired state' is accepted without question, whether for political, anxiety or any other pragmatic reason, then there is very little opportunity to discover the 'real' problem issues. In some industrial projects we have helped the clients to re-examine their 'desired states' and alter them in the light of discussions.

At this stage we can only define the outline shape of, and the rationale for, the prognosis (without content). Once this outline shape is established, we can consider at latter stages what content will support a shape of that nature. However, at this stage we have sufficient knowledge (we assume) of the content that supports the outline shape of the diagnosis.

Let us explain this process using some examples. In Figure 5.5, let us assume the outline shape of the diagnosis to be an organization's (current state) level of profitability or market share or political status or culture, and the prognosis outline (desired state) to be the client's desire to see an increased level of profitability or increased market share or different political status or different corporate culture and so on. The diagnosis includes *content*, affording us some understanding of what functions, roles, product types, market activities etc. contribute to the 'current state' of profitability, market share, etc., and the model DM2 can show specific products, services, persons, etc. performing these functions. However, we do not know at this stage what sets of activities, actions, functions, roles, etc. are necessary to bring about the 'desired state'. Therefore, at this stage the prognosis model can show only an outline. The focus here is not to create the *content* of the prognosis model (that is the role of design), but to understand *why* we need a shape of this nature, e.g. increased market share. These are very legitimate questions to ask, which may very well lead to the termination of the project or give rise to interpersonal conflicts with the client. No one, least of all the client, wishes to be questioned about the *rationale* for his or her expectations, but it is this questioning which helps us to ensure the relevance of subsequent design efforts to the 'desired state'. We can thus appreciate why intended problem solvers abandon their intellectual reasoning and embrace political reasoning when faced with these types of situations.

STAGE 4: DEFINING 'PROBLEMS'

Now that we know (hopefully) the reasons for the 'desired state', our concern now turns to what it is that is preventing its achievement. In other words, this is the stage of a problem-solving process where we attempt to understand

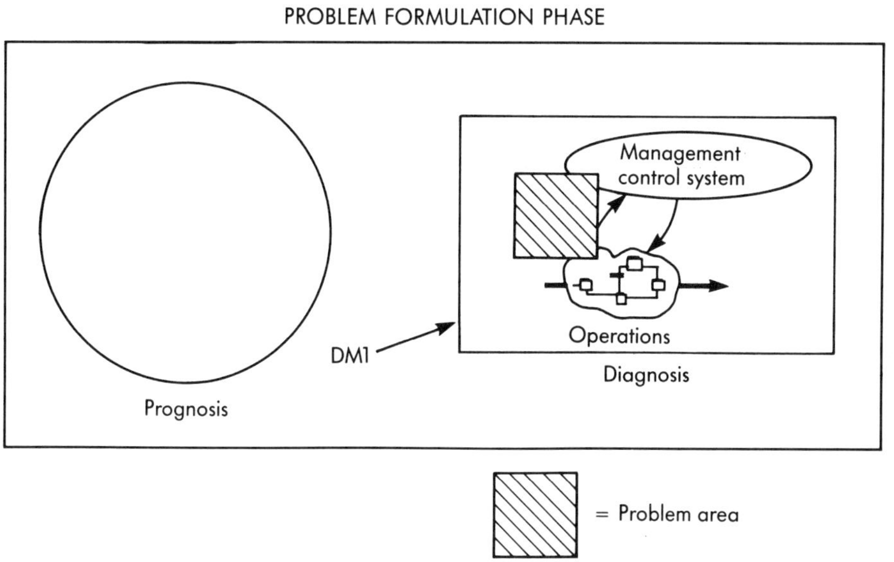

PROBLEM FORMULATION PHASE

Figure 5.6   Problem definition

what is preventing the diagnosis outline (current state) from changing to the prognosis outline (desired state). This process can be described as the conceptual mapping of the two states. (Note that these are perceived states.) Originally termed as inter-gap analysis (Jayaratna, 1979), the task at this stage is to identify and critically examine:

- the *absence* of elements
  - and/or
- the *organization* (current arrangement) of the elements

in the diagnosis model that prevent the 'current state' from changing to the 'desired state'.

In Figure 5.6 we show the result of this mapping process leading to the identification of a 'problem area'. If we wish, we can write these as problem statements.

In information systems domains these statements cover not only gaps or failures of information, but also the associated roles, responsibilities, processes, functions, structures, cultures and relationships. In other domains, depending on the nature of the methodologies, the focus may well be on the gaps and failures of social group functioning, production problems, poor quality

PROBLEM FORMULATION PHASE

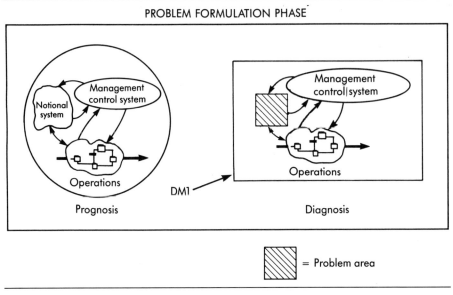

= Problem area

Figure 5.7   Deriving the notional system (s)

products, etc. In order to generate these statements, intended problem solvers need to ask questions of the type *what* and *why*, and not of the type *how* and *whom*.

STAGE 5: DERIVING NOTIONAL SYSTEMS

The mapping, as an activity, is not complete until it also identifies and defines relevant notional system(s). Notional systems are those systems which need to be developed if the client organization is to overcome the previously defined 'problems', thereby helping to transform the 'current state' to the 'desired state'. In other words, these are 'systems' that can be formulated from our 'mental constructs' as being relevant, and if designed, built and become operational, are believed to eliminate the identified 'problems'. The description of notional systems features and their expected behaviour is called the 'systems specification' or the 'requirement specification' document.

Figure 5.7 shows an illustration of a notional system relevant for overcoming the identified 'problems' and thereby expecting to bring about change from the 'current state' to the 'desired state'. Since the areas outside the problem areas are not considered to be problematical, these models can be transferred from the diagnosis to the prognosis model. However, their links to the 'notional systems' must also be considered.

Situations in which the clients/problem owners are unable to express clear and precise expectations (i.e. in Figure 5.5 there is no shape to the prognosis model) are known as 'ill-structured' situations. They are so called as there is no possibility of mapping the outline shape of the prognosis on the diagnosis. Checkland (1981) describes these situations as:

> situations in which the naming of desirable ends is itself problematical. (Checkland, 1981)

Most methodologies guide their users to accept the client's notional systems at the initial entry stage of the project and let these condition their enquiry and boundary construction. This can have serious and undesirable consequences. If the problems, particularly their contributory factors, remain outside the 'situation of concern' (see Figure 5.2), then no matter what improvements are introduced, the problems will continue to persist.

In most instances, our acceptance of a prognosis outline (a desired state) without critical intellectual examination is brought about because of the weaknesses of the methodologies employed, political reasoning-dominated 'mental construct' (e.g. our self-interest, skills, motives, models), and the state of our interpersonal relationships with clients and problem owners. In effect, we are unable or unwilling to question the rationale of the client.

Discussions here do not intend in any way to suggest that the client's concerns or requirements are to be ignored. Indeed, Vickers (1983) discusses the need for particular attention to be paid to this aspect of problem solving:

> the concerned mind devises possible responses and evaluates them with the aid of criteria set by other concerns. A 'problem' begins to emerge. 'Solutions' are sought. Action may or may not follow. Our technology culture, dominated by 'problem solving', tends to take the problem setting for granted. It is, I think, essential to remember that without concerns there would be no problem and that without criteria (which often conflict) there would be no solutions. (Vickers, 1983)

In keeping with the nature of the framework, the objective here is to make the intended problem solver examine the concerns of the clients and the problem owners in depth, and to make explicit the legitimacy and validity of the prognosis outlines, the 'problems', and the notional systems of the clients and the problem owners.

SYSTEMIC ANALYSIS

What is systems analysis?

Systems analysis, as understood within the information systems field, has come to mean, on the one hand in most general terms, *all* activities to do with systems development, and on the other, the more specific activity of investigation and description of a study of a 'system'. In the case of the latter, it is also considered to be simply analysis—as an activity of breaking-down-to-understand, thus ignoring the term 'system' and concentrating only on the scientific meaning of the term 'analysis'.

The notion of breaking-down-to-understand (i.e. separating something into its constituent parts) originates from the scientific method. It is the method advocated by science to promote understanding and generate enquiry. In so doing science has contributed to a vast knowledge base from which many inventions continue to be made. However, 'reality' cannot be appreciated by one method of enquiry alone. For instance, the characteristic of 'wetness' of water cannot be understood by an examination of its constituent parts: oxygen and hydrogen. The properties that are unique to the level of the 'whole' are defined as its *emergent* properties (note that science does not restrict holistic analysis).

Because of this confused understanding, the activity of problem formulation has remained outside the domain of many methodologies. The moment one accepts a clients requirements (description of the notional systems) as legitimate, then there is nothing left to do other than to *design* 'systems'. All efforts of the intended problem solver are directed towards capturing the client's requirements in precise detail, and designing 'systems' to match these requirements. The methodology thus renders its users ignorant of the reasons for the client's notional systems, i.e. what prognosis outlines the notional system is trying to bring about.

Sometimes, we use the term 'systemic analysis' to cover all the problem formulation phase activities discussed in this chapter. 'Systemic analysis' can be thought of as an 'enquiring process'. 'Systems analysis', as it is currently defined, could be left to mean the study of an *existing* system, while 'systemic analysis' could be considered as a process of *critical enquiry* of situations with the use of the notion of 'systems'. Systemic analysis therefore involves activities which (a) examine and critically evaluate the diagnosis (arrived at from an investigation) against (b) the prognosis outline (arrived at from a critical questioning process and with supporting reasons), (c) derive 'problems statements', which explain what is preventing the transformation from taking place, and (d) derive relevant notional systems which, if designed, developed and operated, will remove the identified problems and transform the 'current state' to the 'desired state'. The notional systems for bringing about the 'desired state' are described in specification documents ('root' definition form in SSM). In systems analysis the use of the notion of 'systems' is taken to be in an ontological sense, (i.e. the existence of a system out there to be understood, explored, documented and changed), while in systemic analysis it is taken to be in an epistemological sense (i.e. construction of boundaries and naming them as 'systems'). In the former, there is a desire to define the *right* system, while in the latter the desire is to name the *relevant* system. These uses were discussed in Chapter 2.

If a methodology is to perform systemic analysis then it must offer many ways of conducting enquiry that will define the change of states and the reasons for the change, but must show the use of systems concepts in the performance of this activity.

SUMMARY

In the problem-solving process, the problem formulation phase can be expressed as including several stages, namely:
- Understanding of the 'situation of concern'
- Performing the diagnosis
  - (Diagnosis Model 1: conceptual logical expressions)
  - (Diagnosis Model 2: physical expressions)
  - 'state' of the 'situation of concern'
- Defining the prognosis outline
  - 'Desired state' with supporting reasons
- Defining 'problems'
  - mapping the two states (the outline shapes)
  - identifying problem issues
- Deriving notional systems

Within systems methodologies, the problem formulation phase can be thought of as the 'systemic analysis' phase because of the use of 'systems' concepts.

> Systemic analysis can be defined as the critical enquiring process using the notion of 'systems' for defining notional system(s) that is (are) considered as relevant to the 'situation of concern'. The problem formulation phase activities involve the critical examination of the rationale for the current and the desired states, formulation of problem statements and hence the identification of relevant notional system(s). Systemic analysis is simply the use of 'systems' notions in the problem formulation phase of a problem solving process.

The methodology user needs to ask how specific methodologies help to perform the problem formulation phase. If they do not help to perform this phase, then methodology users have to adopt other methodologies or devise their own ways of carrying it out at a conscious level. How three well known methodologies attempt to do this will be examined in Chapters 8, 9 and 10.

6

NIMSAD FRAMEWORK (THE PROBLEM-SOLVING PROCESS: contd.)

INTRODUCTION

In this chapter we examine the solution design and design implementation phases of the problem-solving process of the framework. The starting point for solution design phase is the purpose, nature and features of the notional system(s). These are described in the systems specification document. As the design activities have to take into account the nature of the existing situation, details of the diagnosis should accompany this document. The document should also state any constraints (limits of freedom) within which the design models, when operational, have to perform. It would be useful to give the design tasks as much freedom as possible before constraints are brought to bear.

SYSTEMS DESIGN OR SYSTEMIC DESIGN

Systems design is defined as:

> ... the drawing, planning, sketching or arranging of many separate elements into a viable unified whole. Whereas the systems analysis phase answers the questions of what the system is doing and what it should be doing to meet user requirements, the general systems design phase is concerned with how the system is developed to meet user requirements.
>
> (Burch and Grudnitski, 1989)

This definition in some ways reflects many of the misconceptions about information systems analysis issues already discussed and critically evaluated in the previous chapter. In the context of the above definition, these issues are:

- What the system is doing—this is described in the diagnosis (the description of and the reasons for the 'state' of the 'situation of concern')
- What the system should be doing—this is the output of the problem formulation phase (systemic analysis)
- User requirements—this is not external to, but very much a part of, the problem formulation phase
- If we replace the ontological use of the term 'system' as employed within the definition with its use in an epistemological sense of the term, then there cannot be just *one* system but many possible 'systems' whose boundary construction has to be very much a conscious intellectual activity
- The design phase is *not* concerned with how the system is developed, but how the system is designed. How the system is developed is the concern of systems implementation
- The most important question in systems analysis is *why* there is a need for the change of 'states' and the relevance of the notional systems to these 'states'.

If we applied the same arguments and paradigm shifts to the definition of 'design', we could define systemic design (solution design using 'systems' notions) as a creative activity of constructing many elements and organizing them into not just *one* but **many** viable unified wholes, each one capable of realizing the notional system(s). Because the activity set is seen as a set for improving or changing *the* system, the current use of the term 'systems design' is also inappropriate to describe the 'true' nature of the activities. If systems concepts are used as the philosophical basis for designing solutions, then we can use the term 'systemic design' to cover the activities of the solution design phase.

Thus, solution design can be defined as:

> . . . the creative activity of constructing elements and organising them into integrated wholes, each capable of realising the notional system(s). If this activity can be guided by the notion of 'systems' taken in its epistemological sense, then we can call the phase 'systemic design'.

This meaning of systemic design is what the conceptual model construction in

'Soft' Systems Methodology attempts to do (Checkland, 1981; Checkland and Scholes, 1990).

The guide for solution design is the notional system(s) as proposed by the problem formulation phase. This guide should be accompanied by information from the diagnosis and its *context* (environmental conditions—see Figure 5.7) in which the design models, when implemented, will have to perform. Taking the notional system(s) as given, our new role is to engage in creative activities that can help to identify and express the logical and physical elements that are necessary to support the notional system(s).

Note that the questioning of the notional system(s) and/or its relevance to the 'problem situation' is not the role of solution design. If this is to be the case (which so often happens), then it reveals the shortcomings of the problem formulation phase. Failures or weaknesses in conducting one phase inevitably causes problems for the subsequent phases, thus resulting in the iterative undertaking of the phases at a practical level, but this should not be confused with current understanding by some to mean that 'analysis contains design' and 'design contains analysis'.

The role distinction between systemic analysis and systemic design described in this book should help to clarify any confusion about the two phases of the problem-solving process. The following should help to illustrate the distinctions between the two phases conducted with the use of 'systems' notions.

SYSTEMIC ANALYSIS vs SYSTEMIC DESIGN

Systemic analysis is essentially the process of deriving notional systems (using the notion of 'systems') and understanding their relevance to the situation in which 'problems' are perceived. Systemic design is the process of deriving models (using the notion of 'systems') that are expected to bring about the behaviour of the notional systems—see Table 6.1.

The solution design phase consists of two related stages, namely the conceptual/logical design and the physical design. Some methodologies may combine these into one integrated stage.

Table 6.1   Systemic analysis vs. systemic design

Criteria	Systemic analysis	Systemic design
Role	Problem formulation using 'systems' notions	Solution design using 'systems' notions
Function	To identify relevant notional system(s) to the desired state	To identify relevant elements of the notional system(s)
Primary concern	To define the *context* relevance of 'systems'	To define the *content* relevance of 'systems'
Addresses questions	'What' and 'Why'?	'How' and 'Whom'?
Measures of performance	Contribution of notional system's performance to the desired state	Contribution of the integrated elements to the notional system's performance
Primary skills required	'Critical thinking'	'Creative thinking'

STAGE 6: PERFORMING THE CONCEPTUAL/LOGICAL DESIGN

The role of conceptual/logical design is to create or make changes (when compared with Diagnosis Model DM1) to the structures, roles, tasks, functions, information, and attitudes of the notional system(s). When undertaking this activity, it is important to consider the links of the notional systems to the 'situation of concern'; for example, the design of elements for a sales monitoring system (i.e. a notional system) may have implications for the order processing activities in the 'situation of concern'. It may be necessary to record sales transactions in order to produce the necessary inputs for the sales monitoring system (see Figure 6.1). If this is the case, then the conceptual boundary of the notional system should incorporate the recording of sales activities.

Apart from the inherent limitations of our 'mental constructs', the conceptual/logical models developed at this stage should simply and comprehensively specify the logical elements. 'Logical' means that the elements can be argued as being useful and essential to the realization of the notional system. (Note that the viability, practicality or achievability of these elements are to be considered for the physical design stage.)

In order to perform this activity, we need to draw on our experience-based

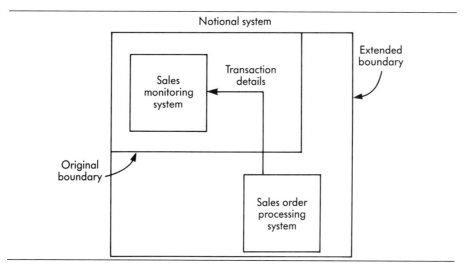

Figure 6.1   Boundary extension

Figure 6.2   Simple systems model

knowledge, rely on implicit models or develop explicitly useful conceptual models. Here we look for methodologies to provide us with effective conceptual/logical modelling techniques for undertaking design. The latter is what models embedded in the methodology would help to formulate. The most basic model for guiding formal information systems design is the simple input–process–output model as illustrated in Figure 6.2. In design, the logical sequence of construction is from output–process–input.

This simple model by itself is not sufficient, but is certainly useful in organizing our experience-based knowledge into a coherent creative form. However, where we do not have experience in the application environment, the possibility of generating relevant solutions is limited. In order to address this shortcoming, we, as the intended problem solvers, may have to develop our ability to use general abstract and conceptual models. We have used these models in the design of many information systems which led to the alteration of already defined notional systems, thus exposing the weaknesses of the problem formulation phase of the existing methodologies.

The integrative function of the logical/conceptual design elements is to

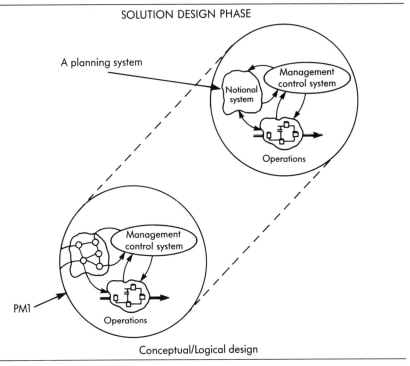

SOLUTION DESIGN PHASE

A planning system

Notional system

Management control system

Operations

Management control system

PM1

Operations

Conceptual/Logical design

Figure 6.3   Logical design

support (at a logically demonstrable level) the notional system(s). Figure 6.3 illustrates the relationships of logical elements of a notional system. It consists of several functional elements which have to operate as an integrated whole in order to make the notional system's performance match its expected behaviour as listed in the systems specification document.

For example, if the notional system is a planning system, then the conceptual/ logical design stage may identify the following logical functions as being necessary:

- Scanning the environment
- Collating operational performance data
- Comparing performance data with planning criteria
- Evaluating new target data for management and control
- Creating planning criteria against corporate goals and environment data

Figure 6.4 shows the conceptual/logical design elements of a typical planning system (notional system). It illustrates only the functional activity sets, but

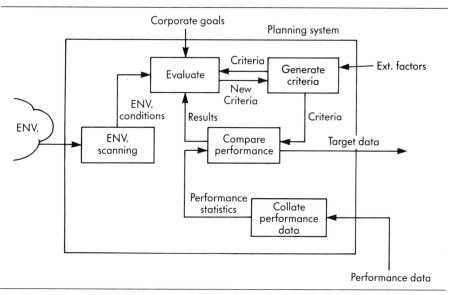

Figure 6.4   Planning systems

could be expanded and extended to include many other related activities and links.

Most structured methodologies devote their entire logical design stage to the construction of logical data flows/processes and/or entity-relationship modelling (see descriptions in Martin and McClure, 1988; Kendall, 1992, Korth and Silberschatz, 1986; McFadden and Hoffer, 1991), and yet they ignore the associated functions and role responsibilities of individuals.

The outcome of this stage is the production of an agreed and acceptable logical design specification which states the nature and the function of the logical elements. These logical elements may also include structures, role descriptions, skills, attitudes, facilities and resources, in addition to the logical task activities and information flows. The conceptual/logical model, which is similar in nature to the Diagnosis Model DM 1, can be termed Prognosis Model 1 (PM1). PM1 can now be compared with DM1. During the implementation phase the comparison helps to determine the extent to which changes may be required. (Please note that this is the reason why we suggested that it would be useful to maintain the separation of logical and physical expressions in the form of DM1 and DM2 during the diagnosis stage.)

Some methodologies simply substitute DM1 in place of PM1, as they offer improvements only in the physical performance of the current operations. We call these *provision-oriented* methodologies (Jayaratna, 1988). Others use DM1 as the basis for undertaking design modifications using a client-given specification.

Once we have designed the logical components and their relationships, then we can move on to physical design.

STAGE 7: PERFORMING THE PHYSICAL DESIGN

Physical design can be considered as the deliberation and selection of 'ways and means' of realizing the logical design. Through this process, we can create several physical design models to realize the features of the same logical model within a given set of physical resources and constraints. These physical constraints may be in the form of policies formulated by management as to what products or tools are to be used (e.g. 4 GL software tools and languages) or what standards are to be introduced (e.g. hardware/software platforms) or as to whether to preserve the working conditions of all those affected, etc. In addition, they may dictate the nature and type of information systems, i.e. distributed systems, network systems, etc. Resources may also include funds to acquire or develop new products, enhance existing facilities and/or recruit new personnel.

The physical design process has to take into account the economic, social, political, technological and cultural environments in which the proposed design models are expected to operate or perform. Some of these environmental conditions may be imposed (constraints, as discussed earlier), while in other cases the physical design may include changes to the environment (opportunities). In order to generate these design elements, we need to raise questions of the type 'how?' and 'whom?' In other words, we need to address such questions as: 'How do we translate the logical models into a physical form within a given set of resources, facilities and other environmental factors?'

Given that a range of physical design models are possible for realizing the conceptual/logical models, some additional criteria need to be used to guide the physical design process. The most dominant criterion seems to be efficiency; however, other criteria may include:

- Reliability
- Accuracy

SOLUTION DESIGN PHASE

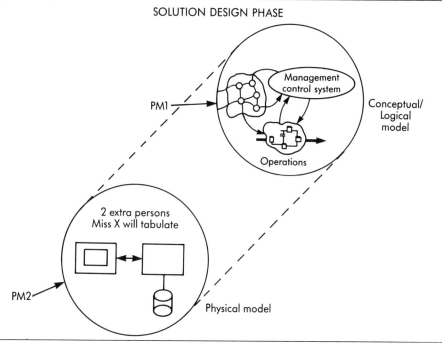

Figure 6.5   Physical design

- Security/safety
- Expansibility/enhanceability
- Availability, etc.

The ultimate set may be a compromise among these criteria. For example, in the design of a process control system for a pharmaceutical company, criteria such as accuracy and reliability may dominate the physical design choice, while in the design of a criminal record system for the police, the criteria of security and safety may override other considerations. The issue of Enhance-ability may already form part of the information and systems management and control policies within the organization. Figure 6.5 illustrates a physical design model generated from the logical model of the previous stages. We call this Prognosis Model 2 (PM2).

Some of the contributions to the improvement in usability of computer-based information systems have come from the Human Computer Interactions (HCI) field. For example, concepts of user-friendly dialogues, WIMP (*W*indows, *I*cons, *M*enus, *P*ictures) interfaces, WYSWYG (*W*hat *Y*ou *S*ee is

What You Get) are already familiar terms in the physical design of computer-based information systems (Shackel, 1990).

The eventual Prognosis Model PM2 should state the particular technology to be used, input and output formats, document standards, data store organization and access methods, screen layouts, persons to be involved, work procedures, documents, etc. For example, if the logical design identified the role of an individual (manager, designer, etc.) then the physical design will help to identify their physical or role characteristics specific to the situation (should the manager be a woman or a man, how many years' experience, whether this experience should have been gained in a chemical environment, etc.).

STAGE 8: IMPLEMENTING THE DESIGN

This is the third phase of the problem-solving process. The resolution of problem issues (as defined previously) or the measurement of success or failure of the outcome of the problem-solving process can be demonstrated only if this stage is completed and managed successfully. In the context of Figure 1.2, implementation can be considered as the most visible and critical link between the **information systems development function** (its output) and the **processing and usability function** (its input).

Implementation is concerned with the realization of the notional system within the context of the 'situation of concern'. The task may become extremely difficult, however, if we have to introduce the changes in a rapidly evolving or politically sensitive 'situation of concern'.

Implementation is also significant in an applied sense of the word. The problem formulation and solution design phases can be considered as merely intellectual human activities, since apart from developing interpersonal relationships and influencing the thought processes of the problem owners, clients and others, very little else in the 'situation of concern' may have been changed during these phases. However, the completion of the implementation phase brings about physical changes (both planned and unplanned) in the 'situation of concern'. Figure 6.6 illustrates this link to the 'situation of concern'.

This phase not only provides an opportunity for us to demonstrate the validity of the previously generated conceptual/logical and physical design models in practice, but also serves as a test of our competence in the translation of the models from the 'thinking world' into the 'action world'. It

DESIGN IMPLEMENTATION PHASE

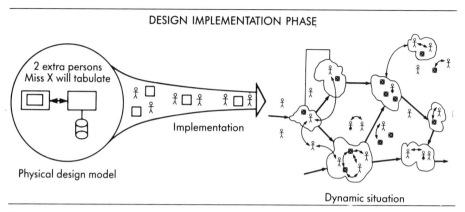

Figure 6.6   Implementation

is also a test for assessing the validity of the assumptions on which the models have been based. Swanson (1988) mentions three aspects that should be considered in systems implementation:

1. Systems realisation is necessarily a process of collaboration between designer, implementor and client,
2. The essence of the implementation task is to bridge the gap between design and utilisation. The role of the implementor is basically that of an intermediary in the systems realisation process,
3. Integration of the roles in the systems realisation often enhances the prospects for success.

(Swanson, 1988)

(Note that these roles are included in the role of the intended problem solver.)

The essence of Swanson's message is clear: the intended problem solvers, the problem owners, stakeholders and clients need to collaborate and liaise in order to make the implementation a success. We suggest that this collaboration is also essential for addressing the following issues:

- However comprehensive the models and however successful the modelling process in the previous phases of the problem-solving process, there is no way that models can capture the richness of any situation. Therefore, collaboration is a useful strategy for refining the models (diagnosis and prognosis) in the light of emerging information, but this should ideally be undertaken before the implementation stage.

- Since most of the previous modelling processes tend to be performed in a different environment (more relevant for information systems design), sometimes remote from the problem stakeholders, we may not observe the continuous changes taking place in the 'situation of concern'. Thus, changes to the models may have to be made with the help of the problem stakeholders.
- We have little or no direct control over many aspects of the 'situation of concern'; hence we need the support and the cooperation of clients and stakeholders to make our designs realizable.
- Since the aim of systems development is to bring about effectiveness in organizations, there is a need to ensure that design solutions are not only implemented but that they actually contribute to organization effectiveness. This can only be achieved through the *actions* of the stakeholders.
- Lastly, this is the stage when the ownership of the design models (if they are ours) and their manifestations in 'action systems' are transferred from us to the stakeholders.

(Note that different methodologies handle these issues at different stages.)

The extent of the design implementation task can be ascertained by mapping two sets of models, assuming, of course, that diagnosis models still reflect the true nature of the 'situation of concern'.

First, the conceptual mapping between DM1 and PM1 highlights the differences and therefore the extent to which there will be changes to information flows, attitudes, beliefs, roles, functions and associated activities. For example, some of the issues that may arise include, the nature and quality of user training, and improvements in decision-making processes, models, roles and, responsibilities. It is very important to work out the extent to which changes are necessary for the planning of the implementation.

Secondly, the mapping between DM2 and PM2 helps to identify the nature of the physical elements that need to be changed. For example, this mapping may establish the changes to staff numbers, file creation/transfer activities, actual role-holder's physical characteristics, etc. (see Figure 6.7).

The major tasks of the implementation phase consist of three essential parts: the 'situation of concern'; the models generated from previous phases of the problem-solving process; and the need to find a way of bridging these two parts (see Figure 6.6). These three parts can be organized into five sets of tasks, as follows:

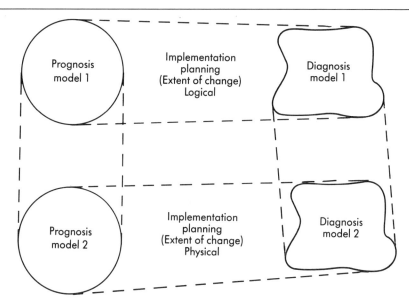

Figure 6.7   Mapping between 'states'

- *Environment preparation*: to identify those parts and connections in the 'situation of concern' that we need to prepare and adjust to accommodate our design models when they become operational, e.g. changes to existing buildings, cabling, training of existing users, etc.
- *Systems development*: to identify the tasks involved in the acquisition of resources and facilities for developing the parts and the interconnections as implied by the design models, e.g. recruitment of new personnel, acquisition of hardware/software, construction of programs, testing, creating databases in information systems development, etc.
- *Changeover*: to consider the 'ways and means' by which we can integrate the new development with the prepared environment in order to help realize the functions of the relevant notional system(s), e.g. ways of introducing changes, whether they should be phased in or introduced at the same time, etc.
- *Strategy and planning*: to identify and adapt a strategy for sequencing the activities, given the nature of the 'situation of concern', developments in it, and the environmental demands prevailing at the time, e.g. whether the activities should be funded in stages, estimation of completion dates, listing the order in which to carry out activities, etc.

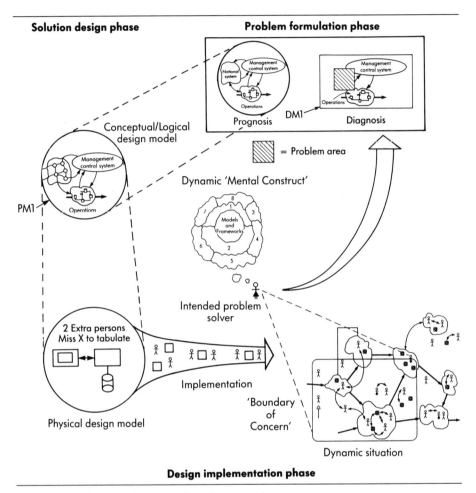

Figure 6.8   The complete NIMSAD framework

- *Management and control*: to establish structures, set up management and control functions to help supervise the implementation
  tasks, e.g. setting up steering committees, coordinating committees
  and controlling the activities, etc.

In the actual implementation phase, the last two tasks have to be in place
before the first three can be undertaken.

THE COMPLETED NIMSAD FRAMEWORK

Figure 6.8 illustrates the connections of the elements of the NIMSAD
framework. As discussed in Chapter 4, there are four essential elements,

namely: the 'problem situation' (methodology context); the problem solver (the methodology user); the problem-solving process (the methodology); and the evaluation. Evaluation will be discussed in Chapter 7. The problem-solving process was further conceptualized to contain three essential phases, namely: problem formulation, solution design and design implementation.

SUMMARY

This chapter discussed the design and implementation phases of the problem-solving process element of the framework, with the rationale for their inclusion. It also established the need for using the term 'systemic design' as a way of understanding the nature of the design task, comparing it with 'systemic analysis' established in Chapter 4. This was followed by a discussion of the importance of structuring and organizing the implementation of design in order to solve 'problems'.

7

NIMSAD FRAMEWORK (THE EVALUATION)

INTRODUCTION

In the previous chapters we discussed the first three elements of the NIMSAD framework and the reasons for their inclusion. We are now ready to look at the last and most important element of the framework.

No problem-solving process can be considered complete until evaluation has been carried out. It is the evaluation which helps us to measure the effectiveness of the problem-solving process and the problem solver in the 'problem situation'—unless this element is considered there is no way of establishing that the 'problems' have been successfully resolved. Despite the importance of evaluation, however, we find that very few methodologies incorporate it into their steps.

If the evaluation is to be effective, it must be well structured. We have chosen the first three elements of the NIMSAD framework—namely, the 'problem situation', the problem-solving process, and the problem solver—as the basis for evaluation. By doing so, we not only consider the importance of the elements (they are all relevant and need to be evaluated for learning), but also the systemic nature of the framework, i.e. the interconnections of the elements. This evaluation has to be carried out at three stages: before intervention in order to maximize our efforts and effectiveness; during intervention because of the dynamic nature of the elements; and after intervention so that lessons can be learned about the three elements.

This chapter is full of questions. This is deliberate. The aims of these questions are twofold.

First, our designed system affects the performance, profitability, survival and growth of organizations. Therefore, problem solving in any organizational context is a serious and responsible activity and not simply the execution of a set of methodology steps. Any methodology that is offered for problem solving must help to bring about efficient and effective transformation of situations and always for the better. The role of the framework is to help question the methodologies as to *what* they attempt to transform, *why* they try to transform it, and *how* they help us to undertake the transformation. If methodologies are to offer effective means of transformation then they must stand up to scrutiny and that means to *critical evaluation*.

Secondly, the questions have to be levelled at methodology users. We, as methodology users, have a serious and ethical responsibility to those in the organization. By our interventions we directly or indirectly affect the organization members' lives, job satisfaction, working conditions, career developments, remuneration, relationships and many other factors. In the end, it is we who bring about successful or unsuccessful transformations of situations, and not the methodology. Any weakness of the methodology will have to be overcome by us, either through our own efforts or with the help of others. In order to decide what and when to substitute our own ideas, we need to know about the nature of the methodology, its purpose, its steps, its claims, etc. We can undertake evaluation only if we ourselves are prepared for the task.

This chapter is full of questions, but with *no* answers. Having to go through questions without answers can be a very frustrating and uncomfortable experience. We believe, however, that it is better to be uncomfortable at this stage and develop our intellectual reasoning processes than to undertake a transformation in the 'action world' and then look for political justifications to cover up our mistakes, shortcomings, failures and disasters. Every time a question causes us frustration it means that we do not have a ready answer for it, and every such question will result in considerable implications for the users of the designed systems. It is our role to find the answers and to justify to ourselves the rationality, soundness and ethical status of the answers. Some of the specific questions that can be asked about the three elements will be listed later in the chapter. If readers feel frustrated by these questions then they should use the opportunity to examine their intellectually desirable thoughts. (At a political level, they can always blame the author for raising questions. Although painful, he is well conditioned to negative feedback.)

EVALUATION OF THE 'PROBLEM SITUATION'

This evaluation is primarily concerned with the resolution of clients' concerns in the 'problem situation'. Given that the clients and the problem owners have invited us to undertake problem solving, are prepared and have invested resources, time and effort, we have a serious ethical and moral obligation to ensure that client's and other stakeholders' concerns are successfully resolved. In order to achieve this, the evaluation has to be conducted at three stages.

BEFORE INTERVENTION

This is the initial assessment of the situation and the client's concerns about it. One of the most essential tasks is to understand the reasons for the client's concerns and expectations. Sometimes clients may indicate their 'desired states' and expect us to identify relevant notional systems that would bring about those 'desired states'. At other times they may keep the 'desired states' well hidden from us and only state the notional systems, expecting us to design and implement 'action systems' to help realize them. Yet on other occasions they may not be able either to define the notional systems or to work out their 'desired states', making the situation appear 'ill-structured'.

Next we need to consider the relevance and validity of clients' needs and their commitments to those needs. On most occasions they may give a clear appearance of being sure of their 'desired states' and notional systems, but this may not last for any reasonable length of time. We should therefore probe clients' concerns in order to establish their understanding of the issues and their commitments to action. The lesser the commitment the more likely they are to change their minds about the 'desired states' and hence the notional systems during the project.

Lastly, we need to select a methodology for use in the situation. Some may already help us to define client management issues while others may help us to perform tasks which enable us to meet the already defined needs. In order to match the methodology to the situation, we need to know the purpose, structure, steps, rationale, models, techniques and skills demanded by the methodology. Organizations are very complex entities, and we cannot expect a methodology to offer explicit ways of structuring our thinking and action on all dimensions. However, we do expect them to comment explicitly on what they can or cannot do, so that we can assess the implications. For every domain and aspect not covered by the methodology, we may have to seek help from other sources or invent our own methodology steps.

DURING INTERVENTION

No matter what methodologies we may use, we cannot guarantee that those involved in the situation will cooperate or support the steps we take to identify and solve 'problems'. We need to ensure that clients continue to be committed to the project and support our intervention. Sometimes the characteristics of the situation may change, thereby forcing us to modify the methodology steps or alter our actions. These changes may be due to circumstances outside our 'situation of concern' (especially those elements of the 'action world' which are not under the control of the client or the methodology user). For instance, we have been in 'industrial project' situations where clients have changed their priorities during the project, thus affecting the outcome of our intervention drastically. An information systems development project in a manufacturing company had to be abandoned because the managing director (the client) moved to another company during the project, and the political system was such that all projects under the direction of that managing director were abandoned by his successor. Threats to the organization from outside (i.e. rationalizations, takeovers, mergers, sell-offs) may also force the client to take drastic action, in which case the project may be seriously affected. On other occasions, the changes in the 'action world' may very well be due to a client's change of direction for no apparent reason. In another 'action research' case study, the regular progress feedback to the client made him take action without waiting for the final phase of the methodology to be completed. This forced us to alter the methodology in the light of his actions.

AFTER INTERVENTION

This is one of the most important aspects of evaluation and needs to be carried out for several reasons:

(1) To assess whether the designed systems were implemented within the limits of resources, time and efforts. This helps to establish the effectiveness of the project management tasks and to measure project performance. A solution which is not timely may not help to solve 'problems' in the 'action world'. For instance, in the context of design and implementation of an order processing system we could ask whether the implementation was completed within the cost and time constraints for the 'action systems' (notional systems in operation) to be of any value to the organization. Some projects have caused delays to their output to the extent that the final solutions have come far too late to be of use in the transformation of the 'problem situation'.

(2) To assess whether the 'action systems' do what they are supposed to do, i.e. whether the features of the notional systems have been realized. This establishes the effectiveness of the design and implementation phases. For example, in the context of the order processing system example to meet the needs of customer demands, a legitimate question that can be asked is: 'Does the order processing system's performance meet the level of customer demand (*effectiveness*) and operate within the resources–cost ratio (*efficiency*) that were defined in the description of the notional system?'

(3) To assess whether the 'problems' have been resolved. This establishes the *relevance* of the 'action systems' to the 'problem situation'. It also helps to measure the effectiveness of the problem formulation phase of the problem-solving process. For example, if the client (or the methodology user) had identified an efficient order processing system as being the notional system to help reach increased profitability ('desired state') then the questions here would be whether that 'state' has now been realized and whether indeed it was reached owing to the sales order processing system. Of course, if this evaluation is to be meaningful then there needs to be a reasonable period for the operation and the performance of the 'action system'.

Taking the order processing example once again, the evaluation here is whether the order processing system helped to resolve the 'problem situation'. For example, an efficient system may help to improve the flow of goods and invoices, but if the market culture is one of delayed payments then the investment in order processing may not solve the problems of cash flow even though it may improve the distribution flow of goods and paperwork and help to focus management knowledge on particular areas that may need attention. Solving the wrong 'problem' is an activity that frequently takes place in many fields.

To summarize, three levels of client satisfaction need to be evaluated, namely:
- 'systems' have been developed and have become operational within the time, cost and other constraints ('model systems' have become 'action systems' within the constraints and policies). *These relate to project management.*
- 'systems' do what they were supposed to do ('action systems' operate as intended by the 'notional systems'). *These relate to operational performance of designed systems.*
- 'systems' have transformed the situation ('action systems' have proved their relevance). *These relate to problem solving.*

It is this last point that will show the effectiveness of the problem formulation phase.

To our knowledge, there is no single public methodology that performs this kind of explicit evaluation, i.e. evaluation of the relevance of its assistance after the event as part of its steps. Of course, if the client's or the methodology users' problem formulation process has not been rigorous and they have conveniently abandoned or changed their 'desired states', then the *relevance* of the solutions developed at enormous cost and effort cannot be established. However, evaluation of this kind would help those performing the problem formulation phase to improve their level of learning and competence. As discussed in Chapter 4, it is political thoughts-driven reasoning that prevents the discussion of these issues.

EVALUATION OF THE METHODOLOGY USER (INTENDED PROBLEM SOLVER)

This is (and should be) the second most important evaluation, but one that is not advocated in any problem-solving process or methodology. This evaluation should help us to understand our strengths and weaknesses. It should also assist us in identifying training needs and ways in which we can improve our competence; yet very few problem-solving processes and methodologies alert us to the need for this. The identification of necessary levels of skills is one lesson that could be derived from this situation; for example, the self-critical reflections performed by the author after interventions in the 'action world' consistently show up his lack of political skills and judgement.

Using the 'mental construct' model we could ask very specific questions of ourselves before, during and after intervention. Examples of specific questions are listed at the end of the chapter, but these are by no means exhaustive. The framework enables us to ask these questions because it has a much wider context than those of the methodologies. The answers to these questions may make us become more effective and competent problem solvers.

EVALUATION OF THE METHODOLOGY (PROBLEM-SOLVING PROCESS)

This is concerned with the assessment of the methodology and the degree of assistance it provides in terms of models, concepts, techniques, structure, etc.

EVALUATION OF THE METHODOLOGY BEFORE INTERVENTION

Each methodology that is offered for undertaking the problem-solving process reflects its creator's philosophical views, his or her appreciation of issues in the 'action world' and his or her own successful experiences. The evaluation here is to examine whether the decision to use the methodology is justified and whether we, as potential methodology users, understand the structure, steps and philosophy of the methodology as intended by its creator.

Many of those who are concerned with problem solving look for specific methodologies in order to help them undertake the problem-solving process. The role of methodologies is to offer many different ways (through their philosophy, structure, steps and ways of performing the steps) of undertaking this process. However, an examination of methodologies reveals that their creators *do not* provide criteria to help us to decide why we should use their methodologies—therefore, we need to acquire knowledge *before* we use a methodology, as to what situations it would be suitable for, how it is to be used and, most importantly, how the benefits can be measured. This whole book is concerned with raising issues that we should take into account *before* selecting or using a methodology. In Chapters 8, 9 and 10 we shall apply these to ask questions about three well known methodologies.

EVALUATION OF THE SELECTED METHODOLOGY

In the process of selecting a methodology we may have already interpreted and changed the philosophy, form, nature, structure and steps of the methodology. This may be a conscious or unconscious effort. This evaluation examines whether the changes or interpretations which were applied to a specific methodology at the time of adoption are justified. Changes may be necessary, given our knowledge of the 'problem situation' and our assessment of our abilities to use a methodology.

Note that if we make changes to the original methodology, then we are in a position to examine the reasons for the changes. Checkland and Scholes (1990) criticisms of those who have misapplied the notions of 'systems' in the 'root' definitions is an example of this type of evaluation. If those who use SSM do not appreciate the epistemological notions on which it is based, then the chances of bringing about changes intended by the methodology will be very remote. The evaluation here is to examine the effects of the changes to the original methodology and the soundness of those changes. Many lessons can be learned from this evaluation for future use.

EVALUATION OF THE METHODOLOGY-IN-ACTION

Despite all good intentions and the 'right' choice, no methodology, whether in its original or adapted form, can be expected to operate according to its predetermined structure when applied in a given situation. Organizations in which methodologies are applied are not laboratories; Organizational members have their own individual and unique 'mental constructs' just as we have ours, and cannot be expected to behave like mice in a maze under experiment. (Note that, in many instances, the regard shown by us to powerless groups within organizations is no different in essence from the regard shown by those to chemical elements under experiment.) Organizational members try their very best to protect and promote their own interest in the situation, which means that the chance of following the structure and steps of any methodology in a situation is as remote as climbing a mountain in a straight line! It is possible to enforce a predefined methodology and its steps rigorously based on authority, power or punishments; however, our experience demonstrates that even in those situations many informal modifications are made by those using the methodology to complete its essential structure. By raising questions during use we are able to operate at a conscious level, thus understanding the need for the predetermined structure and steps, the incorporation of new steps or changes to the steps or structure of the intended methodology in the 'action world'.

This evaluation is, of course, about the effectiveness of the methodology-in-action. By asking questions at this stage we would be able to learn about the changes that we make because of the practical and political difficulties of the situation, e.g. activities of the clients that prevent our actions and their implications for problem solving.

EVALUATION OF THE METHODOLOGY AFTER INTERVENTION

This evaluation is about the lessons we can gain from the original methodology, the adapted/adopted methodology and the methodology-in-action. The focus here is to accumulate lessons that we can abstract from our experience of using methodologies. These can help to establish whether to use the methodology again and, if so, for what situations, in what modified form and so on. It is these experiences which led us to write this book. The evaluation is critical for developing competence in the use of methodologies for problem solving.

CONDITIONS OF USE

The NIMSAD framework is not a template, i.e. it is not to be used for judging whether methodology steps have one-to-one mapping with the framework stages. It is to be used for asking questions of the methodologies as to what elements of the framework they address, in what order and how they address them. The use of the NIMSAD framework to help formulate questions in a potential methodology user's mind makes it an epistemological device. The framework requires its user to *consciously* consider the rational basis and the relationships of the activities suggested by the steps of any methodology. When using the framework, we would also like the user to consider the following related issues:

- The stages discussed in Chapters 4, 5 and 6 and in this chapter take place within the 'action world'. Since these stages, undertaken (or not) by methodologies through their structure and steps take place in the 'problem situation', the sequence and the performance of the steps are going to be seriously affected by situational factors.
- The complexity of the 'action world' and the limitations of human ability to comprehend complexity means that no models are rich enough to map that complexity. It is this fact that makes the methodology-in-action take on different structures, i.e. cyclical, sequential or iterative. Therefore, there is a clear need for continuous examination of the models to ensure that their relevance is considered (i.e. to avoid blind faith in the models used).
- The dynamic nature of the 'situation of concern' implies that we as intended methodology users need to have communication and monitoring links with those involved in the situation and to ensure that the relevance of our methodological activities to the situation is maintained.
- The individual 'mental constructs', self-needs and interpersonal skills that we use in this undertaking have a considerable impact on the way methodologies are practised in the situation.
- NIMSAD is a conceptual framework. Its elements were constructed in stages to illustrate the rationale of the complete framework, i.e. why these elements should be included in the framework. However,

the order of construction does not imply that the framework is relevant only to those methodologies that conform to a similar order. Structuring order is not an important characteristic of a framework, but it is of a methodology. Indeed, in Chapters 8, 9 and 10 three methodologies which do not follow the same order are compared to demonstrate the use of the framework.

- The NIMSAD framework is *not* a methodology. It can only become a methodology if the users of the framework decide to select the stages of its problem-solving process and create a structure in which to carry out the chosen steps. If this is to be the case, the users must justify to themselves the rationale for undertaking the steps, in that order (structuring their thinking and action) as being appropriate to the 'situation of concern'. It is they who should take credit for the success of any transformation.
- For any framework or methodology to be useful, we must be prepared for critical self-reflection. This should include not only an examination of our own 'mental constructs', but also of our influence on the problem-solving process, on others and on the situation as a whole.

The framework should be used as a means for debating the rationale of the steps of a methodology and its structure in the same way as the notion of 'human activity system' is used for debating and giving meaning to purposeful human activity in an organization within the 'Soft' Systems Methodology.

SPECIFIC QUESTIONS ABOUT THE 'PROBLEM SITUATION'

So what questions does the framework help to raise about the 'problem situation'? Some of these are as follows:

Who are the clients? What grasp have they of the 'problem situation'? (A very arrogant but nevertheless a very relevant and intellectually desirable question to raise! In our experience, many clients do not think through their 'desirable states' before inviting us to *design* solutions.) Are these problems self-evident? What degree of commitment do the clients have in order to see through the implementation of our solution to these problems?

Does the methodology help its users to identify the problem owners? How does it help its users to bring the problem owners within the problem-solving process? What are the implications of such action? Does the methodology help its users to assess the legitimacy of their client's concerns? How does the methodology help to assess the client's grasp of or commitment to their needs? If not, does the methodology accept the client's needs as the starting point? What if these needs do not help to resolve the client's problems? Does the methodology help to identify these?

What types of situations are the methodology users facing? Are the situations well structured, less well structured or ill structured? How are the methodology users to assess the nature of the situations they face? D'Arcy (1991) has suggested a number of criteria which could help to diagnose whether a situation is ill structured or not. These are listed in Appendix B. What situation does the methodology claim is the type for which it is suitable? Does it make any comment about the situation at all? or does it claim it can transform *any* situation? Are these claims justified? What evidence and explanations are offered?

What does the situation demand?—to identify 'problems'? or to design solutions for already identified problems? or to implement an already designed solution? or all three? In this context, what is the purpose of the methodology? What does it claim that it is able to do? Are these claims justified?

What type of culture and politics dominate the situation? What is the management style—participative or authoritative? What does the methodology advocate as its style of operations? Do these match the styles practised in the situation? If not, what would be the implications? What risks do methodology users have to take in using the methodology? What additional help will they need from outside the methodology to address these?

What type of 'reality' do the clients and other stakeholders perceive? What are their assessments about the situation 'reality'? What philosophical views does the methodology promote or assume as its view of 'reality'? How does this match the views of those in the situation? What are the implications of these views?

What are the dominant perceptions in the problem situation? Are they expressed in technical, political, social, cultural or functional terms, or are they a mixture of these? (Experience of the frequent use of a methodology may help to derive answers to these questions, but experience is a very time-, effort- and resource-consuming way of learning, not only for methodology users but also for those involved in the situation. Asking questions at this stage may help to reduce costs and undesirable outcomes for self and others.)

SPECIFIC QUESTIONS ABOUT THE METHODOLOGY USER

What specific questions can we raise about methodology users?

What are the methodology users' value sets? What beliefs do they hold as being 'good'? For example, which of the economic, political, social, cultural or technical values do the methodology users consider as uppermost? How committed are they to these values? Can they sacrifice these in the situation because the situation offers solutions to their personal needs? In this context, what values do the methodologies advocate? How congruent are these with the methodology users' values? For example, if the methodology advocates social values and the methodology users' values are political, then how can it ensure 'true' participation is achieved as intended by the methodology? (In these contexts, the methodology may be used for extending one's own control over others while claims may be made for participation. The methodology users may adapt the methodology steps and its structuring features to suit their own needs. Here we have the first indication of a methodology step change, i.e. how the methodology users substitute, change or ignore some of the methodology steps in the light of the situation characteristics.)

What about ethical behaviour? Does the methodology advocate any particular ethical standards? Does it show how these can be maintained? If indeed there are ethical standards advocated in the methodology, how do these match with the methodology users' own standards? (In the author's experience, these issues are raised continuously and the author is often called upon to make very difficult personal and sometimes painful decisions. These cause severe interpersonal difficulties with those involved in the situation. While ethical issues can be discussed explicitly, which particular ethical stand to take should be left to the methodology users as it is only they who can interpret a given situation and experience the status of that situation. The role of the methodology is to bring these issues to the conscious thinking level of the methodology users and offer them means by which to resolve the conflicts.)

What level of abstract and technical thinking does the methodology demand from its users before they are able to practise it? or does the methodology operate at a level where it can be used by anyone? Could the methodology users' fate become the same as that of the workers on a production line? Computer Aided Systems Engineering (CASE) tools are beginning to create this type of environment for structured methodology users.

How do the philosophical views advocated by the methodology match its users' philosophical views? What are the implications of the mismatches? (In our experience, we find it difficult (not impossible) to train scientific- and engineering-based practitioners to appreciate the epistemological notion of 'systems' or to train social- and political-based practitioners to appreciate the ontological notion of 'systems'. For example, the epistemological notion of 'systems' advocated by SSM requires its users to approach systems design in a different way. Yet expressions such as 'I found *the problem*, when we analysed *the system*' in published literature indicate that those SSM users have failed to grasp the epistemological nature of 'systems' notions. We feel that methodology creators should inform their intended users about the nature and type of concepts they need to be familiar with before applying the methodologies. Methodologies should therefore provide 'health warnings', since they have a responsibility to alert their users to these dimensions.

Similarly, what knowledge sets and skills do the methodology users possess? What knowledge sets and skills does the methodology expect from its users before they can become effective users? For example, ETHICS methodology requires its users to engineer the participation of a wide range of organizational members. While this may be most desirable (the author agrees with the intention), its practice requires users to possess both interpersonal and political skills. Attempts to open up free-flow communication channels in an environment where there are already restrictions (authoritarian management styles) may raise a whole range of interpersonal and emotional difficulties for the methodology user. What assistance, if any, does the methodology offer its users in managing these difficulties? How can a methodology user who has little knowledge of interpersonal skills practise a methodology of this type?

What motives do the methodology users have? Just the mere entry of the methodology users into the situation may have already given them a chance to assess how their personal needs are going to be satisfied. Phenomenologically-based methodologies may help their users to bring potential challengers to their power under control, where their actions can be monitored and restricted, while the application of scientific-based methodologies may also give the same level of control to their users through the exercise of their knowledge, design skills and technical know-how.

(The framework helps us to examine these issues so that we are clear as to whose problems we are actually solving!)

What models and frameworks does the methodology offer for the situation? What models do the methodology users need to have in order to manage the situation? For example, we have found that most models offered by methodologies are wholly inadequate for understanding the situation.

What level of experience do the methodology users need to have? Can it help even if they do not have experience in the domain of the 'problem situation'? If so, how does the methodology help its users to generate solutions?

What role does the methodology expect of its users, i.e. as an expert, an advisor or a facilitator? What characteristics accompany these roles? What are the implications for the successful use of the methodology of not having for these role characteristics?

SPECIFIC QUESTIONS ABOUT THE METHODOLOGY

So, what questions can we raise about methodologies at this stage?

UNDERSTANDING THE 'SITUATION OF CONCERN'

Our first question is, what specific assistance does the methodology offer for boundary construction? Does it rely on the methodology users' abilities to define the 'boundaries of concern' thereby identifying the 'situations of concern'? If not, does it help its users to select or exclude elements of the situation? What criteria does it offer in this process ? What are the implications of this selection or exclusion for its users? for those in the situation? and for the practice of the methodology? Most methodologies do not alert their users to boundary construction, and implicit boundary construction without any help from methodologies has severe implications.

What is the role of the client with respect to the methodology? Does it recognize the inclusion and/or the participation of clients? or does it treat them as external to the methodology? Does it assist clients and its users to collectively comprehend the situation? or does it accept the overriding authority and power of the client in problem formulation? (Please note that clarifying diagrams or carrying out client walkthroughs is not participation. Participation involves more than mere communication.)

Does the methodology help its users to identify the sources of information, i.e. those which are likely to offer the most relevant and useful information? Does it provide any criteria for selecting these sources?

Does it discuss any particular method(s) of investigation? Does it recommend any particular way as being more suitable given the philosophical nature of the methodology? Are these to be followed in every situation?

What skills does it highlight as being relevant or useful for conducting this stage? Is it explicit about these? Does it warn its user about the need for these skills?

PERFORMING THE DIAGNOSIS

(As readers will note, there are so many questions for which methodology users have to find answers. These may or may not be provided by the methodology and yet methodologies are supposed to help structure their users' thinking processes.)

What modelling notions and techniques does the methodology offer for expressing situation characteristics? To what extent do these restrict or assist the expression? Can all the information be expressed accurately? What happens to the information for which modelling techniques are not provided? Are the methodology users to retain this in their minds? or express it using techniques of their own? If the latter, how can this information be incorporated in or linked to the formal expressions using the methodology?

What level of expressions does the methodology advocate? Are they conceptual/logical expressions? or are they physical expressions? Does the methodology distinguish between these two levels or does it combine them? What guidance does it offer for the construction of these expressions? or is the task left up to the methodology user? What are the implications of these for the subsequent steps of the methodology?

What environmental (context) information is captured or expressed? Is the expression sufficient for understanding the 'action world'? Can this be used from now on as the basis for problem solving? Does the expression have to be updated? and, if so, how often does it need to be updated in order to keep it representative of the situation? Does the methodology alert its users to the need for these updates?

What tools and techniques are available for this expression? Are these tools independent or closely linked to the methodology? Do the techniques *influence* what information is captured from the situation, i.e. instead of simply being techniques for recording already gathered information?

The previous questions are about *describing* the 'situation of concern'. The most important question is 'Does this expression in its form provide sufficient information to help gain a feel for the situation?' Can it, by itself, convey the *state* of the 'situation of concern'? Is this reliable as the basis for proceeding with the subsequent methodology steps?

If the clients or other participants disagree with the expression, how are the methodology users to respond? What guidance does the methodology offer? Are these questions for which the methodology users have to find pragmatic answers outside the methodology?

DEFINING THE PROGNOSIS OUTLINE

Does the methodology offer any help in defining this? If not, which 'desired states' does it accept as legitimate? If there are more than one, how does it help to resolve the differences? If it does not help to perform this stage, what criteria does it offer for establishing the legitimacy of the 'desired states'? Does the methodology alert its users to this stage at all? If it does not, then the methodology users remain at the mercy of those defining 'desired states'. What are the implications of not assisting in this task? In most cases the clients themselves are not clear about their own 'desired states'.

DEFINING 'PROBLEMS'

What 'problems' or problem types are the concern of the methodology? What criteria does it offer for defining 'problems'? How does it help its users to derive 'problem statements'? Of course, if it fails to ascertain or consider the 'desired states', then there will not be any problem definitions either. In this case, how does the methodology help its users to ascertain 'problems' or to evaluate the stated 'problems statements', or does it help to avoid them altogether? Some methodologies only provide the means for recording 'problems' without question—any questions that are levelled at the clients are only for clarification.

DERIVING NOTIONAL SYSTEMS

Does the methodology derive notional systems from the 'problems' identified? or does it take clients' notional systems as given? If the latter, how does it alert its users to the client's 'desired states' or 'problems'? Does it offer any way of formulating the notional systems? and, if so, how does it derive the notional systems without 'desired states'? Does it use the client's notional systems as the starting point for all its activities? Does it simply provide the means of *recording* the notional systems?

In most situations, the client's notional systems dictate the direction and the way in which almost all methodology users' activities are conducted, particularly in the areas of boundary construction, selection or exclusion of elements for investigation, design activities and so on. Clients who provide notional systems may not have used effective ways of defining 'desired states', 'problems' or notional systems. In many instances, as our industrial activities show, the formulation of 'desired states' remains a private and implicit activity conducted by the client. Often, even the clients themselves are not able to justify the rationale for their 'desired states'. Constrained by the political systems and methodologies, their users do not seek involvement in the problem formulation process. Once a methodology suggests acceptance of the client's notional systems, it can only help its users with the design activities. Accepting the client's notional systems without question therefore may lead to many different 'problems'.

If the methodology offers the means of performing problem formulation (i.e. defining 'desired states', 'problems' and notional systems), does it alert its users to the need for developing 'critical thinking' skills? Does it offer any concepts, models or techniques for formulating these? or do the methodology users have to rely on their experience to determine 'problems' and notional systems? If this is the case, does it offer any techniques for structuring their experiences?

The framework helps us to ask these and many other questions. In addition it offers guidance in examining the steps of a methodology and in comparing how these steps match the stages of the problem formulation process. In this context, the framework also assists us in to making the following observations.

When we examine the private and personal activities of clients' problem formulation processes, we may find that with every significant change in the 'action world' situation there may be a change in the clients' perception of the 'desired state' for that situation. With every change in the 'desired state' and/ or 'current state', there may also be corresponding changes to the problem definitions and notional systems. This may result in changes to the initial specification.

This is the reason why so many clients change their minds over the features of the notional systems. The methodology users who invest their time and effort in the design and implementation may feel very frustrated with these changes to the specification. Some methodologies try to address this problem by producing ever more improvements for capturing the requirements in an accurate and precise form, i.e. to find mathematical, contractual or formal means of *recording* the initial requirements in precise terms, leaving very little room for flexibility and holding the client responsible for the stated requirements. This is understandable from a solution-driven perspective to problem solving, but a disastrous way to undertake it. Clients live in a dynamic and often unpredictable 'action world'. The more dynamic and complex the situation, the more difficult it is to derive relevant notional systems. One solution to this is to understand the process of problem formulation in explicit terms, as was explained in the NIMSAD framework.

What factors prevent this activity from happening now?

First, most methodologies do not provide assistance for problem formulation, thereby clearly separating the tasks of the methodology users and the clients. This makes the methodology users perceive the clients as *specification givers* or *output receivers*.

Secondly, the different roles enable the clients and the methodology users to keep their shortcomings to themselves. They also offer flexibility to both groups to minimize their losses in the political thoughts driven reasoning processes discussed in Chapter 4. In this context, the methodology may become an instrument for the justification of change or a type of change. A breakthrough can occur only if the methodology users and the clients can increase their abstract/conceptual skills to perceive the essentials, their critical thinking skills to undertake problem analysis, and their interpersonal skills to manage their relationships. Political skills in this situation can only lead to solutions for a different set of problems, i.e. maintaining or extending their relative power positions.

PERFORMING DESIGN IN GENERAL

Does the methodology accept the client's notional systems as its starting point? Does it alert its users to the implications of taking this as the starting point?

Does it rely on its users' experience or expertise for design of the solutions? Does it distinguish between logical and physical design stages? If these stages are combined or separated, does the methodology alert its users to the possible implications?

Whose solutions are going to be taken in this process? What steps or techniques does the methodology offer in the formulation of solutions? Does it provide means of capturing the stakeholders' views? If it is the methodology users' models, how does the methodology ensure that these will be represented or be acceptable (at a logical and physical level) to other stakeholders? Does it provide any means for either the communication or participation of others in the design process? If so, how will the participants be chosen?

PERFORMING THE CONCEPTUAL/LOGICAL DESIGN

What particular design skills does the methodology expect its users to possess before it can be put to effective use? What concepts and theories does it offer its users for structuring solutions at a logical level? Does the methodology alert its users to the needs for these? Does it expect its users to be experienced in the solution domain? If so, how can it help its users to ensure that these models are suitable? (A successful experience in one situation does not necessarily help to achieve success in other situations.) If not, does the methodology warn its users to acquire knowledge, skills and experience before using it?

What aspects of the situation are excluded by the methodology in its design support? What are the implications of these exclusions? Does this leave the methodology users to find their own models and ways of designing the excluded elements and dimensions? What techniques are offered for the design? Does it concentrate only on the permanent, static or regular aspects of the situation characteristics, e.g. order processing, stock control, IT?

PERFORMING THE PHYSICAL DESIGN

What external models or physical elements (e.g. technology) does the methodology bring to the design process? or does it expect its users to acquire the knowledge and skills independently? If so, does the nature and the relevance of the solution remain with the methodology users? and at what level of knowledge and skills?

If the methodology accepts the notional system as its starting point, what physical design concepts will methodology users employ at this stage? Does the methodology become an instrument through which its users introduce the latest technical or management styles or work practices? Does the methodology alert its users to accept or ignore the current physical features? Both are legitimate approaches to design, but each has implications for the end solutions. The former is systems improvement, while the latter is systems innovation.

What assistance does the methodology offer its users in handling stakeholders' views? How does it help to accommodate these views? If accommodation is forthcoming, then what skills do the methodology users require for handling potential conflicts of design ideas? Does the methodology alert its users to these? (This is the reason why the rationale of the framework elements were discussed in detail in this chapter and in Chapters 4, 5 and 6. This way, the reader will understand the reasons for the elements and the stages of the framework.)

If the methodology advocates 'systems design' or 'systemic design', does it lead its users to appreciate the different use of the 'systems notions? or do its users draw implicit design boundaries and name them as 'systems'?

IMPLEMENTING THE DESIGN

What help does the methodology offer for the implementation of the design solutions?

Does it alert its users to the possibility that there may be several strategies for implementation? For example, the implementation could be sequenced in such a way that income/savings gained from one area could be used for financing another area, e.g. implementing stock control systems may reduce stock levels and increase cash flow which may help to finance the implementation of the sales order processing systems.

What steps does the methodology offer in the development of the physical systems? What does it offer in terms of techniques for ascertaining resources and facilities for the development task? How does it help to transform the physical models to physical 'action systems'? Does the methodology rely on its users' experience and interpersonal skills to ensure the success of the implementation?

If the methodology was centred around its users (i.e. no participation), then what steps does it offer them for handing over the 'action systems' to those in the situation? How does it help its users to handle major conflicts or disagreements in this transfer? How does it help them to handle major changes to notional systems features at this stage? How are the methodology users going to obtain the cooperation of others in the implementation?

SUMMARY

The framework helped to structure the questions in this chapter by focusing our mind on different aspects of problem solving. The methodology user must consider which of these could be asked within the cultural and political environment in which they operate. However, there is no reason why they cannot question themselves, for that questioning will help to develop a conscious level of awareness and may save the methodology users from making potential mistakes in the situation.

This chapter showed the importance of the evaluation element of the framework. Questions based on the evaluation need to be raised before, during and after intervention in the situation.

The completed NIMSAD framework elements arc listed in Table 7.1.

Table 7.1   NIMSAD elements and stages

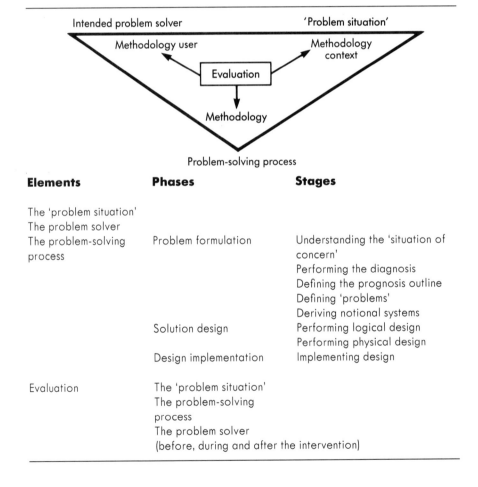

Elements	Phases	Stages
The 'problem situation' The problem solver The problem-solving process	Problem formulation	Understanding the 'situation of concern' Performing the diagnosis Defining the prognosis outline Defining 'problems' Deriving notional systems
	Solution design	Performing logical design Performing physical design
	Design implementation	Implementing design
Evaluation	The 'problem situation' The problem-solving process The problem solver (before, during and after the intervention)	

PART 3

8

CRITICAL EVALUATION OF STRUCTURED ANALYSIS AND SYSTEMS SPECIFICATION

INTRODUCTION

Structured Analysis and Systems Specification (De Marco, 1979) is one of the most well established and widely used methodologies in practice. While there are many structured methodologies, in essence they have similar structures and steps and tend to concentrate on formal data and data-related activities. Structured methodologies were devised to focus our thinking on the tasks that need to be understood before we consider the technology. Methodologies with this focus have been categorized as 'task'-oriented' methodologies (Jayaratna, 1988). This chapter evaluates the Structured Analysis and Systems Specification (SASS) of De Marco (1979). (Note that in SASS, all steps that lead to the production of a target document are called 'analysis'. This use of the term is different to its use as defined within the framework.) Figure 8.1 illustrates the outline of the methodology.

ELEMENT 1: THE 'PROBLEM SITUATION'

SASS is concerned with formal data and data-related activities of the situation. In this context, the methodology's use is to help develop highly maintainable computer-based information systems.

SASS is underpinned by 'positivistic' paradigms. These paradigms bring

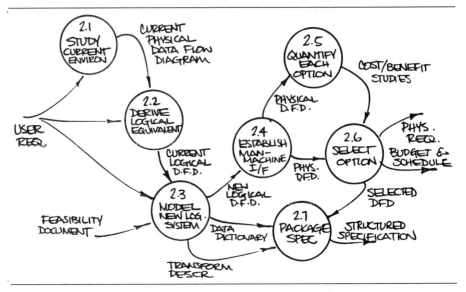

Figure 8.1 Structured analysis and systems specification outline (Tom De Marco, *Structured Analysis and Systems Specification*, © 1979. Reprinted by permission of Prentice-Hall Inc., Engl. Cliffs, NJ.)

increased rigour to the task of systems development. The activities help us to focus attention on the formal aspects of data that can be subjected to rigorous analysis and through which regular and consistent patterns can be extracted and used for building information processing systems. In this way, SASS aims to improve the effectiveness of performing data–related activities in organiza-tions. The scientific perspectives help to disconnect the data from the users and their interpretations and by so doing, help to uncover data relationships and partitioning rules. They also assist in promoting enquiry and in the discovery of 'correct' ways of doing things. Of course, this means that irregular or changing patterns of data are left out of the domain of SASS and similar methodologies.

In SASS, the organization (methodology context) is considered as a purposeful system, albeit implicitly. It recognizes the role of business analysis and suggests that although SASS is not a way of performing it, it can contribute to the process. How it is able to do this is not made clear apart from assisting one's understanding of how formal data are used within an organization.

SASS operates at a very practical level. The emphasis is on data and related tasks which match the features of the techniques and tools employed. The view that data constitutes the most important aspect of the situation is transposed to the methodology users implicitly: they remain unaware of the boundaries they derive with the help of the methodology. In doing this, SASS users automatically exclude many features of the situation which do not match the features of the methodology. SASS achieves this by excluding many of the important elements of the situation and treating them as political processes or client domain areas. We shall examine these later.

SASS recognizes three levels of users (this should not be confused with the role of the methodology user); the 'hands-on' user, the responsible user, and the system owner. It also recognizes that these three roles could be performed by one or many persons. This is an important classification and has implications for systems design. Methodology users have to consider the needs of different types of users in their designs, and SASS also discusses the role distinctions between the users and the designers. However, with respect to clients, the methodology does not discuss the legitimacy, authority or other considerations which we have considered in Chapters 4, 5, 6 and 7; in fact, it believes that by concentrating everybody's attention on the structured techniques advocated in SASS, it can help to minimize the disruptive aspects of politics!

> Political problems are not going to go away, and they won't be 'solved'. The most we can hope for is to limit the effect of disruptions due to politics. Structured Analysis approaches this objective by making analysis procedures more formal.
> (De Marco, 1979)

The creator of SASS does not define what is meant by politics nor how SASS helps to limit its disruptiveness. Helping to concentrate users' attention on formal aspects of data does not necessarily remove the issue of politics; it may, however, help those who resort to politics to find a new basis for legitimizing their reasoning. This is part of the reason why it warns its users to expect changes to the specification during the life of the project.

Clients' needs serve as the starting point of the methodology. The rationale for clients' needs is not considered as they are treated as part of the political process. The users of SASS have to devise their own methods of assessing the commitment of clients to the project.

ELEMENT 2: THE METHODOLOGY USER (INTENDED PROBLEM SOLVER)

This stage examines first how SASS helps us to assess our own 'mental constructs' and secondly, whether it discusses the need for developing these 'mental constructs' to a desirable level in order to apply the methodology successfully. One of the assumptions made by the methodology creator is that those who use the methodology will have the same or similar insightful levels of knowledge, skills and competence as he does.

EVALUATION OF THE 'MENTAL CONSTRUCT'

SASS at no stage alerts its users to their 'mental constructs', nor does it help them to examine the high level of preparation they should have in order to use the methodology successfully. In keeping with the philosophical paradigms, it is evident that SASS assumes that the use of its techniques will yield the same results irrespective of the nature of the 'mental constructs' of its users.

The strong focus on techniques and tools makes SASS fail to consider many of the 'mental construct' elements discussed in Chapter 4. Given the rich and complex nature of the 'mental construct' and the significance of the methodology user in the problem-solving situation, this lack of focus on the methodology user raises many important questions. For instance, given the same situation, two different, technically competent SASS users may derive two different sets of data flow diagrams! This is a fairly common problem that practitioners working in groups experience every day. The group leader's decision or a consensus or a compromise decision cannot necessarily derive the 'correct' diagram, as the processes of compromise are political, emotional and power driven. The development of data flow diagrams in industrial contexts teaches us that most 'action world' operations cannot be captured neatly in this way. The more rigid and formal the procedures in a given situation, the more flexible the informal systems will have to be in order to cope with the changes in the environment. A heavy concentration on techniques fails to uncover the informal information flows or sensitive non-verbal information which may be critical.

DESIRABILITY LEVELS OF THE 'MENTAL CONSTRUCT'

At this stage the consideration is to establish the desirable level of the 'mental constructs' of the methodology users (in the author's judgement) before they can become effective users of SASS.

An examination of the role of SASS users helps to determine that they need either experience in the user application environment or in the use of *general* conceptual models for structuring their thinking in the situation. Since SASS provides only simple input-process-output models and techniques, its users have to rely on their own experience or knowledge (mostly implicit) or on others' knowledge to be successful in bringing about transformation in situations.

The most dominant knowledge and skills required to undertake this methodology are technical. SASS does highlight the need for these skills. Without a high level of technical competence it is difficult to imagine how a potential SASS user could undertake the activities of data modelling and process specification.

SASS recognizes some of the problems of analysis to be political and interpersonal. The techniques it advocates are supposed to keep the political processes external to the activities of systems development. While SASS does not explicitly acknowledge this, in practice it has to rely on its users' interpersonal, political and social skills to make the methodology effective. In other words, it may have to rely very heavily on its users' non-technical skills to draw out information from those in the situation in order to build the context, functional and operational level diagrams. For example, imagine the problems that one would experience in trying to obtain information from people who may be made redundant or whose power may be diminished by the potential designs resulting from the use of SASS. SASS deals with these issues by treating them as political processes outside the domain of its users! This means that SASS users have to devise their own methods of dealing with their interpersonal relationship activities. No matter what techniques are used, there is no possibility of avoiding organizational relationship issues, and the more SASS tries to externalize these as political the more its users have to devise their own ways of addressing them. We urge the creator of SASS to extend the methodology to capture the essential information from the political processes.

SASS promotes technical values. It discusses the need for user participation, but neither its structure and steps nor its rationale provide any means for bringing this about. This is one of the most common claims made by methodologies: however, while graphical presentation techniques may help to improve communication with the clients, they do not necessarily bring about user participation! User participation requires considerable interpersonal and political skills and a commitment to compromise, as we have experienced. See also discussions on participation in Chapter 9.

SASS does not provide explicit conceptual models to help its users capture and structure their understanding of the situations, but it offers a set of very *useful* techniques for understanding the flows, relationships and structural properties of data as well as flows of data that match the features of the techniques. In other words, users will have to rely on their own conceptual models for structuring the situation.

SASS docs not enter into any discussion about ethical and moral values. Since the role of SASS users is presented as that of a technical one, these issues have to be dealt with by the clients as part of their politics.

SASS defines the role of its users as being concerned with *how* to accomplish things, while its clients define *what* needs to be accomplished.

> Logical considerations include answers to the question *What needs to be accomplished*? These fall naturally into the domain of user. Physical considerations include answers to the question *How shall we accomplish these things*? These are in the domain of the analyst. (De Marco, 1979)

This clarification is at odds with the promotion of SASS as a logical process and a way of carrying out systems analysis. Note that in the context of the NIMSAD framework, the 'what' issues are the role of systemic analysis and the 'how' issues are the role of systemic design. If the 'what' issues fall into the domain of the user, how can SASS claim to be an analysis methodology? As discussed in the context of NIMSAD, clients' requirements may not necessarily solve the 'problems'.

ELEMENT 3, STAGE 1: UNDERSTANDING OF THE 'SITUATION OF CONCERN'

SASS does not alert its users to the conceptual construction of boundaries or identification of a 'situation of concern'. Boundary construction is trial and error within SASS.

> The first sub phase . . . is a complete study of the affected user areas. Before this process can begin, you must make an *early guess* [my italics] at the scope of the project. (De Marco, 1979)

SASS offers little useful guidance to its users in identifying the areas for study.

In terms of guessing scope, how is one able to guess the scope? What are the implications of this guess covering too wide or too narrow an area for investigation? In practice, of course, the client requirement list and client-expressed problems serve as the basis for defining the boundaries of *the system for investigation*.

SASS, assumes that techniques of data flow diagramming can help to construct a systems boundary and establish the context for information systems design. However, the lack of discussion of these conceptual issues forces SASS users to rely on their own implicit assessment of the situation in order to define the scope of the study.

From the examination of SASS, it is clear that its interest lies in the flows and structures of formal data and data-related activities, while any aspect beyond this (e.g. responsibility, decision frames, etc.) remains outside its areas of concern. In so doing, it helps its users to draw an *implicit* boundary around a 'situation of concern'. This boundary is considered to be between the logical and physical activities. SASS states:

> the analyst and the user ought to try to communicate across
> the logical-physical boundary that exists in any computer
> systems project.   (De Marco, 1979)

The statements and the reference to the description of *the existing system* confirm the ontological use of the term 'system' and the search for an independent system out there to be identified and documented. Once again, how are we to discover the logical-physical boundary? SASS does not help to locate this boundary nor does it help its users to draw explicit boundaries or to identify the 'situation of concern', clients also carry out physical and logical activities. The non-conceptual boundary construction may lead its users to:

- ignore much essential situational information that cannot potentially be computerized, e.g. many informal information flows may not be recognized as being either relevant or useful
- concentrate exclusively on the *formal* characteristics of situational information that match the essential features of information technology whether this is desirable or not. In data flow and data analysis examples, the emphasis is on the *formal* characteristics, e.g. relationships between order–item–stocks

- exclude many organizational features and dimensions that may be critical to the effective performance and use of information processing systems (i.e. roles, functions, structures and relationships).

INVESTIGATION MODELS AND TECHNIQUES

Given the discussions on methodology support for the evaluation of 'mental constructs' and their assistance in boundary construction, we now examine what help SASS provides for the actual gathering of information.

This topic is not discussed in an explicit way by SASS other than to suggest pragmatic hints, i.e. working around the users. There is reference to user interviews, but no discussions as to what models are to be used or how this process is to be structured. This lack of attention to investigation methods is consistent with the positivistic views of SASS that truthful information about a given situation (or the 'existing system' in this case) is independent of the medium of collection. Therefore, data collection is not given significant methodology attention. This viewpoint is not surprising, given the following statement:

> Working closely with the users, you learn and document the way things currently work. Rather than do this from the point of view of *any one user or set of users*, [my italics] you attempt to assess operations *from the viewpoint of the data.*   (De Marco, 1979)

In this case, SASS fails to acknowledge that data cannot have viewpoints, only humans can. What really happens (although SASS does not recognize this) is that the data collection is achieved through the viewpoint of the methodology users or the client. Since there are no explicit conceptual models advocated within SASS for conducting the investigation, the data captured are those which are meaningful to SASS users, those which are considered by the SASS users to be relevant to the requirement list, or those which the clients insist on as being relevant for their *systems*. The importance of this viewpoint is now recognized by other structured methodology creators (e.g. Yourdon, 1989) who have developed modified approaches.

The lack of attention to methods of investigation has very serious implications for systems development. It means that SASS users may not become alert to the different nature of problems, opportunities, or the effects that methods of investigation may have on the nature, content and subsequent interpretations attributed to data. The factors which influence these interpretations are interpersonal relationships, influence and authority of individuals, personal motives and prejudices.

ELEMENT 3, STAGE 2: PERFORMING THE DIAGNOSIS

SASS makes one of the *most useful* contributions to this stage. The use of data flow diagrams, levelling and balancing techniques, data dictionaries, consistency checking facilities and data modelling techniques provide very clear ways of expressing the flows of formal data—see Figure 8.2. This form of expression is a vast improvement over others, and contributes to a very clear understanding of the use of data for operational activities in the situation. Each process symbol in this description is known as a *bubble*.

Since SASS does not offer explicit conceptual models for structuring the investigation it tries to extract the logical description of a 'system' in the situation by constructing the physical data flow diagrams first. Its arguments for constructing 'current' physical data flow diagrams are that they help to identify real users, documents, equipment, communication and walkthroughs. SASS also provides *very useful* practical hints on how to ensure that the sets of diagrams are consistent. Other structured methodologies, such as Gane and Sarson (1979), do not distinguish between the physical and the logical aspects, while Ross (1977) incorporates both control and operational activities in the same diagram. Once the physical data flow diagrams have been drawn (partial Diagnosis Model 2—DM2), attempts are then made to extract the logic of the physical checkpoints.

There are problems with this approach which SASS does discuss. Basically, the removal of physical document names or numbers cannot always help to abstract the logic of the activities. Imagine an order processing system in which there is reference to a data store. The removal of a name may not make sense, as the activity may be meaningful only in the physical context in which the data store is used. In fact, the removal of the physical characteristics may make it more difficult to understand the logic of why the file is being referenced! This is the reason why SASS suggests the examination of each bubble, data store or data flow in order to determine whether they can be eliminated from the logical model. In effect, it is the users' knowledge of what is possible with current technology that implicitly helps them to pass logical judgements on the diagrams. For example, the reference to a customer accounts file by a salesperson when having dinner with the customer in a restaurant can become a very logical activity only if the salesperson has the

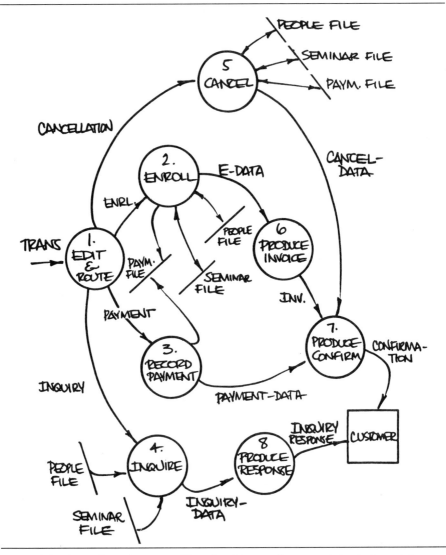

Figure 8.2 Data flow diagrams (Tom De Marco, *Structured Analysis and Systems Specification*, © 1979. Reprinted by permission of Prentice-Hall, Inc., Engl. Cliffs, NJ.)

appropriate technology to take that action. The distinction between logical and physical is not easy to maintain unless we use concepts to help clarify the meanings: what makes logical sense tomorrow may not make logical sense today. It would be more useful to suggest an abstract approach, but SASS does not offer any conceptual models for undertaking this activity. An abstract approach to the development of logical models prior to the development of physical models is insightful but difficult—the difficulty arises from the need to understand the rationale, concepts and philosophy underpinning the models. However, we have found models such as those of Beer (1981) to be extremely useful for both structuring the investigation and expressing the 'diagnosis' (see Figure 8.3).

Problems of logicalization have now been recognized by Coad and Yourdon (1989). Commenting on the problems, they quote McMenamin and Palmer (1984) who state 'Many analysts fell into the "current physical tarpit", never to emerge.' Coad and Yourdon (1989) now advocate the use of the term 'essential'. The approach is similar but not the same, i.e. construct the physical model and then abstract the essentials. They recommend that we build current physical models based on one bubble for each event.

The current logical diagrams form the Diagnosis Model 1 (DM1) expressions as discussed at the 'diagnosis' stage of the framework. Also useful is the notion of 'levelling'. SASS advocates the use of a context diagram, which can then be expanded to understand the detail levels (the terms 'de-composition' and 'partitioning' are used). In SASS, these numbers of levels may be many, depending on the situation, and may continue until they show a lowest level which is defined as 'functional primitives'. SASS uses the term 'parent–child' to show these level connections. The notion of 'balancing' is used for ensuring that the different level diagrams are consistent as far as the number of inputs and outputs are concerned. Most of the practical hints provided are *very useful* on the technical aspects of data flow construction.

The construction of logical data flow diagrams is followed by deriving logical equivalents of physical file structures. How is this task performed? SASS states that:

> The most straightforward answer to the question is that we must look at each *use* of the set of files and *somehow* [my italics] derive an ideal file structure from the pattern of use.
> (De Marco, 1979)

This is an activity of abstraction from existing file data. SASS provides a technique for performing this activity, however, it is based on users having to go through each data element. As Yourdon's (1989) comments show, this is a laborious task to undertake at this stage. Besides, here we are supposed to be describing the situation and not defining 'ideals'. Construction of ideal data structures is a design activity and should be undertaken only after the

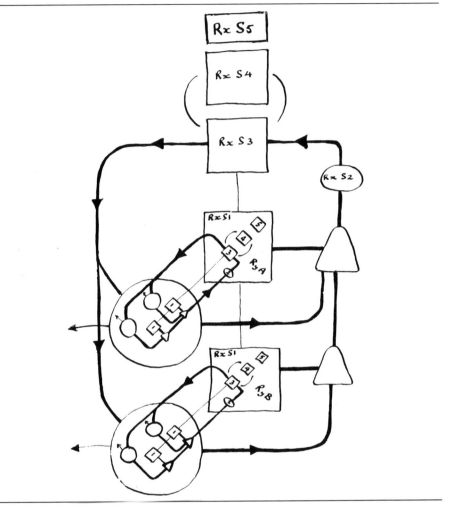

Figure 8.3   Systems' five model (Stafford Beer, *Brain of the Firm*, © 1981. Reprinted by permission of John Wiley & Sons, Ltd.)

methodology users are aware of what they are trying to achieve. In other words, ideal data structures should be constructed only after passing judgement on what 'ideal' information processing systems we are trying to design.

In SASS, a lot of details are left out of the 'diagnosis'. For example, there is no information on role characteristics, structure or responsibilities of the users of information. The techniques of SASS are *very effective* and powerful for describing some aspects of the situation (formal data and related activities); however, this information is *not* sufficient for obtaining an impression of the *state* of the 'situation of concern'. From the perspective of the NIMSAD framework, there is not enough information to complete the diagnosis. Any judgement is based on the methodology users' 'mental constructs', i.e. past experience and subjective interpretation of the situation. The methodology relies on its users' considerable experience for gaining an impression of the *state* of the situation, and yet it does not recognize this experience as a necessary requirement for its user.

SASS, while providing useful techniques for recording data and related activities, focuses its users' attention on the discovery and expression of explicitly recognizable, definable and repeatable patterns of data. These techniques influence the users to look for signs of regularity and consistency in the data and associated activities at the expense of related roles and functions. While these data are useful for database and software design, the exclusion of other information has serious implications for evaluating the relevance and usefulness of information. For example, in an order processing system, the orders, invoices and their flows are easily recognizable; they occur frequently and therefore the pattern of the flows can be recognized. However, most information which does not show this level of visibility and characteristics is not captured, i.e. telephone calls from a sales clerk to a supervisor about work progress, etc.

SASS suggests that these diagrams are used for 'structured walkthroughs' with the users for establishing consistency in understanding:

> . . . walkthroughs with the user to verify correctness.
> (De Marco, 1979)

Certainly in our 'industrial work' the diagrams helped to establish the relevance of information rather than their 'correctness'. Correctness is possible only where it involves human agreement or proof of demonstrable consistent characteristics, i.e. the design of logic circuits, operations of a chemical process, etc. In some situations, people may agree to a particular data flow diagram as 'correct' because that is how it is supposed to operate or because failure to agree may create political problems for them. In SASS it is the client who determines the 'correctness' of the diagrams, and yet why should humans be consulted when the data flow diagrams are drawn from the viewpoint of data?

The data flow diagram is documentation of a situation from

the point of view of data. This turns out to be a more useful viewpoint than that of any of the people or systems that process the data, because the data itself sees the big picture.

(De Marco, 1979)

If it is the data which see the big picture, then it must show how this view can be extracted.

ELEMENT 3, STAGE 3: DEFINING THE PROGNOSIS OUTLINE

As SASS does not make its users aware of this formation, it cannot help them to understand or, more significantly, question the *rationale* for the clients' 'desired states'. SASS simply relies on the clients to be clear about the rationale for their requirements. It does not offer any steps for examining the validity of these expectations; it considers these to be the domain of political processes. Because of the lack of awareness of the problem formulation activities SASS is unable to help its users consider the reasons for the clients' expectations.

ELEMENT 3, STAGE 4: DEFINING 'PROBLEMS'

As SASS does not concern itself with the clients' 'desired states' (prognosis outlines), it simply has no means of performing this stage either. It relies on the ability of the client to conduct the mapping of the two states and deriving of problem statements. These issues do not enter the domain of the methodology. SASS treats this also as part of the political process.

Of course, analysis is an intensely political subject.

(De Marco, 1979)

Despite this acknowledgement, SASS is presented as an analysis methodology.

ELEMENT 3, STAGE 5: DERIVING THE NOTIONAL SYSTEM

As SASS does not help its users to participate in the definition of 'desired states', it cannot define problems nor can it arrive at the notional system(s).

The concern of the methodology is to record the features of the notional system(s) expressed by the client in a concise form in order to facilitate its

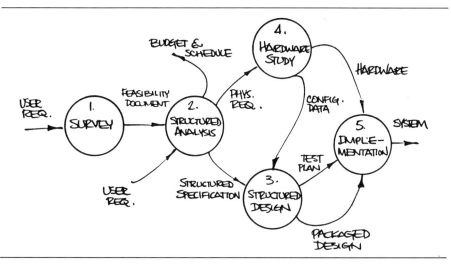

Figure 8.4 Requirements model (Tom De Marco, *Structured Analysis and Systems Specification*, © 1979. Reprinted by permission of Prentice-Hall, Inc., Engl. Cliffs, NJ.)

design tasks. Any questioning of the client is only for clarification and to ensure that the SASS users have *correctly* understood and recorded his or her *exact* requirements. Figure 8.4 shows how notional systems features (user requirements) enter the SASS methodology process. In practice, user requirements guide the whole methodology process and they are taken into account at the beginning of the project.

Of course, as SASS suggests, the problem formulation process (analysis) is an intensely political activity, but it is also an intellectual activity. By treating it as a political process, SASS also leaves itself out of the potential intellectual activity of understanding or questioning the rationale for the clients' 'desired states'. We are not trying to underestimate the politics of problem formulation, but to highlight the need to understand the intellectual rationale for the requirements.

Avoiding politics by recording and using client requirements as the basis for systems design does not exclude SASS users from the implications of the political processes either. The lack of intellectual focus on the problem formulation and requirements definition may result in many unwanted and expensive changes to the original requirements. Some of the changes to requirements made by clients are very legitimate, as they are made in response to changes in the environment, i.e. legislation, customer preferences or competitor activities. These changes are recognized by SASS. However, many are due to weaknesses in clients' problem formulation processes and their methodologies. Many clients do not spend sufficient time and effort on explicit reasoning about their requirements. In other words, clients very often do not use methodologies for arriving at their requirements. Since SASS does not provide any problem structuring and requirement deriving processes, it treats this as an external political process and takes a pragmatic stand on changes to the specification. De Marco (1979) is explicit on this point and recognizes the pragmatic difficulties and the limitations of SASS in this task. Some of these limitations are performance analysis and conceptual thinking.

SASS's non-involvement in the problem structuring process may lead its users to view clients as 'specification givers' and/or 'output receivers'. It does not consider the analysis phase as being definite. This is a practical problem, but as the NIMSAD framework demonstrates, methodology users must be able to identify the intellectual end-point of the systemic analysis phase.

ELEMENT 3, STAGE 6: PERFORMING CONCEPTUAL/ LOGICAL DESIGN

The boundary domain of the design is set by the client's requirements. In SASS this is referred to as the *domain of change*. The domain is established in consultation with the client.

Some of the *most useful and rigorous* techniques offered by SASS are the data flow diagrams and data dictionaries. In SASS, the designs are usually created by modifying the current logical diagrams (Diagnosis Model DM1) using the user requirements and feasibility document as a guide. Techniques of levelling and balancing enable the SASS user to maintain consistency between different levels of diagrams. Data dictionary concepts help to store the details of data and procedural aspects used within the data flow diagrams. SASS considers the transformation of current logical data flow diagrams (DM1) to a new logical data flow diagram (PM1) as part of its analysis phase. (It is for this reason that we used earlier chapters to clarify the terminology of analysis and design.) It recognizes that PM1 could start from new, but suggests the use of the current logical data models (data flow diagrams, data dictionaries, data structure diagrams) and determining the domain of change, i.e. the parts of the existing model to be changed. It also advocates the examination of each process symbol (bubble) of the current data flow diagram and asking whether it can be automated, semi-automated and so on. Figure

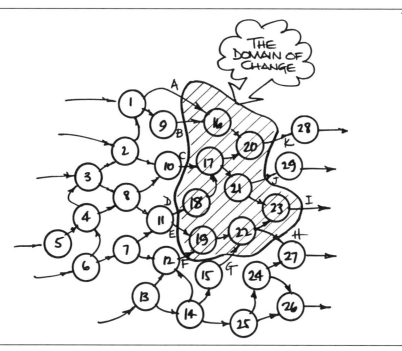

Figure 8.5 Domain of change (Tom De Marco, *Structured Analysis and Systems Specification*, © 1979. Reprinted by permission of Prentice-Hall, Inc., Engl. Cliffs, NJ.)

8.5 illustrates this boundary construction. This is applying *physical* characteristics to help determine areas for change! (In the framework this is considered to be part of physical design because it is dealing with issues of *whom and how*.) The area thus marked is treated as a collective domain for a new context diagram. While SASS considers design to be a top-down partitioning, in this case it is clear that bottom-up physical characteristics are being considered for determining the areas for design. SASS proposes this approach as it does not offer any conceptual means of undertaking designs. In fact, SASS is very explicit about this process when it says:

> This is where he invents the new system. I won't tell you how to go about this. I have restricted myself to teaching tools for analysis, and no tool that I could think of would aid the invention process. When you have come up with your invention, however, the tools of Structured Analysis are exceedingly useful for documenting it and trying it out.   (De Marco, 1979)

We agree with the honest admissions of the creator of SASS. The techniques are extremely useful in describing the design models (PM1). SASS offers assistance in performing data modelling by extracting the structural features of static data. It calls this the construction of data structure diagrams. In data structure diagrams, the data elements and structures are rationalized and organized so that their relationships can be well defined.

SASS is *extremely helpful* when it comes to structuring the operations on the data. Its use of structure charts helps to partition the operations of the processes into logical modules, which can then be easily transformed into software modules. The cohesion and coupling techniques help to design the software modules so that they can be easily maintained in a changing environment. These are systems concepts applied at a technique level. The objective is to design systems in such a way as to strengthen the connectivity within the modules and reduce the connections between them. The latter is really the concept of 'de-coupling' (rather than coupling), the use of which leads to the design of relatively independent software modules. Designs of this type can help to reduce maintenance activities during the life cycle of information processing systems. What is most interesting is that SASS uses a number of 'systems' concepts very effectively without alerting the users or discussing the nature of the concepts with them. The implications are very obvious to an effective systems thinker: the notions of cohesion and coupling help to test the modules that are already designed, because the designers do not understand the concepts, they are unable to decide on issues such as how many modules to construct for a given function. In SASS, software module construction is called *structured design*.

Unfortunately, SASS does not extend this level of rigour to designing other associated roles, functions, decision-making methods, etc.. In effect, it does not take any interest in those aspects beyond the organization of formal data and data-related activities. This is not surprising when you examine the views promoted within SASS.

> A data flow is a pipeline through which packets of informa-
> tion of known composition flow.   (De Marco, 1979)

The whole design process is based on the view that the design of information processing systems is no different to the design of, for example, parcel delivery systems! SASS should show interest in how the information processing systems it helps to develop, affects the 'problem situation'.

ELEMENT 3, STAGE 7: PERFORMING THE PHYSICAL DESIGN

SASS provides guidelines for transforming logical data processes, flows and models to a state closer to computerization. However, it does not offer any physical design guidelines; its original demarcation at the logical design stage determines the areas for physical design. There are two problems which arise when logical models are transformed into physical models.

The first is the problem of selection of an area for computerization. The boundary content identified can cause problems for other non–computerized areas of the design. For example, computerization of the A/C receivable data store (considered as part of the domain for change) may create problems of duplication, inconsistency and practical difficulties if manual access is also to be gained to this data store in another part of the organization. Boundaries for automation cannot be established easily in this way. In Figure 8.5 none of the bubbles identified within the domain of change should be changed until we are sure about the implications for the bubbles outside the boundary.

These difficulties arise because SASS does not provide any conceptual approach to the identification of areas for computerization. Letting the client determine the areas for change without offering assistance for considering the implications of these decisions can lead to expensive revisions.

The second problem is how to decide on alternative configurations, e.g. distributed, de-centralized, mainframe/micro systems. There are simply no guidelines on how decisions on physical design options are to be made, since physical design is also considered to be part of the analysis phase in SASS. It is here that all previous activities are packaged in one document called the target document. SASS suggests the addition of configuration-dependent features to the logical design, but offers no guidance as to how this could be undertaken. However, it does list them as being outside the scope of the methodology.

ELEMENT 3, STAGE 8: IMPLEMENTING THE DESIGN

This is the weakest stage of SASS. To expect that the design models which are generated by great human effort can be implemented with little support from the methodology is a serious underestimation of the implementation task. SASS does not provide guidelines as to what criteria or strategies to adopt for the implementation of design models. However, it cannot be criticized for this as it claims to be an analysis methodology and recommends the use of structured techniques for that task only.

ELEMENT 4: EVALUATION

SASS does not offer any evaluation steps. In the context of the evaluation focus of the framework, this is not effective. Since SASS provides only a set of techniques and excludes many of the problem formulation activities as being political, it can offer to measure only the applicability of these techniques.

SUMMARY

SASS is one of the most popular methodologies for the design of information processing systems. It offers a range of very useful techniques for describing and designing computer-based information processing systems. However, it excludes many factors, such as why clients need the systems, how the information helps to resolve the problems facing clients, etc. One of the most salient features is that it is very clear and honest about its limited role. The creator of SASS (De Marco, 1979) sets its role very explicitly as being one of analysis, yet the methodology avoids the analysis issues as discussed in the context of NIMSAD by treating them as part of the political process. SASS guidelines are very practical and easy to understand. Its strength is in the practical help it offers for documenting data and data-related activities, while its weakness lies in the lack of conceptual support for undertaking analysis activities. Potential SASS users may have to seek the support of other methodologies and their own 'mental constructs' in order to undertake success-ful problem formulation. In the context of the discussions in Chapters 4, 5, 6 and 7, SASS does not address many of the problem-formulation issues (discussed in the context of the NIMSAD framework) which are essential for an analysis type methodology.

The creator of SASS is one of the few to openly admit the limits of the methodologies. The exclusion of many issues as being political prevent us from further critical evaluation. We urge the creator of SASS to include user requirement and political process in the new version to help the users.

9

CRITICAL EVALUATION OF 'ETHICS' METHODOLOGY

INTRODUCTION

ETHICS methodology (Mumford, 1983a, 1983b) is well known for its emphasis on and interest in the human side of systems design. It was classified as a 'process-oriented' methodology in the methodology classification (Jayaratna, 1988). ETHICS is an acronym for **E**ffective **T**echnical and **H**uman **I**mplementation of **C**omputer-based **S**ystems. While the acronym may imply ethics, however, the methodology is not about formulating or resolving ethical issues—it subscribes to a particular ethical stance which will be discussed in this chapter. The title also implies a focus on implementation, but the major concern of the methodology is the process of design. The methodology steps and structure are outlined in figure 9.1.

ELEMENT 1: THE 'PROBLEM SITUATION'

Here we examine what ETHICS has to say about the situation.

ETHICS is concerned with the design process and in encouraging the participation of those organizational members whose lives may be affected by the design. Because of this interest it is underpinned by 'phenomenological' paradigms which make designers appreciate that 'reality' is very much an interpretation of the phenomena perceived. ETHICS attempts to reconcile multiple interpretations by helping to form collective groups and extracting consensus viewpoints about their psychological and social needs. The balancing of collective human needs within management set goals for an organization means that ETHICS is less rigorous and more subjective when compared with scientifically-based SASS discussed in the previous chapter.

Table 9.1   ETHICS methodology steps

Step 1:	Why change?
Step 2:	Systems boundaries
Step 3:	Description of existing system
Step 4:	Definition of key objectives
Step 5:	Definition of key tasks
Step 6:	Key information needs
Step 7:	Diagnosis of efficiency needs
Step 8:	Diagnosis of job satisfaction needs
Step 9:	Future analysis
Step 10:	Specifying and weighting efficiency and job satisfaction needs and objectives
Step 11:	Organizational design of the new system
Step 12:	Technical options
Step 13:	The preparation of detailed design work
Step 14:	Implementation
Step 15:	Evaluation

ETHICS is pragmatically oriented and relies for its success on the practical abilities and the commitment of the participants to arrive at consensus decisions. It aims to build computer-based information systems which provide job satisfaction and meet the efficiency needs of the organization.

This raises three issues for discussion.

First, the definition of efficiency. The methodology does not make it clear about the distinction between efficiency and effectiveness.

> Efficiency needs can be identified by looking for *variances*. A variance *is a tendency for a system or part of a system to deviate from some expected or desired standard or norm.*
>
> (Mumford, 1983b)

The deviance against expected norms or goals of a system is a measure of its effectiveness. Efficiency is the measure of the cost/benefit ratio in achieving a system's goals. While the two measures are interrelated, it is important to clarify conceptually the differences between the two them.

Secondly, the notion of organization needs. Throughout the explanation and discussion of the methodology, there is reference to organizational needs. As discussed in Chapter 4 in the context of organizational mission statements, organizations *do not* have needs—the needs, objectives and goals are formulated by powerful groups or individuals (management) for the organization. Even the changes depend on how management views the organization's role, survival or growth in the particular environmental context. By defining these as organizational needs, the methodology effectively removes any debate or discussion of the relevance, validity or viability of these needs, and the participation advocated by it becomes limited to the best *ways* of performing operations within the constraints and goals laid down by the management. For ETHICS these issues should be central to its intervention process. Ultimately, the job satisfaction, rewards and career development of many participants depend on the nature of the decision-making processes employed within the organization.

Thirdly, organizations tend to have a mixture of management styles, but the main ones depends on the type of market, products or services, time scales of operations, measures of performance, reward systems, etc. These eventually dictate the form of organizational culture that is formed. The type of management style and organizational culture dictates how easy or difficult it would be to practise participation. For example, within an authoritarian management style it would be extremely difficult to bring about participation advocated by ETHICS. Yet there is no discussion as to what context factors and conditions are essential or need to be in place before the methodology can be introduced.

Mumford states:

> an argument based on values which states that people have a moral right to control their own destinies and this applies as much in the work situation as elsewhere.
>
> (Mumford, 1981)

Most people (including the author) agree with this value statement. However, organizations consist of people who have a considerable interest in promoting their own destinies. This tends to conflict with the desire to let other people pursue their destinies. Each attempt to achieve one's own destiny can come only at the expense of some other person's destiny in an environmental context which is both constraining and finite in resources. Therefore, those who have access to resources and power reach their destinies much more quickly and easily than those with less resources and power. What one expects from a methodology of this kind which has set itself the goal of empowerment is some assistance in how to bring about a reconciliation of the legitimacy and desirability of these destinies.

(Readers should note that this is not an evaluation of the desirability of democratic values advocated by the methodology, but of what help it offers the user in the understanding of the context factors and how to bring about the conditions for ensuring that methodology goals are achieved.)

What about the role of the client? In ETHICS, the client is the management which defines the needs for the study, the boundary of the design and becomes a member of the steering committee.

ELEMENT 2: THE METHODOLOGY USER (INTENDED PROBLEM SOLVER)

First, we need to examine how ETHICS helps its users to assess their own 'mental constructs'; and secondly, whether ETHICS alerts its users to the need for developing their 'mental constructs' to a desirable level in order to apply the methodology successfully.

EVALUATION OF THE 'MENTAL CONSTRUCT'

ETHICS alerts its users to the role expected of them in systems development as one of teaching.

> Instead of being designers they will be teachers, advisers and
> learners   (Mumford, 1983a)

This is a fundamental role shift for the methodology user. While this is essential for those practising the methodology, ETHICS does very explicitly alert its users to the different role they may have to perform but does not discuss the different values, motives, prejudices, needs or potential problems that they need to manage when bringing about participation or when working in a participative environment. This shift requires the methodology users to be responsible for bringing about change using design models owned by others. This approach is a direct converse of the one advocated in structured methodologies where the methodology users expect organizational members to operate and live with the 'action systems' designed by the methodology users. In this context, ETHICS advocates that consultants should seek a transfer of their knowledge to the design group.

> By the end of the design exercise the Design Group was both
> confident and expert and had little need for the consultants.
> The consultants' skills had now been transferred to members

of the Design Group and the Consultants were superfluous. The Consultants looked on this transfer of knowledge as a major achievement.　　　　　　　　　　(Mumford, 1983a)

This raises further issues for discussion.

First, the methodology users' role is seen primarily as one of transferring knowledge. This expectation is consistent with the role of teacher discussed earlier. However, many of those who acquire knowledge about systems development will not be prepared to part with it if it has been derived from experience and personal investment.

Secondly, the transfer of knowledge may affect the methodology users' future marketable skills within the organization. A methodology user also has personal needs to satisfy on a continuing basis. Once their knowledge is transferred, methodology users have very little to offer to that organization— in other words, the methodology is asking its users to achieve their job satisfaction at the risk of redundancy! In addition, there are financial, psychological and emotional problems that need to be overcome in order to continue in this vein, yet the methodology does not discuss how its users can adapt themselves to this new role.

Thirdly, what is being advocated is not a transfer of knowledge about the methodology, but of the methodology users' own knowledge and skills. If this is to continue, methodology users will need to continuously acquire new relevant and useful knowledge and skills in ever shorter time scales to remain in viable occupation or consultancy position.

We must commend these high ideals and aspirations, but there are, nevertheless problems with their practice. What is not discussed here is how one is to resolve the political, emotional and psychological problems of undertaking this kind of role shift.

The role shifts advocated in ETHICS have other implications for the skills of its users (see, for example, the nature of the problems in the Rolls Royce case study (Mumford, 1983a)). Opening up participative consultations and discussions over shortcomings and problems inevitably focuses on individuals and groups within the organization, and ETHICS users need considerable skills in order to handle these conflicts. Given that discussions and debates are diverted from the technical issues to the human relationship issues, methodology users require a high level of political and interpersonal skills to manage these emotional expressions. ETHICS discusses the need for such skills but does not provide any models or techniques. This is not a criticism of the methodological values, but one of ETHICS' failures to explicate the methods by which a potential user can manage the processes.

DESIRABILITY LEVELS OF THE 'MENTAL CONSTRUCT'

At this stage we wish to consider what should be the level of appropriateness of the 'mental construct' (in the author's judgement) before ETHICS can be used effectively.

To practice ETHICS, its users require to adopt social values, to have knowledge of social processes and to possess considerable interpersonal and political skills in order to manage the social interactions and interpersonal conflicts which may arise as a result of opening up a free flow of information exchange. ETHICS users will need considerable training in and use of these skills if they are to perform in less dominant and more supportive roles.

ETHICS has not explicitly recognized the need for its users to have a high level of technical skills. However, without this level of technical competence, its users will be unable to maximize the advantages of available technology. ETHICS has, nevertheless, acknowledged that the pace of technology development has a considerable impact on the designed solutions, and since this is the case, it would be advisable for ETHICS users to keep themselves up-to-date with the developments in information technology. Without an understanding of the *capabilities* of the technology (application potential and not necessarily the logic or architecture—see Chapter 1 for a discussion on the skills of information specialists) ETHICS users are limited to designs which may fail to increase organizational efficiency or members' job satisfaction, enlargement or enrichment.

ETHICS is not explicit as to how it can help its users to manage the participation of members who may be made redundant. Most cost justification for introducing information technology has been at the expense of the human side of systems. Structured methodologies deal with these issues by treating them as political processes outside the domain of their users. Since ETHICS is very much focused on the human aspects of the design, it is very surprising that it does not offer any assistance for dealing with these issues. Those who intend to pursue ETHICS would be well advised to adopt *genuine* social values, to develop effective long-term interpersonal relationships with potential users and to become involved in the action domain of organizational members on a regular basis.

Since the methodology does not provide any explicit models for managing social processes, we would like to suggest the use of interpersonal dynamics models of the type advocated by Schon (1983), Argyris and Schon (1974), Schein (1969), Lewin (1958) and Kolb et al. (1991).

(Readers should note that the creator of ETHICS has considerable experience, skills and competence in handling interpersonal problems, and unless methodology users are able to exercise similar skills intervention can be very problematic. The role of this book is to alert potential methodology users to these dimensions. In fact, unless the methodology user can develop interpersonal management skills, have models for addressing different situations and be competent in handling human conflicts it is best that they be cautious of using ETHICS. Emotional and interpersonal problems can be far more difficult to manage than technical problems.)

ETHICS provides simple systems input–process–output models to help with investigation. Its use of the cybernetic models of Beer (1978, 1979, 1981) does not extend to the more sophisticated notions of homeostasis or their recursive interlocking nature. The use of systems models here is of the ontological kind discussed in Chapter 4.

What ethical and moral values does ETHICS promote? It explicitly states that it is morally right for those people who ultimately have to operate the developed 'systems' to participate in their design. The methodology is to be complimented for taking such a stance. On the question of ethics, it claims to be an ethical approach to systems design because it assists designers to maximize human gains while achieving business and technical excellence (Mumford, 1983b). This raises further questions for discussion.

First, the methodology objective is to achieve a balance between people and information technology, therefore invariably it will have to sacrifice some of the excellence in technology in order to achieve this.

Secondly, it cannot maximize human gains (here we refer to those who have to operate the designed 'action systems') as it operates within the constraints of management objectives and policies. Despite the attempts to promote participation, the weaker power groups can participate only on the *means* of achieving the ends, while the *ends* have been set by the stronger power groups. Within this *unequal* power distribution context, it does not show how power can be transferred from the stronger groups to the weaker groups nor does it provide evidence on how even the power within the weaker groups can be equally shared. This means that the weaker members may not have control over their own destinies. The methodology certainly provides opportunities for improving their conditions, but not the freedom to determine their destinies.

Thirdly, if this distribution of power is to be achieved, then the facilitator has to demonstrate an extremely high level of political skills. Politics, which attempts to focus on people without being open about its intentions, however noble they may be, raises conflicts with ethics. (See the discussions on politics in Chapter 4.) ETHICS does discuss some of the practical difficulties of politics but does not offer any models for reconciling the ethical issues.

Lastly, ETHICS users (facilitators) also have to maximize their own personal rewards (promotions, consultancy fees, etc.); thus, there will be great difficulty in maintaining the open participative status of their intervention. In fact, the methodology does not engage in any discussion of the ethical dilemmas that may arise for its user when trying to balance or resolve conflicts among the various groups, the management (including the clients), and their own personal needs.

(Readers should note that the evaluation here is based on the published descriptions of ETHICS. The intention of the evaluation is to alert potential methodology users to the issues they need to consider before using the methodology.)

However, the methodology has to be *commended* for raising the issue of ethics for consideration, even though how the different ethical issues can be resolved is not discussed. It is for this reason that the issues of ethics were incorporated into the 'mental construct' of the NIMSAD framework so that potential methodology users can examine their own positions.

ELEMENT 3, STAGE 1: UNDERSTANDING OF THE 'SITUATION OF CONCERN'

In ETHICS the boundary construction is influenced by management-expressed goals and policies. Contrary to the phenomenological paradigms it tries to promote at the employee level, the determination of the boundary is guided by management. Management goals are taken as given for determining the system's boundary.

> It is used to find management problems at the boundaries between units of operations and at the boundary between the *system* [my italics] and its environment.   (Mumford, 1981)

While the methodology accepts management-imposed boundaries, it attempts to extend those boundaries along other dimensions by accommodating job satisfaction, enlargement, enrichment and human psychology factors. Thus it can be described as phenomenological in terms of providing opportunities for the participants of the design team to explore their views, but ontological in terms of accepting *the system* to be studied. ETHICS does not show how these philosophical contradictions are to be balanced or addressed at a conceptual level—it is very much a pragmatically focused methodology.

INVESTIGATION MODELS AND TECHNIQUES

Given the discussions on methodology support for the evaluation of 'mental constructs' and their assistance in boundary construction, we can now examine what help ETHICS provides in the actual information gathering (investigation) stage.

There is no explicit discussion in ETHICS on methods of investigation for gaining knowledge of the operations, although the methodology is explicit as to the use of questionnaires as the main form of investigation for collecting job satisfaction data. We attribute this to the following reasons, even though these are not discussed explicitly within the methodology.

Its users are expected to operate in a supportive role as opposed to the more dominant role expected in the case of other methodologies. They are not expected to dominate the design of the *systems*. There is no conscious focus on the methodology users to collect information as they will not be the *owners* of the subsequent design models. Through the principles of participative design, users who participate in the design are expected to bring their knowledge of operations and problems to the discussion meetings. The latter is very much a goal of the methodology.

> ... relates to the location of knowledge and states that the experts on operational factors such as task design are people who do the job. (Mumford, 1983b)

However, it is not realistic to assume that ETHICS users are able to provide technical options or help resolve interpersonal issues without access to additional background information and to assume that this can be gained as a member of the design team is to put ETHICS users in a disadvantageous position. Therefore, they must develop a range of investigation techniques to obtain information that other participants may readily possess.

Unlike other methodologies, ETHICS suggests the formation of two groups. In fact, this is central to the achievement of participative goals. The first group is called the steering committee, which consists of senior management, management of the affected departments, trade union representatives, consultants, etc. The role of this group is to ensure that the design activities of the second group are conducted within the policies, guidelines and constraints laid down by them. The second group is called the design group which consists of representatives of those who will be affected by the design.

ETHICS suggests three different forms of democratic structure models for organizing design groups for gathering information and for undertaking subsequent design activities, namely: consultative, representative, and consensus.

In the 'consultative' form, employees contribute ideas to the design process, but the final decision is taken by the designer or the design group. The second form is the 'representative' form, in which the design group members are selected from various interest groups. In the 'consensus' form, members are elected and there is a continuous exchange of ideas and suggestions by members with their constituents.

Not all three forms suggested can bring about participation. For example, in the consultative form the design group can ignore the information that is collected from the users. This form of action takes place every day in organizations. It cannot ensure that the constituent members' views are translated into decisions. The creator of ETHICS discusses the strengths and weaknesses of all three forms.

What ETHICS suggests are ways of bringing about user *involvement* and not forms of democracy or participation. User involvement is the generic term used to cover many forms of working relationships. There are four levels of user involvement, namely: two-way communication, consultation, participation, and co-determination.

- In the *two-way communication*, decision making remains with management. In this form, information about decisions is communicated to the employees and in turn employees can communicate their views to management. It allows employees to obtain clarification of management decisions.
- *Consultation* is a deliberate action taken by management to solicit the views of the employees. This process takes place before decisions are taken. The purpose is to obtain as many viewpoints as possible so that well informed decisions can be taken. However, the decisions still remain with the management, who may or may not consider the views of employees obtained from the consultative process. This is similar to the definition of consultative form in ETHICS.
- *Participation* is where the employees participate in the discussions and decision making. They play a much bigger role in this process. This is a joint exercise, and decision making is a shared activity, but it is management who take responsibility for the outcome of any decisions. Understandably, management do not like this form of involvement where they alone have to take responsibility for the outcome of shared decisions. Therefore, they exercise subtle political pressure to force others to conform to management-favourable decisions.
- *Co-determination* is where both management and employees participate in the decision-making process. Both groups are responsible for the decisions and also for their outcome. This means that, unlike in participation, both groups have to share in the successes as well as in their failures. They are equal partners. This form of democracy is very rare because of the political nature of current organizational decision making.

Returning to the forms advocated in ETHICS, consultation is not a form of participation as management can ignore the views of those consulted. In the context of the case study, the creator of ETHICS discusses many of the problems that arose in practice with the consultative form. Representative form can become a participative process only if the representatives are elected and the involvement is extended by the representatives to their constituent members, i.e. everyone can share in the decision making. Consensus can be a form of participation as the representatives share the decision making on a continuous basis. Both representative (in elected form) and consensus forms can become participative processes only if management are prepared to share their decision making with the employees. The structural forms of the steering committee and their relationships with the design groups ensure that this cannot be the case, since any decisions that are taken by the design group have to be put to the steering committee for their approval. The discussions surrounding job gradings in the case study is a case in point. (Co-determination is not discussed in ETHICS.)

ETHICS discusses the problems and opportunities for participation, but these do not include discussions about the management of the participative process. Moreover, the strength and quality of information depends not necessarily on these forms of involvement but on the sincerity, commitment and intentions of those involved in the decision-making process. Once again, politics interferes with any chance of building the democratic characteristics of a participative process. Under unequal distribution of power and a lack of commitment to the spirit of power sharing, employees have no chance of controlling their own destinies. Raising expectations and not providing 'real' opportunities for achieving those expectations can help to destroy participants' faith in the democratic processes. ETHICS does discuss the need for trust but does not show 'what' or 'how' to manage a situation where such trust does not exist.

ELEMENT 3, STAGE 2: PERFORMING THE DIAGNOSIS

From the perspective of the NIMSAD framework, there is not enough information to complete the Diagnosis. Any judgement is based on the methodology users' 'mental constructs', i.e. past experience.

ETHICS uses video recordings, minutes and text descriptions for recording job satisfaction data. It suggests the recording of activities and data flows in a horizontal input/output form, as illustrated in Figure 9.1, and in a vertical form showing different levels of work complexity, as listed in Table 9.2. This recording of horizontal physical data flows is based on work study methods. This is the ETHICS approach to the expression of Diagnosis Model DM2 of the NIMSAD framework. As a technique, this is not very useful and has been superseded by other techniques. Table 9.2 also shows the recording of physical activities and operations. However, this document extends beyond the mere recording of operations to the recording of 'problems' as well as

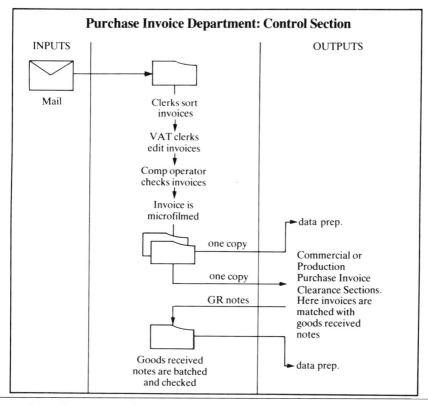

Figure 9.1   Physical data flows

suggestions. It is a mixture of a description of existing and desirable features. In the context of the NIMSAD framework, 'Operating activities' in Table 9.2 is the recording of existing tasks. The problem prevention/solution activities are part of problem analysis. 'Coordination activities' and 'Development activities' relate to notional systems features, i.e. desirable features. 'Control activities' relate to judgement of existing operations. (This is the advantage of using a framework to evaluate methodologies. The framework does not impose a sequence of activity stages, but helps to examine whether and where they take place within a methodology!).

ETHICS could clearly benefit from the use of rigorous structured techniques and models for expressing logical notions and data-related activities, instead of its use of 'work study' techniques which help to illustrate DM2 type but not DM1 type descriptions. ETHICS is very much biased towards physical characteristics of operations.

Table 9.2 Vertical description

STEP 3: Example of vertical analysis of the Purchase Invoice Department
This is a simplified description to show readers examples of what is required.

Operating activities

What are the most important day-to-day tasks?
- a) The receipt, opening, checking and distribution of mail, letters, invoices, credit notes, etc.
- b) The passing of receipts for payment
- c) Dealing with rejected goods. This often involves asking suppliers to send a credit note
- d) The payment of cheques

Problem prevention/solution activities

What are the key problems that must be prevented or quickly and easily solved?
Incorrect accounts being passed for payment
Incorrect payment for goods received
Suppliers' queries

Co-ordination activities

What activities must be co-ordinated within the system?
Passing of receipts for payment with payment of cheques

What activities must be co-ordinated with other systems?
Receipt of goods received notes from stores
Notification of rejected goods by stores or production units

Development activities

What activities, products, services, etc. need to be developed and improved?
Better relationships with suppliers

Control activities

How is the system controlled now? (Targets set, progress monitored, etc.)
There is very little effective control

In one sense, if the democratic values of ETHICS are to be upheld, the methodology should allow the participants to determine which techniques to use and refrain from suggesting *any*. On the other hand, if the methodology relies on the participants own techniques, then it may fail to bring about desirable benefits from the use of efficient techniques and models that are being developed in the field. We recommend that the methodology offer its users several ways of performing this stage and explain their relative merits so that the participants can choose the appropriate techniques to adopt, thus maintaining the aims of user involvement.

We wish to point out that what we are doing here is attempting to critically evaluate the support given by ETHICS for conducting this stage. In 'reality', methodology users gather and store vast amounts of information, particularly of the 'soft' kind which cannot be expressed for client discussion. Given different experiences, methodology users form their own impressions about the *state* of the situation. Since it is the role of the methodology to show how to perform these processes explicitly, our evaluation is to determine to what extent ETHICS helps to explicate and express this information and to what extent that information is sufficient for achieving the aims of the methodology. We feel that the methodology users should know, certainly before they use the methodology, whether the activities they plan to undertake are sufficient for bringing about the transformation claims of the methodology. After all, that is the reason for using a methodology. In the case of ETHICS, it discusses openly many of the problems, but without providing theoretical models or practical ways of addressing these. Therefore, the creators' models need to be made available for the benefit of ETHICS users.

ELEMENT 3, STAGE 3: DEFINING THE PROGNOSIS OUTLINE

In ETHICS, the 'desired states' are determined by the management. The methodology does not offer any means of formulating these expectations. It is clear from the discussions (Mumford, 1983a, 1983b) that the design group has to ensure the continuing interest of management and operate within company policy. ETHICS does not provide either for an understanding or for debating about the legitimacy of or the validity for the (management) clients expectations. From time to time the discussions of the design group may border on questions of expectations, but these are referred to the steering committee who may or may not decide to alter the pre-set expectations.

ETHICS, commenting on the aim of the methodology, states clearly that:

> . . . it has the principal objective, the successful integration of
> *company objectives* [my italics] with the needs of the employees
> and customers . . . Steering Committee *will* [my italics] set
> the guide lines for the Design Group. The Design Group
> must be absolutely clear where its design responsibilities begin
> and end and so it must identify the boundary and the system
> which it is designing   (Mumford, 1983a)

ELEMENT 3, STAGE 4: DEFINING 'PROBLEMS'

In ETHICS, there is an attempt to identify some of the problems of *the existing system*. The link between the new designed system and the client's 'desired state' is not discussed by the methodology. Many of the management assessments as to the validity of the 'desired state' remain outside the domain of the design group, and the management, by setting guidelines for the design group, ensure the limits of the design process.

For instance, in the context of one of the examples quoted, the notional system was:

> to obtain goods and services from the suppliers which are the
> right quality and price and arrive on the date promised
> (Mumford, 1983b)

Many would not find problems with this statement until they begin to question what is meant by the right quality and price. In some environments where there are few suppliers, quality and price will be dictated by them. In others, where there is a wide availability of suppliers, they may be set by the purchasing manager. The point here is that the features of the notional system had already been decided because of the problems experienced by the management. The project was to put this right. Problem definition had already taken place, and the 'desired state' had already been defined by management, albeit implicitly or unconsciously. Step 3 documents (Table 9.2) contains a record of these problems.

ELEMENT 3, STAGE 5: DERIVING THE NOTIONAL SYSTEM

In ETHICS, the features of the notional system are described as *key objectives*. The key objectives (as illustrated in Table 9.3) are to guide the design process.

It is suggested that:

> The Design Group is now asked to forget the existing system
> and to start asking some fundamental questions about the
> areas which lie within the design boundary.

Table 9.3 Key objectives

STEP 4: Example of key objectives of the Purchase Invoice Department

---

Key objectives are to ensure that the company obtains goods and services from suppliers which are of the right quality and price and arrive on the date promised, also to provide a satisfying, stimulating work environment for Purchase Invoice and Treasurer's Department staff.
Relationships with suppliers are in fact very poor due to inaccurate or delayed payment of suppliers' accounts. This is affecting the quality of the suppliers' service.

> The first question is, *why do these exist?* What is their primary role and purpose?
>
> The second question is, *given this role and purpose what should be their responsibilities and functions?*
>
> The third question is, *how far do their present activities match what they should be doing?*   (Mumford, 1983b)

First, there is a contradiction in the above statement. One cannot be asked to forget about the existing system and then pursue questions that relate to it.

Secondly, these questions are focused on the improvements to existing 'taken-as-given' systems. The question of what should be their role has already been answered by the key objectives.

Thirdly, 'Why do these exist?' is a question for the diagnosis stage and should have been addressed before formulating the key objectives.

Fourthly, the list of objectives also includes a mixture of features of the notional system as well as failures of current 'taken-as-given' systems. ETHICS is not clear in terms of separating out the logical differences of the activities undertaken.

As discussed in the context of NIMSAD, this process has to establish the notional system(s) and their relevance to the problem areas which prevent the perceived 'current states' from becoming perceived 'desired states'. The notional systems features are to take account of particular problem areas and express these in terms of features.

ELEMENT 3, STAGE 6: PERFORMING THE CONCEPTUAL/ LOGICAL DESIGN

In ETHICS, there is a focus on an important design step. Before embarking on design, the methodology suggests the formation of design objectives. Commenting on these, ETHICS states:

> Do not confuse these key objectives with objectives for the
> new system in step 10.   (Mumford, 1983b)

This is an important initial step. Before engaging in systems design, the process should consider the criteria that should guide the design activities. These were discussed under physical design (Stage 7) of the NIMSAD framework. The key objectives are followed by the definition of key tasks identification. These are the tasks which must be performed if the key objectives are to be achieved. An example of a key task is:

> The fast, correct payment of supplier accounts.
>   (Mumford, 1983b)

Key task definitions are similar to the functional definitions of other methodologies. If these key tasks are to be useful for later design activities they need to be expressed in more precise terms, e.g. what is meant by 'fast'. For example, 'fast' for an airline seat reservation system may mean a few seconds response time, whereas 'fast' for a planning permission granting system of a local authority may mean several months. ETHICS does discuss the importance of detailed definitions, but these are considered at later design stages.

The next step in the design process (Step 6) is the construction of key information necessary for performing the key tasks. ETHICS suggests that this information can be of the form 'accurate goods received information' Mumford (1983b).

The linking of information to the tasks is one of the *most useful* features of ETHICS. It does not create problems of the kind raised in the next chapter when trying to link conceptual models and information in 'Soft' Systems Methodology. Unlike many methodologies which attempt to build information systems based on what *can be* achieved, the aim here is to consider what *should be* achieved. Linking enables the design group to understand the use of information, i.e. its relevance to the activities.

The next step in the design process is to identify variances of the 'existing system' or sub-systems. The creator of ETHICS states:

> *Key variances* are potential problem areas which cannot be eliminated although they may be effectively controlled. . . . Operating variances are not so deeply embedded in the system and are weak links.   (Mumford, 1983b)

In other words, key variances are structural weaknesses, while operating variances are operational weaknesses. According to ETHICS, operating weaknesses arise from previous design failures.

This raises further issues for discussion.

First, ETHICS accepts the boundaries of the given situation. For example, in the case study the department boundary is taken-as-given and it forms the basis for identifying key variances which it considers unsolvable. But these boundaries, although physical, are nevertheless human-designed boundaries. If there are undesirable variances then they indicate structural weaknesses. They are also the effects of previous design efforts, but of different kinds. For example, the case study in Mumford (1983a) uses the production and sales departments as examples to illustrate the unsolvable key variances. In some engineering organizations, these weaknesses have been resolved by allocating specific customer accounts to the production engineers. In others, department boundaries have been redesigned based on project teams or product types. Yet in other organizations, multiple structures have been created, i.e. product manager-, marketing manager- and production manager-based units. There is no reason why existing boundaries have to be taken-as-given.

Secondly, the variances discussed are based on existing boundaries. These may or may not appear in any designs as the design boundaries can avoid many of the problems with existing variances. In any case, this analysis should have been carried out *before* defining the key objectives (Step 4) so that problems of variances could have been taken into account.

Finally, the methodology is focused on problems of physical organization of operational and monitoring activities. This makes it accept, and operate within, the existing physical power structures. For example, managers are incorporated into the steering committee automatically. By accepting current management structures and reinforcing their legitimacy within the steering committee, ETHICS is not in a position to challenge the existing department boundaries; hence the reason for two-tier team structures. We urge the creator of ETHICS to consider opening up the methodology to the structural dimension. By using Beers (1979, 1988) VSM models, ETHICS could address both human relationships and their structural interconnections not just at employee level but also at management level, i.e. reorganize departmental boundaries to address unsolvable variances.

The next step (Step 8) is to conduct a questionnaire survey on employee job satisfaction. This is called *diagnosis of job satisfaction needs*. As the name implies, this should have been undertaken at the diagnosis stage before the key objectives are formulated. In addition, this analysis, which is defined as Analysis of Social Needs (Mumford, 1983b) has the categories 'Should be incorporated in the new system' and 'Must be improved in the new system'. If these are considered important, they should be performed *before* the formulation of key objectives (Step 4) unless, of course, they are considered as secondary to the main objectives.

The survey does not address one of the main tenets of the methodology, i.e. ethics. It is not specific about the ethical issues facing the employees, and does not ask questions about the circumstances under which employees are compelled to carry out activities which they consider to be unethical or immoral. The ethical stance of the methodology is explicit and clear: it believes that employees have a right to determine their own destinies but, as discussed earlier, these destinies must fall within the constraints set by management. The methodology does not attempt to discover or raise existing ethical conflicts for discussion. For example, in relation to suppliers it could have asked, does the supplier payment system discriminate against small suppliers? Are the ethical issues arising from these explained to the employees? Does the system exploit the supplier's credit position? Are the employees compelled to follow these procedures or policies? None of these questions have been raised in the case study nor are they included in the survey questionnaire. In structured methodologies such issues remain external, as they neither consider them to be important nor offer any means of addressing them; however, since ETHICS has declared itself as an ethical methodology these questions do need to be asked. In fact, in the Analysis of Social Needs this area is consciously omitted. It says:

> The Ethical Fit has not been included as it is more relevant to personnel policy than to systems design.   (Mumford, 1983b)

This simply cannot be the case. Systems design raises many ethical issues for explicit consideration.

The next step is to undertake Future Analysis (Step 9). According to ETHICS, Future Analysis is conducted at this stage to ensure that the designs are able to adapt to changes expected in the future. These include changes to legislation, technology, economic factors, etc. If these changes occur, they may affect not only the designs but also the key objectives, e.g. what type of service the organization would be able to offer. However, it is difficult to see how flexibility can be built into the design when the nature of the changes is not known, and in the case study there are no examples of how these have been incorporated. Besides, if the changes are fundamental, then they will have severe effects on the already incorporated efficiency and job satisfaction needs, thus requiring another cycle of design effort.

Step 10 is where weighting is allocated to different goals by different design groups. The intention here is to seek consensus. The most favoured objectives are ranked in order so that they can guide the design process. The personal needs of various groups will be manifested through these objectives and their ranking; thus, this stage will generate both political and interpersonal difficulties. The compromise process will therefore require considerable skills on the part of the methodology users. While ETHICS recognizes the difficulties, it does not explain how this process can be handled by a potential user of the methodology. There are no models, criteria or ways of reconciling these differences. In any collective process, some individuals have to sacrifice more of their personal needs than others in order to reach consensus. Thus, what this process does is to enable the most articulate, vocal and power-based individuals to realize their needs at the expense of others unless the methodology user can guarantee that all individuals needs would be satisfied. Thus, while the methodology may attempt to improve the needs of a representative group it cannot satisfy every individual's job satisfaction needs.

ETHICS does not consider logical and physical designs as separate activity sets. It attempts to design systems which take account of management requirements and job satisfaction needs. Unfortunately, it does not offer suggestions as to how the ranked objectives are to be realized in the design process. While understandable (in keeping with the philosophy of user involve-ment it needs to encourage users to put forward their own design techniques), the methodology should nevertheless have some outline design methods to offer, since the knowledge and skills level within the design group may not be sufficient to consider different options. ETHICS does not offer any techniques or ways or models of how the objectives could be turned into a design. As discussed under 'diagnosis', the work study methods used in the case studies cannot capture the essential characteristics of information flows. ETHICS recommends simple flow charts. However, both work study formats and simple flow charts are inappropriate: they are too rooted in historical work flow documentation to be of much use for design with emerging technology.

ELEMENT 3, STAGE 7: PERFORMING THE PHYSICAL DESIGN

The next stages of the design process are where the actual design activities are undertaken. These are Steps 11 and 12 of ETHICS where Organizational design and Technical options are considered. Again, no design help is offered either on how technical options can be incorporated with employer requirements and job satisfaction needs or on how the various groups could be brought together to derive satisfycing solutions. ETHICS relies on the members of the design team to determine the balance between technical options and human needs, but unless the participants have good technical backgrounds (not just in terms of how they work but rather in terms of what technology options are suitable) how this step is going to be performed is not clear. In ETHICS, information technology is considered as a means:

> Again, it must be stressed that technology is always a 'means'
> to greater efficiency and higher job satisfaction, and never an
> end in itself. (Mumford, 1983b)

It is true that technology is not an 'end' in itself, but it is not just a 'means' either. This is a serious underestimation of the role and the nature of information technology. As discussed in Chapter 1, information technology is not just a means to an end. The capabilities of information technology have created new ends which would never have been envisaged had the technology not been available. Complete new communication systems, banking services, multi-media applications, etc. have emerged because of these capabilities. Design group members must be aware of these possibilities.

ELEMENT 3, STAGE 8: IMPLEMENTING THE DESIGN

This is the weakest stage of ETHICS; despite the term 'implementation' being used in the acronym it does not discuss the problems nor how to manage this stage.

> The best designed system is not going to achieve its objectives unless it is successfully implemented, and many good systems encounter problems at the implementation stage.
>
> (Mumford, 1983b)

This attitude to implementation is in the belief that users will manage this stage effectively, given that they have participated in the design and that it incorporates their job satisfaction needs.

> Commitment is facilitated by involvement in the design process and by a belief that the system will increase job satisfaction and provide an improvement to previous work methods.   (Mumford, 1983b)

But this stage is about realizing the dreams. Raising high expectations and not satisfying them can create even more frustrations. The methodology must show how the stage is to be organized, how priorities can be allocated, how systems can be tested and how the implementation can be managed. Leaving it to the design group is not much help to a methodology user.

ELEMENT 4: EVALUATION

ETHICS has an evaluation stage (Step 15) which is a very valuable stage for any methodology. Here, evaluation is carried out to establish whether efficiency and job satisfaction needs have been achieved and is focused on key variances which were identified as weak links of *the existing system*. These are described as 'endemic' to the objectives and tasks of the department, but the evaluation is unfortunately not extended to examine whether the key objectives have been achieved or whether there are lessons to be learned from the use of the methodology. As we discussed earlier, key variances occur because the methodology accepts taken-as-given existing physical boundaries. They can be removed if the more conceptually oriented models are incorporated into its design process. Given the problems discussed in the case study

(Mumford, 1983b), should have been extracted for use by potential methodology users.

We urge the creator of ETHICS to restructure this stage. The evaluation can be focused not just on the situation but, more importantly, on whether the 'what' problems (systemic analysis) have been resolved. As the methodology has a human focus it naturally evaluates the fit between job satisfaction and the new work structures. We also recommend that evaluation of the methodology and its users is undertaken to discover what persistent and essential changes may be needed in the long term.

However, we need to acknowledge that this methodology, unlike many others, has an evaluation stage built it. What we are suggesting here is an improvement to its set of activities, for example why should there be a mismatch between the job satisfaction and new work structures when the design models were developed and implemented by the same people!

SUMMARY

ETHICS is one of the pioneering and most well known methodologies for undertaking human-centred systems design. By focusing on human needs, it alerts designers to the practical implications of their designs on people working in the situation. This chapter used the NIMSAD framework to examine what level of support ETHICS offers in this transformation process. The examination revealed that the methodology offers many design guidelines *useful* for the understanding and the design of human-centred systems, but that it does not offer models or ways of performing many of the steps. Nor does it provide any models for handling the interpersonal and political conflicts that may arise from opening up human feelings and emotions. In effect, the success of the transformation depends very much on the commitment of the participants and, more importantly, the interpersonal and political skills of the methodology user. While ETHICS is committed to a particular ethical stance, it does not offer any means of discussing or resolving many of the ethical dilemmas that could arise in systems development. In effect, the creator of ETHICS has not abstracted the knowledge, models, skills and abilities of herself (in the role of facilitator) and made these available to potential methodology users. Potential users must not underestimate the level of knowledge and particularly skills required for practising ETHICS. The success of ETHICS is largely due to the personal knowledge, and competent interpersonal skills of its creator.

10

CRITICAL EVALUATION OF 'SOFT' SYSTEMS METHODOLOGY

INTRODUCTION

'Soft' Systems Methodology (Checkland, 1981; Checkland and Scholes, 1990) is one of the most thought-provoking methodologies to emerge in recent years. It was classified as an 'issues-oriented' methodology in Jayaratna (1988). Its strength is that it makes its user approach problem-solving situations with an open mind and with a powerful set of conceptual notions. SSM, as it is popularly known, has undergone a revision of its steps and structure, as outlined in Figures 10.1 and 10.2.

The new version is based on the former one and incorporates many lessons learned from the application of the former in 'action research'. The critical evaluation of SSM in this chapter will mainly cover the revised version (the creators of SSM claim that this has superseded the seven-stage SSM), but will also make reference to the former version.

ELEMENT 1: THE 'PROBLEM SITUATION'

Here we examine what SSM has to say about the situation.

SSM is concerned with improvements to problem situations and lessons that can be learned in the problem-solving process. It assumes the 'action world' to be an interpretative one, and hence is underpinned by hermeneutic paradigms. This view is confirmed by its creator:

> The 'heroic' mood of the Singerean inquiring system is taken

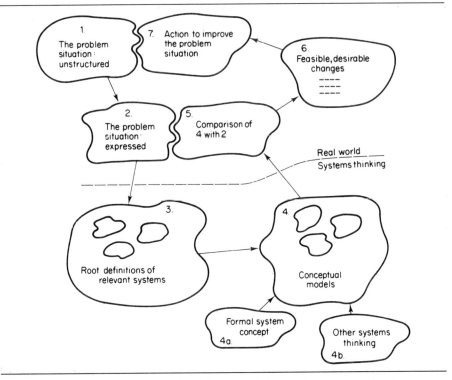

Figure 10.1 'Soft' systems methodology (original) (Peter Checkland, *Systems Thinking, Systems Practice*, © 1987. Reprinted by permission of John Wiley & Sons, Ltd.)

> to be central to SSM, which is used to analyse organisations
> from a hermeneutic stance.   (Checkland, 1981)

It is a methodology which recognizes the role of the individual's 'world images' and the influence of historical background on the interpretation of 'reality'. As can be seen in Figure 10.2, this history is now included explicitly within the methodology outline. Oliga (1988) states that:

> the interpretative paradigm and its hermeneutic methodology
> underwrite the 'soft' systems methodologies.
>   (Oliga, 1988)

Whereas structured design methodologies are concerned with the discovery of a single 'truth' state (i.e. there is only one correct definition), SSM with its underlying hermeneutic paradigms makes its users search for many states, any or all of which can be argued to have the same 'truth' value. Whereas the rigour in positivistic methodologies is on the extraction of rules governing the

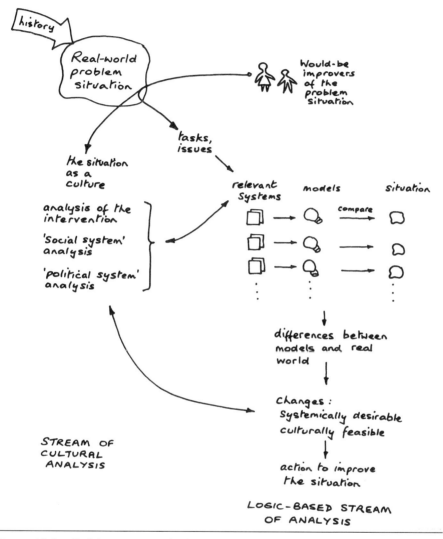

Figure 10.2 'Soft' systems methodology (revised) (P. Checkland and J. Scholes, *Soft Systems Methodology in Action*, © 1990. Reprinted by permission of John Wiley & Sons, Ltd.)

behaviour and relationship of formal data, in SSM the rigour is found in the debate which attempts to establish the relevance of stakeholders' world images and their desires. From this perspective, data alone has little relevance. It is the user's subjective interpretations that give meaning to them.

SSM is explicit about the role of 'systems' paradigms underpinning its structure and steps. It discusses the use of the notion 'human activity system' (based on 'systems' concepts) which helps its users to understand and make sense of purposeful activities of the organization.

It is also different in its outlook. SSM is abstract, conceptual and philosophically oriented. Its interest lies in learning from the situation and in involving members in a debate by exploring their 'world images', even if this process does not lead to a transformation of the 'action world' in practice. Despite this, as the SSM 'action research' case studies show, it is highly relevant to practical problem solving.

In SSM, however, there is a conscious attempt to prepare its users to develop new perceptions of organizations through the use of 'human activity systems' models and the use of 'systems' notions applied in an epistemological sense of the term. Nevertheless, practice reveals that many methodology users find these notions difficult to absorb and even more difficult to apply. This will remain so until potential SSM users are prepared to invest their time in learning about the epistemological notions associated with the methodology.

SSM recognizes three categories of role players in the situation: the client; the problem owner; and the problem solver. These may be one or several persons. Unlike in other methodologies, the role played by the client is explicitly recognized by the methodology. It is the client who initiates the study. The problem owner is the one whose *Weltanschauungen* will be used for articulating relevant systems, while the problem solver is interested in using SSM for resolving the client's concerns. The model of problem-solving and problem-content systems of Checkland (1981), provides a conceptually clear way of understanding the interconnections between SSM users (taken to be in a problem solver role) and their clients. In the revised version of SSM (Checkland and Scholes, 1990) the role concept is connected to norms and values, but this is not sufficient by itself in helping us to understand the role ambiguities and conflicts discussed in the context of the 'mental construct' in Chapter 4.

One of the most fundamental notions that is considered to be relevant for problem solving in SSM is that of *Weltanschauung* (world images) originally derived by Dilthey (1931) (see also Kluback *et al.*, 1957.). SSM discusses the influence this has on the interpretations ascribed to 'reality'. However, while it discusses the role that *Weltanschauung* plays in human interpretation, it does not give a clear definition of what it is or how it is formed. The term *Weltanschauung* is used in more than one sense of meaning within SSM. In the context of examples, it is defined as a viewpoint, a world image, a set of beliefs or perceptions and values. It is even presented as belonging to a situation. There is also a reference to *Weltanschauung* of the CATWOE. Almost all examples of *Weltanschauungen* are projected from a *role* point of view, i.e. as a manager, an owner, a user, a customer and so on.

Weltanschauung is not unique because many can share the same *Weltanschauung*. It can be influenced and can vary from situation to situation. Eriksson (1990) refers to there being the possibility of different *Weltanschauungen* at different times by the same person. This possibility is crucial for bringing about consensus, but the term *Weltanschauung* does not convey this changing nature of an individual's perception. It is for this reason that we developed the concept of a 'mental construct' as a fundamental element of the framework. Using the 'mental construct' it is easy to understand how even people with emotionally strong beliefs can be susceptible to financial incentives and power inducements or that they can form alliances with strange bedfellows or that, given the 'right' circumstances, they can quite easily abandon their strongly held and expressed *Weltanschauungen*! Methodology users also bring their *Weltanschauungen* to the situation through which they attempt to interpret others' *Weltanschauungen*.

SSM is one of the few methodologies that has comments to make about the 'problem situation'. It used to be known for its applicability to ill-structured situations, and for over a decade, was promoted as such. However, in the revised version of SSM, its creators state that:

> There the white lie is that SSM is a seven-stage problem-solving methodology applicable to problems of a certain kind, namely messy, ill-structured ones. We can forgive the pedagogues' simplification; after all true complexity of the real world *has* to be simplified for class room consumption.
>
> (Checkland and Scholes, 1990)

We consider this to be unjustifiable for several reasons.

First, the original SSM was promoted and used as a seven-stage methodology for ill-structured situations in its early days. The 'action research' examples of its seven-stage applications were also published in the prestigious *Journal of Applied Systems Analysis*, and it was the publication of the proof of the model that led to its use in the classroom environment. The publication of seven-stage proofs of 'action world' transformation is not confined to academics either. Examples of industrial applications were also published in the same journal.

Secondly, it is the appropriateness of SSM for 'ill-structured' situations that gave its application a special status. In Checkland (1981), the case for SSM, its suitability for application in 'ill-structured' situations and its contrast with 'hard' systems engineering and 'well structured' situations is very effectively argued. The recommendations came from the original version of SSM and can be well justified even today.

Thirdly, there is an unfortunate reference to the classroom environment as being somehow more simple than the real world. This is a belief that is strongly adhered to by those who either cannot or do not want to understand the work carried out in academia and some of the strong links between academic and industrial environments. It is unfortunate that the creators of SSM have chosen to re-inforce this view. Simplification does not have any particular context—it happens in industry as well as in the classroom. For example, the case studies described in Checkland and Scholes (1990) are an example of a simplification of the interventions in highly complex social, political, economic, cultural and technical situations. All methodologies are complexity-reducing mechanisms. Just like the creators of SSM, the author too worked in industry for a considerable period of time, first as a user, then as a designer and finally as an analyst of information before embarking on an academic career. This suggests that the classroom environment can be made as simple or as complex as the industry environment. The division between the academic and the 'real world' (industry by implication) is not a very useful distinction to make based on these criteria, since some classroom discussions can be far more complex than one could envisage in the industry. For example, students who have to defend the ethical and moral justifications of their decision models in a classroom environment face far greater complexity than industrial practitioners who may not permit discussions about or challenges to their decisions from their subordinates by creating artificial political barriers. Students have very little power to avoid these pressures. Similarly, industrialists who have to achieve results through the work of others face greater complexity than students or academics. The degree of simplification/complexity depends on individual 'mental constructs' and the specific situations in which they operate. Both groups can simplify situations. It is for this reason that we use the term 'action world', which can refer to all situations that are considered problematical whether in industry, the public sector or academia.

ELEMENT 2: METHODOLOGY USERS (INTENDED PROBLEM SOLVERS)

In SSM, the user is considered to be a very important factor. SSM points out that the user can also be the client, or the problem owner or an outsider i.e. consultant.

Here we examine what SSM has to say about its users.

EVALUATION OF THE 'MENTAL CONSTRUCT'

SSM focuses the attention of its users on their role in systems development. It encourages them to drop the role of an expert and assume that of a facilitator of debate and learning. This is a considerable role shift for the SSM user. SSM also discusses the implications of these roles for the outcome of the methodology. As discussed in Chapter 4, the role element of the 'mental construct' has several dimensions, namely: the position; one's own role expectations; others' expectations of that role; and the role holder's behaviour. If the methodology user is also the client or the problem owner, then this may indeed cause role conflicts unless the person concerned can explicitly separate and address these role dimensions. The recognition of the role relationships between clients, problem owners and problem solvers is one of the most useful features of SSM.

When we examine SSM we note that it has recognized the need for reflection. (Issues surrounding evaluation will be discussed at the end of the chapter.) Recent work of Checkland and Scholes (1990) has recognized the contribution of Schon (1983) to this reflection process. Rodriguez-Ulloa's (1988) research has focused attention on the need for a problem-solving system (methodology users' needs as explained in our 'mental construct') to be also considered as part of the problem-content system. In Chapter 4 we discussed these needs, confirming Rodriguez-Ulloa's concerns.

DESIRABILITY LEVELS OF THE 'MENTAL CONSTRUCTS'

What (author's judgement) should be the desirable levels of the 'mental construct' for the methodology users to be effective users of SSM?

SSM relies on its users possessing considerable conceptual, abstract and philosophical skills. It has consciously attempted to build this knowledge, i.e. the epistemological notions of 'systems', the Formal Systems Model and

CATWOE criteria for structuring the systems design process. Recently, more social models have been added to help its users appreciate the values, norms and role dimensions. The case studies and the discussions of their implications help to prepare its users for some of the subtle conceptual differences in the use of the methodology, e.g. one of learning, the use of 'relevant systems' as an instrument of debate.

Since the methodology does not claim to be goal-oriented, it can be adopted by many users with different experiences, backgrounds and values. In effect SSM can be adopted for a wide range of 'ill-structured' situations, from building information systems in voluntary services to developing expert systems in the military. However, despite the paradigms embedded in the methodology and its epistemological direction, it can still be used in a mechanistic sense by those who do not have a grasp of the essence of the epistemological notions of 'systems' that underpin the methodology.

Given that the methodology is concerned with addressing the *Weltanschauungen* of the problem owners, those who use SSM require a high level of political skills in order to manage their relationships with clients and others. The personal needs of those in the situation or their *Weltanschauungen* cannot be easily extracted without subtle complex relationship management. If SSM users exercise their considerable political skills then the chances of generating and debating radically different 'root' definitions may be possible. However, if they attempt to do this without these skills, the chances of their continuing with the project will be extremely low. SSM in its new revised version has at last recognized the importance of politics. This is considered as the context in which the debate of relevant systems for the situation is to be conducted. But we are referring here to the political skills of SSM users who may have to articulately avoid political pitfalls, take evasive action, be selective in what to say, when to say it, etc. If the incorporation of possible problem owners (in a role sense) is dependent on the organizational political context then this would certainly affect what issues can be raised for debate, and SSM users may have to sacrifice their intellectually desirable ideas for politically expedient ones in order to bring about transformation of the situation. In Chapter 4 we discussed the kind of conflicts methodology users may have to face when trying to balance intellectual and political thought-driven reasoning, but SSM does not offer any models for dealing with this dimension.

What ethical and moral values does SSM promote? In the revised version, the question of ethics has been raised and incorporated into the Constitutive Rules. SSM has not, however, declared a particular ethical standard nor does it discuss how ethical values can be extracted from or resolved within the 'situation of concern'. As a methodology, if it includes any elements (in this case ethics) then it should show how to handle these, but if fails to do this. However, SSM has to be commended for at least raising the subject of ethics for consideration. The issues of ethics and morality were incorporated into the 'mental construct' of the NIMSAD framework so that potential methodology users can examine the implications of their own ethical positions.

ELEMENT 3, STAGE 1: UNDERSTANDING OF THE 'SITUATION OF CONCERN'

SSM provides the most insightful contribution to boundary construction. The boundaries, problem ownership, problem content and context issues are all open to question. Because of the danger of its users identifying themselves with clients' and problem owners' defined *systems* (as if they exist), SSM avoids the use of 'systems concepts' at this stage. While this avoidance is understandable, the non-use of epistemological notions of 'systems' deprives SSM users from being able to derive many relevant and useful ways of structuring their understanding of the situation. While the original SSM (Checkland, 1981) did not use 'systems' concepts at this stage, in the revised version there seems to be an acceptance of the ontological notion of 'systems' (taken as given) as a legitimate way of going about systems development. Commenting on Patching's (1987) identification of 'the system' within a rich picture, the creators of SSM state:

> . . . and the assertion that the 'rich picture' (singular) represents a system, rather than a situation, shows that, in terms of the true Constitutive Rules above, what is here being described is a variant of SSM with a strong flavour of hard systems thinking.   (Checkland and Scholes, 1990)

Surely this is inconsistent with the epistemological notions of 'systems' advocated by the methodology. Taking a system as given and using 'systems' as a notion for the construction of a boundary of a potential system leads to different implications! In the former case, the focus is on the *content* of the system, while in the latter the emphasis lies on the *context* of a potential system (the justification of the boundary—why is the boundary there? Why not elsewhere? What important elements have been left out?) How does the methodology then resolve the issues of ontology and epistemology? Does this mean that whatever a potential SSM user does is to be considered as a variant of SSM? This may explain why many methodology users who take systems as given claim to have used SSM. (See, for example, the differences between the use of ontological and epistemological notions in Chapter 2 and Figures 2.6 and 2.7.)

If attempts are not made to consider the boundary domain consciously, then many relevant and useful elements may be excluded from the 'situation of concern'. Political considerations may override intellectual considerations. SSM cannot support the idea of ontological use of the notions of 'systems' and claim epistemological status at the same time! Patching has simply misunderstood the notions advocated in SSM or SSM has broadened its interpretation of the use of 'systems'.

INVESTIGATION MODELS AND TECHNIQUES

Given the discussions on methodology support for the evaluation of 'mental constructs' and their assistance in boundary construction, we can now examine what help SSM provides in the actual information gathering (investigation) stage.

There is no explicit reference in SSM to methods of investigation. However, case studies indicate that interviews have been the primary source of informa- tion collection. The lack of reference to methods of data collection is surprising given the sensitivity and quality of information that is necessary for gaining an insight into critical issues. Considering that the preparation of methodology users to the use of epistemological notion of 'systems', human activity systems modelling and abstraction of 'world images' are highly abstract activities, these methods of investigation have to be highly interactive processes.

This lack of attention to methods of investigation has very serious implications for systems development. It means that methodology users do not become aware of the different nature of problems, or recognize opportunities or realize effects that the methods of investigation may have on the nature, content and meaning they derive in practice. The factors which influence these interpretations are interpersonal relationships, influence and authority of individuals, skills in communication, personal motives, and prejudices.

The methods of investigation for SSM and similar methodologies should be dialectic between the methodology users and the clients/problem owners within a particular problem context. Information of the type necessary for obtaining an insight into the way in which clients and problem owners perceive the situation does not come easily from the normal methods of investigation. Strong interpersonal relationships among the participants are required if methodology users are to extract the innermost concerns of clients and others, and even stronger political skills are required to handle the conflicts of ideas to which their owners may stubbornly hold. It is for these reasons that we have suggested the need for SSM users to have interpersonal and political skills in addition to abstract thinking skills. Since the resolution of 'problems' or 'concerns' is as much behavioural as it is intellectual, methodology users need to have access to considerable intervention models for investigation. The role, values and norm model offered by SSM is not sufficient for understanding or abstracting information about the complex relationships among members in the 'situation of concern'. SSM needs to explain how conflicts between the intellectual and political thought-driven reasoning can be formulated or resolved.

ELEMENT 3, STAGE 2: PERFORMING THE DIAGNOSIS

SSM performs the diagnosis at two levels. First, it attempts to develop a picture of structures, processes, concerns and the *Weltanschauungen* of members in the situation. It calls this the 'logical' stream of analysis. The second stream is called 'cultural' analysis. In the original version of SSM the latter used to be known as the 'climate'. However, since many SSM users have failed to recognize the importance of the context, the revised version has expanded on this analysis, which enables SSM users to understand the meaning of information gathered from the situation. In this sense, SSM is unique as it attempts to link the logical expressions and the cultural context which helps to make sense of the logical analysis. These two streams, although separated for conceptual clarity, are interconnected. Their role and the implications are discussed below.

SSM does not prescribe any particular form of expression, nor does it attempt to distinguish between logical and physical expressions. SSM permits any technique that will help to express or capture the essential aspects of the organization. These may include graphs, text, animation, pictures, charts, tables, etc. These expressions are known within SSM as 'rich pictures' and are illustrated in Figure 10.3.

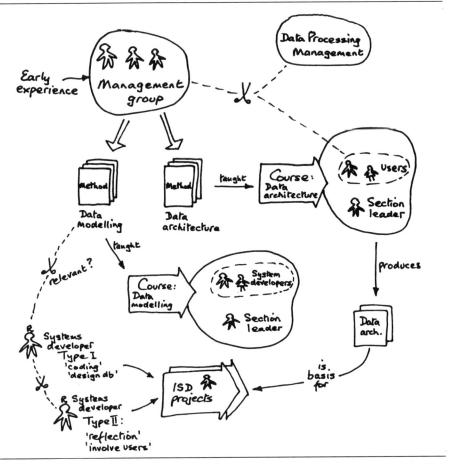

Figure 10.3   A 'rich' picture (P. Checkland and J. Scholes, *Soft Systems Methodology in Action*, © 1990. Reprinted by permission of John Wiley & Sons, Ltd.)

The encouragement of any form for expressing the diagnosis has several implications.

First, it gives SSM users freedom in the selection of relevant tools and techniques which are appropriate to the situation and the understanding of the issues. Secondly, much of the information collected will be of a fairly sensitive nature, e.g. information on clashes and disagreements of *Weltanschauungen*. The expressions in the form of 'rich pictures' enable the presentation of sensitive information in a less emotional form leading to greater client response.

The freedom afforded by SSM to its users in 'rich picture' construction can also be a fundamental weakness for problem solving in the situation. The desire to express this understanding in a few pages, forces its users to abstract the essential messages from the situation for discussion. 'Rich pictures' are one of the most useful ideas to emerge from SSM as they help to develop not just a description but, more importantly, an impression of the 'situation of concern'. However, to use the 'rich picture' as the only basis for undertaking further methodological activities is to simplify a very complex problem-solving activity. The examples of 'rich pictures' published in the literature *do not* provide sufficient information for decisions; most politically sensitive and logically critical information remains locked within the minds of the methodology users and the clients. If SSM users are to benefit from the freedom of 'rich pictures', they need to accommodate as many relevant and useful techniques as possible (data flows, data models, role models, graphs, tables, statistics) that can help to present views of the *state* of the situation from several viewpoints. General systemic models, the Viable Systems Model (Beer, 1988) and the cognitive maps of Eden *et al.* (1987) have proved to be very effective means of capturing many complex features of a situation.

In the revised version of SSM, there is analysis of the intervention (Analysis one), analysis of the 'social system' (Analysis two), and analysis of the 'political system' in terms of power distribution (Analysis three). Checkland and Scholes (1990) have acknowledged the dynamic features of the situation and advise SSM users to continue these analyses throughout the project. If SSM users are to make use of this knowledge, then they should also have sufficient models, skills and ways of making use of this information in their intervention activities.

SSM warns its users about the public visibility of Analysis three, the 'political system':

> . . . if the results carried from Analysis three are all bluntly made public then those results can themselves easily become a potent commodity of power. . . So it behoves users of SSM to be circumspect about the use of the cultural enquiry and especially Analysis Three.   (Checkland and Scholes, 1990)

This is extremely sound *practical* advice. However, this same advice raises several important issues for discussion.

First, if SSM users are to perform political analysis, then the methodology must provide models for understanding the power forces in the interactions.

Who has power? Who are the power brokers? How do they exercise or not exercise these powers? Who are the victims or beneficiaries of this power distribution? How can the nodes of the power network be identified? How does the SSM user enter the network and manage the redistribution of power? and so on. It is important to note that methodology users, through their links with influential power brokers, particularly clients, can also exercise power directly or indirectly, over those in the situation. Note also that while power may reside with those with authority, its exercise may not depend on those with legitimate authority. For instance, a secretary may exercise considerable power over a manager's staff merely by scheduling or rescheduling the manager's diary, acting as a gate-keeper of information, deciding whether to schedule meetings when the boss is in a 'good' or 'bad' mood and so on.

Secondly, by the very act of cautioning its users about public visibility, SSM is accepting the pragmatic political circumstances. Simply alerting its users to politics is not sufficient: if it recognizes politics as an important issue to be dealt with, then it must provide its users with models and ways of handling this power network. After all, every action or inaction on the part of SSM users is going to dictate how the methodology, or indeed, whether the methodology, can be practised in the situation in its intended form. It is here that the structure of the methodology changes, particularly when its users recognize and assess the implications of using it in its intended form. Case studies on using SSM show what political activities were faced, but not how they were resolved, what models were used and why the particular strategy [rationale] was adopted.

Thirdly, SSM users have to consider explicitly what is desirable and what is feasible as far as the methodology application is concerned. In effect, they must consider the intellectually desirable reasons for intervention if they are to benefit from the notions, steps and structure of the methodology. If they become sensitized to the politics of the situation, then they may well pursue feasible options. Once this happens, the users come under pressure to intellectualize their political action! This may explain why so many published SSM examples show the seven-stage implementation and why they were criticized by the creators as being too simplistic. We need guidance from the methodology as to how we can reconcile its intellectual demands with the demands of the political systems. In Chapter 4 we discussed the conflicts that arise when political and intellectual thoughts compete to dictate the reasoning process.

Finally, the analysis of the 'political system' and the private and cautious use of that information is indeed sound *practical* advice when intervening in organizations. However, when entering into this network through the node of the client, the methodology users cannot remain in a neutral position. Unconsciously or unwittingly, they are reinforcing or enhancing the power base of their clients while satisfying their own needs. (This is the reason why personal motives of the methodology user was incorporated as an essential element of the 'mental construct' of the NIMSAD framework.) Each action raises issues such as: Whose needs are being satisfied? Which needs should be given priority? What happens to the position and career development of the potential victims of the change? What are the implications of failing to accommodate the *Weltanschauungen* of those who may not be considered favourably by the clients? Is it more ethical to place one's own needs over those of the other stakeholders? In SSM there is no debate and discussion of these issues despite its concern with ethics. Simply raising the subject of ethics is not enough; the methodology should help its users to handle it.

SSM should be commended for alerting its users to the social and political issues that many other methodologies do not address or pretend as if they do not exist. However, since the critical issues that are to be addressed by SSM are embedded in these interactions, simply drawing the attention of its users to the need for conducting social and political analysis is not sufficient. It must also provide means for understanding and, on that basis, intervening in the situations. After all, that is the reason for using a methodology.

The analysis of the political, social and intervention issues together with 'rich pictures' enables SSM users to form an impression of the *state* of the 'situation of concern', i.e. why does the situation exist in its present form? A rich analysis of the kind recommended by SSM should enable its users to gain an insight into the issues facing the members of the organization. The questions raised here are to help make these intervention issues explicit for discussion and debate. Since the NIMSAD framework was derived from practice, it enables the questioning of the issues facing methodology users.

ELEMENT 3, STAGE 5: DERIVING THE NOTIONAL SYSTEMS

(Note the jump to stage 5 from stage 2 of the framework. That reflects the unique structure of SSM.)

Using the rich information accrued from the diagnosis, the methodology embarks on discovering the most relevant notional systems for discussions.

One way of defining notional system(s) in ill-structured situations is to find processes through which clients and problem owners can derive one or several 'desirable states'. This is what Schein (1969) attempted to do through the mode of 'process consultancy'. However, this particular process is both emotional and difficult, requiring a high degree of political and interpersonal skills. SSM addresses this process in a rather *unique* and *indirect* way. Instead of trying to discover the prognosis outline as the basis for deriving notional systems, it attempts to develop many potentially relevant system(s) expressed in 'root' definition form incorporating the *Weltanschauungen* of the problem owners. Since there are no prognosis outlines to relate to, the *relevance* of all relevant systems that are developed has yet to be established, but that is not the concern of SSM at this stage. The following is a typical example of a relevant systems description, i.e. a 'root' definition:

> An MF-owned system of experienced professionals which both pro-actively and on demand provides Shell companies, joint ventures, third parties and groups within Shell with relevant operational service support and advice, exploiting pooled know-how and specifically generated data in order to enhance the competitiveness of its customers.
>
> (Checkland and Scholes, 1990)

In SSM there is a discussion about two types of relevant systems, namely the 'primary task' systems and the 'issue-based' relevant systems. 'Primary task' systems are explained as the type made by 'hard' systems thinkers where the choice is made axiomatically (Checkland and Scholes, 1990). 'Issue-based' relevant systems are those that are conceptualized to represent a particular *Weltanschauung* and used as a way of generating debate in the situation. In general, the boundaries of the latter would not map to the 'action world'.

There is considerable contradiction in the pursuance of these two types of relevant systems within the same methodology. The 'issue-based' relevant system which represents an explicitly declared *Weltanschauung* is used in a notional sense for generating much valued debate in order to gain insights into the situation. It is used as an *instrument* for discussion and debate, and it is for this reason that the creators of SSM have taken care to emphasize that relevant systems are not ideal systems to be developed by SSM users. The use of metaphors is also to help the SSM users maintain the abstract nature of the development activities of relevant systems. This process is consistent with the epistemological nature of SSM and the intentions of its creators.

However, the incorporation of 'primary task' systems is in direct contradiction to the epistemological notions advocated by the methodology. Writing in the context of the Oxfam case study, the 'primary task' system is described as a system to provide relief (Checkland and Scholes, 1990). The 'primary task' system is mappable either to the organizational boundary as a whole or to a department/function with which the methodology users are concerned. This is a taken as given system. In discussing the accommodation of the 'primary task' system and the 'issue-based' relevant system within SSM, the creators state:

> The distinction between 'primary task' and 'issue based' relevant systems is not sharp or absolute, rather these are the ends of a spectrum. (Checkland and Scholes, 1990)

Writing in Checkland (1981), its author describes a primary-task root definition as:

> A *root definition* of a system which carries out some major task manifest in the real world. Such root definitions give would-be *neutral* (my italics) accounts of public or 'official' explicit tasks, often ones embodied in an organisation or section or department. (Checkland, 1981)

These raise a number of issues for discussion.

First, the 'primary task' system is out there to be taken as given for improvement while the 'issue-based' relevant system, in general does not exist. The latter is used in a notional sense and is consistent with the epistemological notions advocated by the methodology. The former is philosophically at odds with the nature of the methodology.

Secondly, the 'primary task' systems, because of their very existence, focus debate on the *content* and the improvement of the content, while the 'issue-based' relevant systems concentrate debate on the *context*. It is difficult to take a system as given within a methodology that invites its users to operate at an epistemological level and challenge the very nature of that taken as given system at the same time. Most importantly, SSM does not explain how this conflict can be resolved.

Thirdly, when 'primary task' systems are taken as given, their relevance to the situation is *already* established, while the relevance of 'issue-based' systems has *yet to be* established and is open to question, rejection and debate. In fact, rather than the 'primary task' system becoming mappable, the very notions that help to derive the 'primary task' system come from the information collected during the logical stream analysis of SSM. This point is also confirmed by Fitzgerald (1992) who states:

> For example, the Primary Task Model appears to lose all the richness gained in the traditional application of SSM and I suggest that one could arrive at the Primary Task without having made use of SSM.   (Fitzgerald, 1992)

Fourthly, 'primary task' systems are taken-as-given descriptions of systems that exist, therefore conceptually they form part of the 'diagnosis'. 'Issue-based' relevant systems are notional, therefore they belong to the 'prognosis'. One is focused on 'what exists' and the other is focused on 'what should be considered'. The conceptual clarity between the two should be maintained at a methodological level if relevant and useful solutions are to be found for the 'action world'.

SSM also claims that working with both kinds of relevant systems frees thinking. This unfortunately cannot be the case given the above conflicts of philosophy and aims of the methodology. Take, for example, the case of Oxfam once again. In attempting to clarify the two types of relevant systems, the creators of SSM offer the following example:

> Oxfam can be *observed* [my italics] providing relief, providing aid, running retail shops and begging. It would be possible to name relevant systems based on these actions (a system to provide relief', etc.), and we might in the real world *anticipate* [my italics] finding functional divisions of Oxfam which map these choices. Or an overall relevant system with the four named systems as subsystems could map the organisation boundary as a whole. This would be a primary task system for Oxfam with each subsystem being itself a choice of the same kind. But within Oxfam, as in any organisation under-taking a portfolio of different tasks, there will always be debate about its core purposes and about the fraction of resources which should be devoted to each. From this con-sideration we could make the second kind of choice of

> relevant system. We could name as relevant such conceptualisa-
> tions as 'a system to resolve disagreements on resource use' or
> 'a system to define information flows to and from the manage-
> ment committee'. Here we would not necessarily expect to
> find institutionalized versions of such systems in the real
> world. In SSM these are called 'issue-based relevant systems';
> in general their boundaries would not map on to real-world
> boundaries.   (Checkland and Scholes, 1990)

In the context of the above example, if one defined the 'primary task' system as a system to provide relief, then its relevance is not going to be in question. In effect, the familiarization of Oxfam activities during the investigation phase would have already established the relevance of the 'primary task' system. As the above example illustrates, it is not difficult to show the relevance of the 'primary task' system when it is based on a set of current activities. Once the 'primary task' systems are accepted, then the 'issue-based' relevant systems have to concentrate on the periphery of these systems. This kind of accommodation prevents SSM users from considering a possible 'issue-based' relevant system that advocated the abandonment of provision of relief altogether. For example, some believe that the provision of relief from relief agencies helps the governments of both the donor and recipient countries to become complacent about the real issues facing the victims; forces the donors to psychologically prepare themselves to accommodate their guilt; makes them disregard the ethical and moral implications of their other activities that may very well contribute to the undesirable conditions of the victims; disconnect themselves from the situations facing their fellow human beings; causes the recipients to abandon faith in their own energies, strengths and abilities and become highly dependent on the donors; leads the governments to neglect their responsibilities; helps fuel the repressive practices of some recipient governments and military regimes to maintain their power over the victims; and enables the relief agencies to act as big conglomerates exercising power at a global level while strengthening their power base to act at this level through increased resources generated by sending highly sophisticated emotive messages that are intended to exploit the guilt and emotions of potential donors. None of this may be true or justifiable in the light of massive organized human relief aid activities undertaken by OXFAM, but unless radically different 'root' definitions which promote different *Weltanschauungen* of the primary activities of the organization can be incorporated, the chances of developing worthwhile debates to examine the core activities will be minimal. The epistemological nature of SSM cannot be maintained which takes as given the noticeable and visible 'primary task' system. The creator of SSM is very concerned that many who are engaged in the improvements of 'primary task' systems in organizations consider themselves as users of SSM. The original intention of SSM was to suggest that even 'primary task' systems were to be used for generating useful perceptions for explorations. Because of their mappable status to existing organization or functional boundaries, not much debate can be generated.

If the conceptual and fundamental epistemological contribution of SSM to the development of 'truly' relevant notional systems is to be maintained, we urge its creators to abandon the use of the notion of 'primary task' systems. It distracts attention from problem issues and prevents the raising of *radically* different 'root' definitions central to the creation of debates. An 'issue-based' relevant system can be used both at the primary task level (if indeed, that is an issue) or on any critical issue facing an organization. For example, in the context of Oxfam, a worthwhile 'issue-based' relevant system could be:

> An information providing system owned by its members and subscribers that takes its primary role as the raising of ethical and moral awareness and obligations of society members and their collective organisations (i.e. the governments, local au-thorities, companies, banks, etc.) to those who are either directly or indirectly disadvantaged by their actions. It is to do this by continuously monitoring the general welfare, health and quality of life of target groups; by assessing the methods, decisions and actions through which the undesirable conditions are created and by galvanising its members' activi-ties where necessary for privately and publicly exposing and questioning those who are individually or collectively responsi-ble for bringing about those undesirable and unacceptable conditions.

EXPANDING THE 'ROOT' DEFINITION

SSM is one of the few methodologies to have made a great impact in the use of conceptual thinking. It uses 'systems' ideas in an epistemological sense and was a pioneer in the promotion of this form of systems thinking. This influence has helped many methodology users to consider concepts rather than techniques of the design process. In this context, SSM has developed an *extremely useful* systems model known as the Formal Systems Model (Checkland, 1981). However, in the revised version of SSM, the use of the Formal Systems Model has been replaced by CATWOE (Customer, Actor, Transformation, *Weltanschauung*, Objectives and Environment) on the grounds that the latter is sufficient to guide the construction of 'root' definitions.

> For some years use has been made of a general model of purposeful activity known as the Formal Systems Model (Checkland, 1981) against which conceptual models of activity systems could be checked. It was expressed as a set of entities (boundary, sub-system, resources etc.) and later expressed by Atkinson and Checkland (1988) as an activity system . . . However, its use has declined in the last decade, CATWOE has virtually eliminated it, and in any case its language tended to blur. . . .von Bulow (1989) usefully points out some of the confusions surrounding the use of the Formal Systems Model and it can probably now be cheerfully dropped.
>
> (Checkland and Scholes, 1990)

This also raises issues for discussion. The CATWOE criteria have been extremely useful in focusing the thought processes of SSM users on organizational aspects which need to be considered *explicitly* in developing sound intellectually desirable 'root' definitions. But these criteria are not sufficient by themselves to focus conceptual clarity in the use of 'systems' concepts. As the creators of SSM themselves have criticized, some of the SSM users have not appreciated the conceptual clarity of the transformation process—see, for instance, criticisms of Ryan (1973) and Passos (1976) in Checkland and Scholes (1990). The essence of the epistemological use of 'systems' cannot be grasped from CATWOE. The reasons for the decline of the explicit use of 'systems concepts' by SSM users may have more to do with their misunderstanding of the conceptual differences between the ontological and epistemological notions of 'systems'. CATWOE unfortunately does not raise the methodology users' thinking processes to a conceptual level. For example, in what way would the 'root' definition be different if it was owned by the managing director or the deputy if they both happen to subscribe to the same *Weltanschauung*? Apart from maintaining the notion of the owner at a conscious level, the subsequent design steps of SSM do not make use of this ownership issue. What 'systems' concepts enable us to do is to help us concentrate on the *specific* nature of the integration which gives the 'root' definition its emergent properties.

CATWOE does not help to focus attention on the *connectivity* nor can it represent the more subtle conceptual clarity of the 'systems' notions advocated in the original version of SSM (Checkland, 1981). For example, compare the formal systems model with the CATWOE definition illustrated in Figure 10.4.

The shortcomings of CATWOE as a replacement of 'systems' notions can be illustrated by examining its very definition. Consider the definition of CATWOE elements given in the revised version of SSM.

Transformation is a 'systems' concept that is used in many disciplines. It is essential to many of the changes proposed in organizations, and is central to the process of thinking advocated by SSM. It focuses the attention of the thinker (using 'systems' concepts) on the *process* of the transformation. Inputs are information, material, ideas, signals etc. which enter the transformation process while outputs are information, material, ideas, signals etc. which have been subjected to it. In the CATWOE examples, the focus is *not* on the transformation. Transformation is described in input and output form, thus focusing the minds of potential SSM users on recognizable changes in the output from those of the input in order to determine the role of the transformation undertaken. The transformation itself is shown as an arrow—see Figure 10.5 for examples. The arrow cannot, however, describe the nature, the form or the organization of the transformation process that help us to understand its unique emergent properties.

Imagine if this approach had been taken by someone to contrast the nature of the transformation process implied by SSM with that of a structured methodology. Using the CATWOE definition, both methodologies would be described in input–output form of the type: 'a methodology user requiring intervention assistance in a situation' and 'that assistance met'. This would not help a potential methodology user to consider the unique transformation characteristics implied in SSM. The essence of SSM is in the transformation (in the thinking and the interactive exchange of thought processes of its participants). What the illustrations of CATWOE show is the notion of a 'Black Box', one that is commonly used in the engineering disciplines to focus attention away from the nature and logic of the transformation. An arrow *cannot* describe the nature, the form or the essence of the transformation implied in SSM.

(Readers should note that CATWOE may help trigger points to be included in the 'root' definition, but for most who do not have an appreciation of the epistemological notions of 'systems', CATWOE terms merely become labels

Formulate root definitions by considering the
elements C A T W O E :

C 'customers' : the victims or beneficiaries of T

A 'actors' : those who would do T

T 'transformation: the conversion of input to output
   process'

W 'Weltanschauung': the worldview which makes this
   T meaningful in context

O 'owner(s)' : those who could stop T

E 'environmental: elements outside the system which
   constraints' it takes as given

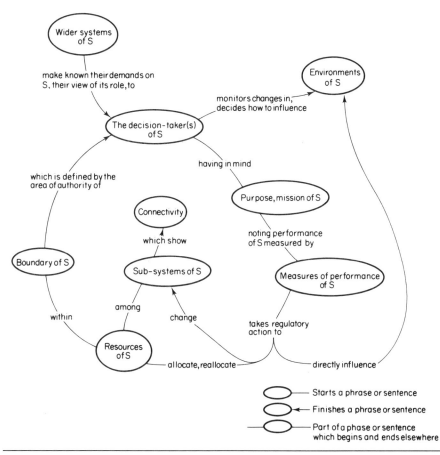

Figure 10.4   CATWOE and the formal systems model (P. Checkland and J. Scholes, *Soft Systems Methodology in Action*, © 1990. Reprinted by permission of John Wiley & Sons, Ltd.)

Example: a public library

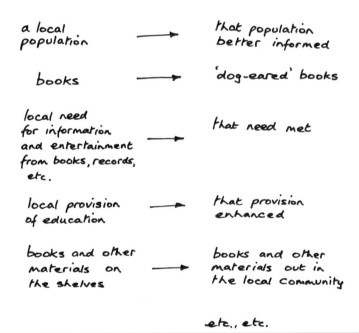

Figure 10.5   Ideas of transformation (P. Checkland and J. Scholes, *Soft Systems Methodology in Action*, © 1990. Reprinted by permission of John Wiley & Sons, Ltd.)

or words used in everyday language. CATWOE cannot illustrate the conceptual clarity of 'systems' notions discussed in the context of the Formal Systems Model in SSM. In some case studies even this use of CATWOE has been dropped.)

Instead of CATWOE being taken as central to the revised SSM, we urge the SSM creators to bring in other more powerful 'systemic' notions and retain the Formal Systems Model or a form of it in order to assist the transformation of SSM users' *thinking* processes. For instance, advanced systems concepts of 'autopoesis' (Maturana and Varela, 1980) and 'homeostasis' (Beer, 1978, 1979, 1981) can enrich the building of 'root' definitions.

(Readers should note that critical evaluation of these notions is possible because SSM has chosen to incorporate many notions which other methodologies have chosen to exclude from their domain of influence.)

ELEMENT 3, STAGE 6: PERFORMING THE CONCEPTUAL/ LOGICAL DESIGN

(Readers are reminded that in SSM, systemic analysis as discussed within the NIMSAD framework has not been conducted as yet, i.e. the relevance of 'notional' systems to the 'problem situation' have not been established.)

The role of this stage is to design conceptual models for each chosen relevant system.

The revised version of SSM suggests the use of the 'root' definition (relevant systems in descriptive form) as the guide for the design process. The methodology is general enough to accommodate many dimensions, including data, role and norm aspects of organizations. The specific designs will depend on the abilities of the SSM users, while the methodology provides the means for structuring these sets of activities. Note that according to the structure of SSM, this stage is performed for each 'root' definition *before* the phase of systemic analysis is undertaken. In the context of the NIMSAD framework this means that the conceptual/logical design is completed before finalizing the problem formulation stage.

SSM does not separate the conceptual/logical and physical activities. It suggests the building of necessary activities which would help to realize each 'root' definition (relevant system)—see Figure 10.6.

Here again we see the clear implications of not keeping the 'systemic' notions at the forefront of design. In many of the examples listed in Checkland and Scholes (1990), the conceptual models of the 'root' definitions as a system do not show any inputs and outputs although, as we discussed earlier, the CATWOE describes the transformation in terms of input and output. If we apply the efficacy test suggested in SSM to the conceptual models, they would not pass the efficacy test. Efficacy is defined as the verification of

Figure 10.6 A conceptual model (P. Checkland and J. Scholes, *Soft Systems Methodology in Action*, © 1990. Reprinted by permission of John Wiley & Sons, Ltd.)

whether the means chosen actually work in producing the output (Checkland and Scholes, 1990). This is done by examining the transformation which converts inputs to outputs, whether they be material, services, information or ideas. Taken from CATWOE, if the conceptual models do not show any inputs and outputs (apart from the monitoring and control), then it is difficult to see how the inputs and outputs described in the CATWOE-based 'root' definitions can be linked to the conceptual model or how the transformation implied in the conceptual model can be judged as workable or useful. In discussing the links between the 'root' definition and conceptual model building, SSM states that:

> What is now done in stage 4 is to make a model of the activity system *needed to achieve* [my italics] the transformation described in the definition. We now build the model which will *accomplish* [my italics] what is defined in the root definition. The definition is an account of what the system is; the conceptual model is an account of the activities which the system must do in order to be the system named in the definition. (Checkland and Scholes, 1990)

In fact, the conceptual model is incomplete if it cannot show how the inputs stated in the CATWOE-based 'root' definition can be transformed into the outputs stated in the same definition.

In SSM, users are encouraged to design the minimum necessary activities in order to bring about the transformation. This focus on the minimum is useful as there is a tendency for many designers to elaborate their designs by building activities that may contribute very little to the achievement of the stated purposes in the 'root' definition.

Finally, a new guideline for limiting the number of activities at any one level has been taken from Miller's (1956) model. As discussed in the context of SASS in Chapter 8, the relevance or usefulness of this hypothesis is not established.

ELEMENT 3, STAGE 7: PERFORMING THE PHYSICAL DESIGN

(Readers are reminded that, according to the structure of SSM, systemic analysis has still not taken place.)

In SSM, physical design activities are combined with logical design activities and are undertaken as a collective function.

SSM does not provide any means of conducting this stage, except to encourage systemically desirable and culturally feasible solutions. It relies on its users' experience, skills and knowledge of the context domain to develop relevant practical solutions.

ELEMENT 3, STAGE 3: DEFINING THE PROGNOSIS OUTLINE

SSM welcomes the opportunities to address critical questions. It operates in

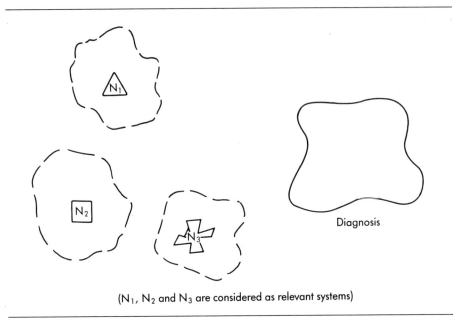

(N$_1$, N$_2$ and N$_3$ are considered as relevant systems)

Figure 10.7   Illustration of notional systems mapping using NIMSAD

environments where there are either multiple 'desired states' and/or the clients are unsure of their 'desired states'. Situations in which clients are unable to express clear and precise expectations are known as *ill-structured* situations. (Note that in diagrammatic terms, these are situations where there is either no outline shape or many competing shapes to the prognosis outline as discussed in stage 4 of Chapter 5.) SSM is uniquely placed for addressing this very kind of situation.

In SSM there is no attempt to construct prognosis outlines. Nor does it attempt to directly discover the client's 'desirable state' for the situation. Each of the completed 'root' definitions (potential notional systems) and related conceptual models (logical and physical designs) imply a particular 'desired state' for which it can be considered as relevant. The construction and association of relevant systems to the 'desired states' of course remains as an implicit thought process, and its relevance is brought to bear at the next stage. The process of structuring the situational characteristics, developing relevant systems and conducting debates with client(s) enables SSM users to understand the context and the *relevance* of relevant systems to the situation which client(s) perceive to be problematical. Figure 10.7 illustrates the use of potentially relevant notional systems in the problem formulation process of SSM using the NIMSAD framework.

The 'rich pictures' in SSM help its users to obtain an understanding of the 'situation of concern' and abstract the 'state' of that situation. However, since there are no clear emergent outlines to the 'desired states', the methodology helps to construct many relevant systems. The shapes (triangular, square, etc.) in the prognosis (Figure 10.7) can be thought of as the relevant systems. Each relevant system supports a particular 'desired state' (illustrated by the dotted outlines), but these shapes remain implicit within the client group. The focus of SSM is to establish the *relevance* of the relevant systems to the diagnosis. However, the clients attempt to evaluate the relevance of the relevant systems to the prognosis outlines that begin to form in their 'mental constructs'.

ELEMENT 3, STAGE 4: DEFINING 'PROBLEMS'

As discussed in Chapter 5, this can be considered as the conceptual mapping of the diagnosis and prognosis outlines on each other for arriving at problem statements and subsequent expression of notional system(s).

Since SSM does not attempt to extract 'desired states' explicitly, it cannot perform the mapping of the two states in any explicit manner either. Because of this it does not attempt to define 'problems' or formulate problem statements. It simply does not focus on any 'problem(s)'. This is a *unique* feature of the methodology.

If this is so, how does it conduct systemic analysis as discussed in Chapter 5?

This is carried out by conducting a structured debate with the participants in order to establish the *relevance* of the relevant systems and their conceptual models to the situation. SSM uses the relevant systems (potential notional systems) expressed in 'root' definition form, together with their supporting conceptual/logical/physical (design) models and maps them against the diagnosis (expressed in 'rich' picture form together with Analyses one, two and three). Direct mapping between the two states is not possible because of the absence of an outline shape to the prognosis; hence the methodology is only able to establish the *relevance* of relevant systems to the current situation. Given that clients operate in ill-structured situations, the presentation of a range of relevant systems may force an intellectual debate and challenge to both the client(s) and the SSM users such that a clear, acceptable relevant notional system(s) is expected to emerge, thus lending structure to those situations. This process, of course, avoids directly challenging the client's implicit 'desired state' or rationalization process. The legitimacy of the 'world images' is established during these debates. In establishing relevance, the participants are implicitly addressing areas which they initially considered to be problematical.

Because there is no explicit mapping of 'desired states' with 'current states', the *relevance* of the relevant systems in general cannot be established in one iteration. The debate gives rise to changes of 'root' definitions and their conceptual models; thus, the cycle of modifying, revising and debating these definitions and models continues until desirable and feasible changes are agreed upon. Thus the whole activity of problem formulation is triggered at an *implicit* level using explicitly constructed relevant systems. This is the *unique* and *powerful* nature of SSM.

In our interventions we usually find that clients have political and emotional difficulty in handling the term 'problem'. In an explicit problem formulation process, inevitably the client is forced to accept the role of problem owner, making it very difficult for the problem-solving process or the use of a methodology to continue. Extracting and making public 'problems' is, of course, not the focus of SSM; its aim is to focus the debate on particular issues. This is the reason why we recognized the need for SSM users to posses extremely high political, interpersonal and abstract skills.

The process of mapping and debating is a critical step in the methodology. It suggests a matrix model for conducting this debate. After all, the debate is to establish the relevance of the models to the situation. Since these are not in any comparable form, different models are proposed for structuring the debate and discussion. Mathiassen's and Nielson's (1990) idea is to use contradictions as a way of forcing this debate. SSM does not, however, discuss any particular models that would be useful for managing the potentially emotional and political relationship processes which may arise in the debate between SSM users and their clients or between the clients and others. The debate is critical if SSM is to be applied successfully. It is also a process where ethical and moral issues are bound to emerge, but SSM does not offer guidance here either.

ELEMENT 3, STAGE 8: IMPLEMENTING THE DESIGN
Surprisingly, this is the weakest step of SSM.

There is no any particular strategy for implementation in SSM. It assumes that desirable and culturally feasible changes incorporated in the design models will ensure clients' support for implementation. However, in the revised version, there is a recognition of the need for some guidance on the implementation stage of the desirable and feasible choices made within SSM. It suggests the use of SSM to structure the implementation as if it was another situation to be handled.

> This implementation is, of course, itself a 'problem situation' and it is not unusual to use SSM to tackle it.
>
> (Checkland and Scholes, 1990)

In other words, the implementation can itself be considered as a 'transformation process' to deal with the output of the 'transformation process' from the previous use of SSM. Commenting on this, the creators of SSM state:

> We may conceptualise and model systems to implement the changes, and do that according to several relevant Weltan-schauungen. Finally, we may pinpoint 'a system to make changes' whose activities can then become real-world action.
>
> (Checkland and Scholes, 1990)

This exploration of different methods of bringing about changes is similar in form to the implementation strategies discussed in the NIMSAD framework. However, the use of SSM at this stage raises several issues for discussion.

First, if the application of SSM for resolving issues in a 'problem situation' (after a number of iterations) results in a desirable and feasible relevant notional system, then its application during the implementation stage cannot have the same relevant notional system as a point of debate. The output of the first cycle of SSM *must* be implemented (without question) in the second cycle of SSM if learning about the situation has to be achieved.

This leads to the second cycle having to accept the relevant notional system from the first cycle as a taken as given system. Once this is accepted, the epistemological nature of SSM cannot be maintained in the second cycle. What is being used here is what Checkland (1981) originally defined as a 'hard' systems task, i.e. the task is to find the best *means* of achieving a given end.

If this is the case, those responsible for implementation cannot discuss the desirability of the notional systems as it has already been established. The involvement extended to this group is participation in determining the best 'means', in other words, feasible options. This cannot be considered as the use of SSM.

Secondly, the recursive use of SSM in this way poses further points for discussion. Note that the recursive use of systems has been applied successfully by Beer (1978, 1988) in the context of Viable Systems Model applications. However, the recursive mode applied within VSM is about the modelling of 'systems', while the recursive mode advocated in SSM is on the methodology itself. The latter is much more difficult to maintain without losing the essence of SSM.

Apart from the recommendation of the use of SSM there is very little discussion about problems involved in implementation. The case studies give very little indication as to how this stage has been performed using SSM.

Thirdly, in the revised version, the creators state:

> Implementation of changes will take place in a human culture, and will modify that culture, at least a little, and possibly a great deal. But the changes will be implemented only if they are perceived to be meaningful within that culture and within that world view.   (Checkland and Scholes, 1990)

This creates further points for discussion.

As explained earlier, if the first cycle of relevant systems and their conceptual models lead to desirable and feasible changes, they should then proceed with the implementation of the relevant notional system. In order to facilitate these, the revised version of SSM contains Analyses two and three which enable its users to consider the cultural context of the change situation. If, on the other hand, further cultural analysis is to be conducted at the implementation stage in order to consider the best options, this implies that the cultural context of establishing the relevance of desirable and feasible notional systems is different from that in which these systems have to be developed and operated. If the latter is the case, the initial cultural analysis in SSM should be extended to incorporate both environments, i.e. the environments of the client groups and other users, beneficiaries or victims. Our experience shows that what clients consider to be desirable and feasible may not necessarily be what is considered as desirable and feasible by those having to operate and live with the changes thus creating difficulties. SSM does not discuss how these issues are to be resolved i.e. can those involved in the implementation disagree or challenge the status of previously agreed relevant notional systems?

LINKS TO INFORMATION SYSTEMS DEVELOPMENT

Links to information systems development can be considered at two levels.

First, information processing systems development can be incorporated into the cycle advocated in SSM. In this mode, information systems that are necessary for bringing about relevant notional systems are incorporated at the conceptual model building stage. According to the revised version, data flows that can support the conceptual model activities can be constructed and followed by the development of data structures. Attempts to link data flow diagrams to conceptual models or to replace conceptual models with data flow diagrams raise a number of difficulties. These are mainly on the meaning of the lines linking the conceptual activities, i.e. whether they can be taken as information, influences, dependencies, material, etc. The creators of SSM have acknowledged the difficulties of the philosophical changes these impose.

Secondly, information processing systems development can be considered as a separate process whose role is to develop information systems to support the relevant notional systems arising from the use of SSM. In this mode, structured methodologies can be deployed to develop information processing systems without changes to the conceptual models as the relevance of the notional systems has already been agreed. This is known as *grafting* while the first form described above is termed *embedding*. Multiview is a methodology which attempts to do the grafting (Wood-Harper, 1989; Avison and Wood-Harper, 1991). The use of SSM however may or may not lead to the design of information processing systems.

Whichever approach is taken, it is difficult to avoid the conceptual difficulties arising from linking two methodologies with different philosophical and conceptual emphases. In the embedding mode, the positivistic paradigms of the structured methodology components have to be sacrificed in order that they can be accommodated within the phenomenological paradigms of SSM. In the grafting mode, the users have to *terminate* the epistemological nature of SSM and switch to the ontological nature of a structured methodology. These present difficulties of justifying (explain the rationale) of how these links are achieved in practice while maintaining the philosophical nature of SSM (Miles, 1988).

FURTHER ANALYSIS

SSM is so rich in its discussion of the context issues that we need to discuss some of the changes in the revised version as they raise many points of interest and implications.

HOW SOFT IS 'SOFT'?

There is a clear departure from the nature, philosophy and use of SSM between its first version (Checkland, 1981) and the revised version (Checkland and Scholes, 1990). One of the most noticeable observations is the disappearance of the quote marks surrounding the terms 'soft' and 'hard' in the revised version. If SSM is a methodology aimed at a learning epistemology, then the use of quotes reminds its users that they are using the notion 'soft' as a means of learning about a situation. Once the use of quotes are dropped and at the same time if we include the notion of 'hard' as a special case of 'soft', then everything becomes a special case of 'soft'. The grounds on which 'hard' is considered as a special case of 'soft' are explained by the SSM authors:

> SSM is a systemic process of enquiry which also happens to make use of systems models. It thus subsumes the hard approach which is a special case of it, one arising when there is local agreement on some system to be engineered.
>
> (Checkland and Scholes, 1990)

If the basis for incorporating the 'hard' approach within SSM is simply because it also uses systems models, we could also incorporate all engineering, and many other similar approaches under SSM as being special cases. If this rationale is to be extended, then the 'hard' approach could also claim, quite legitimately, that SSM is a special case of it.

The world is neither 'hard' nor 'soft'. It is we who have chosen to treat it as such. This classification, like all classifications of knowledge, is to help us structure our understanding and knowledge and help determine characteristics which are unique to those classified groups. If we can also develop approaches, methods or solutions that would be appropriate to those categories then we could very well claim that the partitioning (classification) is very useful. This is what 'soft' systems approach attempts to do. By criticizing and discussing the failures of engineering approaches (see Checkland, 1981) as being inappropriate for certain classes of problems, the SSM creator established the legitimacy for treating these problems in a different way. Thus, the terms 'hard' versus 'soft' came to be promoted. Therefore, it is difficult to understand how the 'hard' approaches with all their failures can become a special case of 'soft', thereby making the use of SSM not an epistemology but a term for encompassing all approaches using systems models.

The problems for the information systems field are that many who come to the field attach themselves to one or more labels given their background, interests, values, etc. A 'hard' systems methodology user deals with all 'soft' issues implicitly without any help from the 'hard' methodology, just as a 'soft' systems methodology user deals with 'hard' issues without much assistance from the 'soft' systems methodology. Once attached to 'soft' or 'hard' approaches, users fail to recognize that they are operating in this way when they look for activities that match their chosen methodology and associated philosophy. An effective systems thinker knows that these are *artificial boundaries* and that the situations he or she faces are far more complex than any type or form of methodology or philosophy could address. The question that a methodology user needs to ask is, 'In what way can this methodology help me to address the complexity of the situation?' What are the implications of using this methodology? (See Chapter 7 for a list of questions that one could ask—readers should not blame the author for the frustrations these questions might create.) A 'hard' systems methodology user who decides to *challenge* the client's requirements is turning it into a 'soft' situation in the same way as a 'soft' systems methodology user who *agrees* to a client's requirement changes that situation into a 'hard' one. The task is to become aware of the philosophical assumptions that underpin the methodologies and to select and use them in the context consciously without treating the world into 'hard' or 'soft' situations. In order to do this, the methodology user must be free as far as possible (at least in an intellectual sense) to reflect in a considered way on the reasons for choosing or constructing a methodology and on the implications of making that choice. In so doing, the methodology user must be prepared to admit that no methodology can work in practice in any human context. It has to be modified, changed, altered and constructed based on the situation characteristics, the 'mental construct' and the dynamic interactions between those in the situation and the methodology user. This is why we identified several versions of methodology in operation, namely the original methodology, the adopted/adapted methodology, and the methodology-in-action.

SSM CONTEXT ISSUES

Unlike many methodologies which are only concerned with the transformation of taken as given systems or situations, the creators recommend that SSM is suitable for use in two modes. These modes have been constructed from their experience and are explained as follows:

> These experiences led to the recognition of a spectrum (in principle) use of SSM from, on the one hand, a formal stage-by-stage application of the methodology (let us call it Mode 1) to, on the other, internal mental use of it as a thinking mode (which we call Mode 2).
>
> (Checkland and Scholes, 1990)

Mode 1 application

Mode 1 use of SSM is what we have examined so far in this chapter. We have used the NIMSAD framework to question how the seven-stage or the two-stream versions address the problem-solving process. This section examines further issues raised by the Mode 1 use.

The creators of SSM are very concerned that those who use it should understand and observe the nature and the spirit of SSM steps. In order to assist this process, they have provided a set of Constitutive Rules. These rules define the terms and the nature of the steps and are intended to guide potential SSM users. The rules are not intended to be of an 'ideal' type to map step by step to the applied version of SSM. In other words, the methodology-in-action need not include all the steps of SSM nor its defined structure. In effect, many of the case study examples demonstrate this use.

This raises a number of issues for discussion.

The creators have acknowledged the need for flexibility and adaptability of SSM. The explicit recognition of this feature is consistent with the role of *Weltanschauung* discussed in Checkland (1981). Not only is this a recognition of different *Weltanschauungen* of different people, but also of the different *Weltanschauungen* of the same persons at different times discussed earlier in this chapter. In some cases, the *Weltanschauung* may depend on the changing nature of the political situation. While this concept of adaptability is both an intelligent and practical recognition (and should be so if it is to be relevant, useful and effective), the changes pose problems for the status of SSM-in-action.

SSM is a 'systems' methodology. Its creators have gone to considerable lengths to establish that this is the case. So why should this adaptability pose problems of a conceptual nature?

A 'system' is a *coherent collection* of parts and not simply a *collection* of parts. It is the coherence and not the parts themselves that give rise to the emergent properties of a 'system'. Part of the coherence is provided by its structure. The removal of parts or changes to the structure must affect the systems' emergent properties, else it will be very difficult to justify that the collection is still the *same* system.

When we examine SSM (both the original and the revised version) we can observe cogently argued structures. In other words, the rationale for its parts (steps) and its structure (order in which the steps are carried out) is well described, discussed and argued by its creators. In fact, it is this *coherent collection* that has given SSM its unique identity and not just the steps.

For example, some of the steps and elements in SSM are not unique to it. The notion of 'systems', *Weltanschauung*, political analysis, social analysis, client management, measures of performance, ethics, efficiency and effectiveness have formed part of discourse analysis in the social science field for generations. They have been used within much of sociology literature. What is unique to SSM is the convincingly well structured and argued way in which these notions have been brought together based on the well founded 'systems' philosophy. But in so doing (as in every boundary construction of systems), SSM has chosen to include some steps (such as political analysis, social analysis, etc.) to construct new 'holistic' notions such as 'root' definitions and exclude others (such as technical analysis, psychological profile analysis, financial analysis, etc.). It is the selected inclusion of steps and, most importantly, their structural connection which has given SSM its unique identity, and it is the emergent properties arising from this coherence which enables SSM to be distinguished from other methodologies.

If, according to the Constitutive Rules, the steps can be performed selectively, then this affects the structure of SSM. While the changes to any structure and steps may be necessary to adopt a methodology to address a given situation, the question that has to be raised here is whether the resulting methodology can still be called SSM? The Constitutive Rules provide guidelines on how parts, if used, need to conform to the spirit of SSM. They do not, however, explain which steps (parts) are to be fundamental and what structures are to be used for the methodology-in-action to qualify as being SSM. As illustrated in Figures 10.1 and 10.2, if the structural properties of SSM are disconnected to form a different methodology, can the resulting methodology still be called SSM? For example, the creators of SSM criticize Flood and Gaisford (in Checkland and Scholes, 1990) for misunderstanding the notion of 'client'. Had they defined their clients according to the Constitutive Rules, could their methodology be called SSM? There is a need to be clear as to what minimum steps and structures need to be followed before the resulting methodology can continue to be defined as SSM.

There are two general lessons that can be derived from this discussion.

First, we should not be surprised to find that a methodology is subjected to interpretation within the context knowledge of the methodology user, resulting in an intended methodology. The methodology-in-action may very well be different from the original methodology as described by its creators, or the intended methodology, as interpreted by the methodology user. Because of this, methodology users should refrain from claiming:
- that the methodology-in-action is identical to the original methodology, thereby ignoring the interpretations and changes which they may have introduced to it. Checkland and Scholes, (1990) criticisms of seven-stage applications relate to this
- that the methodology-in-action has the same emergent properties and has brought about the same intended transformation even though it was fundamentally different in structure and content from the original methodology.

What is most important is to question
- the rationale of the original methodology. If it is accepted, why did the methodology user consider it relevant and useful for the situation?
- the rationale of the changes. If the original methodology was modified, why did the methodology user make these changes?
- the rationale for the methodology-in-action. Why were changes made and, if so, what are the implications for future interventions?

As discussed in Chapter 7, these issues need to be examined continuously before, during and after the use of methodology. The evaluation should cover not just the methodology, but also the situation and the lessons for the methodology user. It is important for SSM users to know that the only justification they have to make is to themselves and that justification needs to be intellectual and not political. Justification of political action may make us feel secure, but it does not contribute to our intellectual development.

If SSM had been instrumental in developing a methodology for the situation and also the methodology-in-action, then it would indeed have achieved its epistemological goals. If this is the case, then the literature must show how SSM helped to develop these methodology versions. Under these circumstances it is not desirable to justify that the methodology-in-action is the same as SSM. It is these conceptual differences that led Argyris and Schon (1974), Argyris (1982) and Schon (1983) to differentiate between the 'espoused theory' and the 'theory-in-use'.

The implications of these for methodology theory and practice are twofold.

If credibility of transformation remains with the status of the original methodology, then methodology users will attempt to suppress the methodology-in-action and discuss only those steps of the original methodology as a way of achieving credibility. On the other hand, if the original methodology offered is in a loose structure (i.e. any parts can be removed) then the practitioners may very well justify their (implicit and not well thought-out) methodologies-in-action to be the same as the original methodology, in this case, SSM. The way to avoid these difficulties is for the methodology users to justify why they accepted the original methodology, why they made any changes and, if so, how they preserved the essential structure, content and philosophy of the original methodology in the methodology-in-action. On the other hand, if the methodology-in-action is identical to the original methodology, the methodology users must demonstrate how it was possible to achieve this in a complex human interaction situation, i.e. explain the authority structures, management styles, rewards/penalties, group commitments, etc. that enabled them to maintain the characteristics of the original methodology in the 'action world'.

Mode 2 application

This is considered to be the thinking mode, in which the methodology user undertakes reflection using SSM. With reference to mode 2, the creators of SSM state:

> We have to accept at the start of such re-thinking that the extreme ideal type of 2, as a purely internal mental process, is

> publicly untouchable by testing against Constitutive Rules of
> any kind.   (Checkland and Scholes, 1990)

The creators have dismissed this kind of use of SSM as being incompetent. We agree. We also suggest that, since the process is purely internal and its rationale cannot be demonstrable, this kind of thinking is not considered even as an extreme case of Mode 2. The whole reason for using a methodology is to make the rationalization process *explicit* so that useful lessons can be learned by its users in addition to transformations. As defined in Chapter 2, a methodology is an *explicit* way of structuring one's own thinking and actions.

For Mode 2 use of SSM, the creators provide guidelines in addition to the Constitutive Rules in order to help evaluate situations. In this mode of use, SSM is presented as a framework of ideas. These raise further questions for discussion.

As discussed earlier, parts (steps) of SSM are comprehensively covered elsewhere in the literature, e.g. political analysis, social analysis. Even those who have never been introduced to SSM are able to use their acquired theory and knowledge to undertake reflection. Therefore, simply using 'parts' to undertake reflection cannot be claimed as using SSM, i.e. the 'whole', and since the users are selecting 'parts' and not the 'whole' of SSM for reflection, it is difficult to justify that this is the use of SSM in Mode 2. The role of a methodology is to structure one's *thinking* in this case. If this is to be so, then that structure and steps must be demonstrable as being instrumental in the reflection.

Take, for example, someone who has been introduced to political theory. Engaging in reflection after the events using the concepts of power may reveal how the methodology user realized his or her goals. This can be undertaken without much assistance from SSM. If SSM is to be useful, then it must offer *explicit* guidance in the reflective process. In this context, SSM considers its contribution to be in the form of a framework of ideas. The case studies confirm the use of selected ideas. This is the use of *systems ideas of SSM* and not the use of 'Soft' Systems *Methodology*. The reflection process must show how the structural aspects and steps were used to guide the reflection if it is to claim to have used SSM.

ELEMENT 4: EVALUATION

Learning is considered central to the role of SSM. This is the case whether SSM is used in Mode 1 or Mode 2. This role of learning raises a number of issues for further discussion.

Intervention in the 'action world' is a complex activity because it affects not only the usually functional and technical aspects of organizations, but also the psychological, political and emotional aspects of their members. Learning, therefore, is an extremely important and fundamental development process, particularly for management of industry. In fact, many industrial problems can be attributed to the lack of attention given to learning by management. Therefore, the role of SSM in attempting to focus attention on the learning process is a very commendable one. The emphasis of SSM is on debate and discussions, but therein lie some of the fundamental problems that need to be addressed.

SSM, unlike many other methodologies, requires its users to invest considerable time and effort in developing their thinking processes. In addition, if improvements are to be gained, clients are required to invest resources with implications for their status, positions and personal reputations. Because of these heavy investments, clients' primary concerns will most often be about pragmatic benefits (i.e. improvements to the situation) and not learning about the methodology. For SSM users who are committed to the learning epistemology there will be considerable philosophical, political and pragmatic difficulties when trying to shift their clients' expectations from one of seeking improvements to one of learning. This is so *unless* the SSM users can successfully make their clients to expect different outcomes. This is a very challenging task and politically risky. (In our industrial work we have taken these risks and have, on occasions paid heavy penalties. But these were worthwhile penalties for the lessons we have learned.) Lessons become even more difficult to learn when one considers that the methodology users have their own personal needs and internal motives to satisfy.

Clients' concerns for improvements to the situation are very legitimate. Apart from satisfying their own needs, they have an obligation to other organizational members and stakeholders to ensure that the resources used and changes resulting from methodology intervention are desirable for the work practices, working conditions and life-associated activities of the members. SSM users, too have an interest in learning about the methodology. In order to learn, the methodology needs to have an explicit step aimed at learning.

An examination of SSM reveals that it does not have an explicit step (see Figures 10.1 and 10.2) built into the methodology to enable its users to reflect or focus on this learning (in addition to any lessons they may have learned during methodology use). If clients' and methodology users' concerns are to be addressed, we urge the SSM creators to include an evaluation stage (similar to the debate step) where a joint discussion can take place on the results of the methodology application. Using the NIMSAD framework, this reflection can be conducted at three levels:

- the problem situation (the methodology context)
- the problem-solving process (the methodology)
- the problem solver (the methodology user).

But before we examine this, we need to know something about the learning. After all, if a methodology user is to benefit, it must encourage open and free discussion. The case studies must examine both successes and failures. Indeed, failures are more important than successes, both for understanding the reasons as well as for maintaining the ethical status of the interventions. We urge the creators and users of SSM to incorporate a critical self-reflection as the final step of the methodology as this is one of the few methodologies to have a learning epistemology as its focus.

What about the learning modes? We suggest structuring this based on the NIMSAD framework evaluation discussed in Chapter 7.

LEARNING ABOUT THE 'PROBLEM SITUATION'

When considering lessons that can be derived from the evaluation, we need to first of all consider the 'problem situation'. Evaluation of the situation for lessons can be conducted at three levels.

First, we can examine whether the relevant notional system(s) were implemented within the resource and other constraints set and agreed with the clients. Failure to *realize* the notional systems within time and resource constraints may negatively affect clients' satisfaction. Clients expect to see that resources utilized are used efficiently in bringing about the realization of relevant notional systems. This is the reason why criticism was levelled at the lack of support given in the implementation stage of SSM.

Secondly, the relevant systems in operation ('action systems') that have been created at the expense of resources and efforts must perform according to the 'root' definitions. In effect, the systems which were notionally set and agreed must be realizable in practice: lessons cannot be learned if their operation is not successful. In SSM particular attention is paid to the monitoring and control aspects of the relevant systems in operation.

Thirdly, there is a need in SSM to question the *relevance* of the relevant notional systems to the 'problem situation'. This final point leads to questions on what improvements were sought and achieved in the situation. The current focus of SSM is on lessons learned from methodology use.

PROBLEM SOLVING PROCESS

The second focus on learning is on the methodology itself. Most SSM case studies concentrate on this aspect, which has invariably led to its revised version. What we would like to suggest to the creators of SSM is that the evaluation of the methodology is also conducted using the NIMSAD framework at four levels, namely:

- Why did the methodology users select SSM? What are the implications of this decision?
- How was SSM interpreted by its users in the context of their knowledge of the situation, the client and other factors? What changes, if any, were made? Were the changes fundamental such that they altered the nature, form and philosophy of SSM? In other words, can it still qualify as SSM? If not, what are the implications? Case studies in SSM show these changes very clearly (see the non-use of CATWOE and 'rich pictures').
- What were the changes made to SSM during the action stages? What were the implications of these changes? For example, choosing not to make the 'root' definitions explicit is an example of such a change.
- Evaluation of SSM after intervention. In the case study examples, its creators have explicitly acknowledged changes made to SSM by engaging in reflection. It is only by raising questions at this stage that methodology users are able to abstract further lessons. Unless this level of questioning can take place, it will be very difficult to refine the methodology. (The discussions in this book are aimed at helping to improve methodology refinement.)

EVALUATION OF THE METHODOLOGY USER

The third focus of learning should be on the SSM user. This is by far the most neglected part of learning in SSM; yet this focus is critical if SSM users are to examine and learn how their skills, needs and motives affect the problem-solving process and the situation. It would help to assess the training and the development of skills necessary for improvement of self-performance and competence (e.g. skills in the use of the epistemological notion of 'systems'). As discussed in Chapter 4, no amount of use or perfection of SSM can bring about the successful transformation of situations; they can only *assist* the methodology user. For a methodology of this type which raises its users' level of intellectual reasoning, lessons on self-learning are critical if users are to become effective practitioners. The success of the transformation depends not only on SSM, but also on its users and their ability to manage dynamically their interactions and the expectations of the stakeholders. For example, the use of the evaluation element of the NIMSAD framework by the author led to the conclusion that he is very poor at exercising as this book illustrates political skills in practice. It also helped to establish that no amount of effort is going to improve these skills because they create internal value conflicts and tension between the intellectually desirable statements (what he wishes to say) and the pragmatically feasible statements (what he is allowed to express within the political context). Attempts to express intellectually desirable statements in preference to politically desirable statements have destroyed the author's chances of building a network of powerful political allies.

SUMMARY

Critical evaluation of SSM in this chapter using the NIMSAD framework raised many issues for discussion and debate. Potential methodology users should examine these issues in the context of their own interpretation of SSM and for refining their approach its use. In a way, this chapter is proof of the role of SSM as a methodology for creating intellectual debate and discussion. It confirms the epistemological nature of SSM. The creator of SSM (Checkland, 1981) has always encouraged debate and discussion; for example, through the *Journal of Applied Systems Analysis* he encouraged criticisms of his work by his former students (Jackson, 1982); see also Mingers (1992) and Jayaratna (1993b, 1993c). In the revised version, the creators (Checkland and Scholes, 1990) themselves criticize other users of SSM in the way they have interpreted and used it. This chapter is intended to contribute to that process of refining SSM, which the author still claims is one of the most thought-provoking and intellectually challenging methodology to emerge in the last two decades. The discussions and the length of this chapter is a testimony to the thought provoking role of SSM.

PART 4

11

CONCLUSIONS ON METHODOLOGIES AND FRAMEWORKS

INTRODUCTION

This chapter presents the lessons derived and the conclusions reached from the 'action research' case studies, industrial work, consultancy and methodology evaluation. The conclusions are organized around the four basic elements of the NIMSAD framework:

- the 'problem situation' (the methodology context)
- the problem solver (the methodology user)
- the problem-solving process (the methodology)
- the evaluation.

CONCLUSION 1: LEARNING PHASE OF A METHODOLOGY

Wood-Harper (1989), Avison and Wood-Harper (1990) discuss the time scale for developing their Multiview methodology, both in its theoretical rationale and in its refinement from the lessons derived from 'action research'. Experience from using the NIMSAD framework in practice confirms this conclusion. However, not only do methodologies evolve over time (see changes in ETHICS (Mumford and Henshalls 1979; Mumford, 1981, 1983a, 1983b SSM (Checkland, 1981; Checkland and Scholes, 1990) and SASS (De Marco, 1979; Yourdon, 1989; Page-Jones, 1980, 1988)) and reach a level of 'perfection' in the eyes of their creators, but as our experience demonstrates, users of the methodology too take time to learn and appreciate the strengths and weaknesses of methodology features. For example, some of the implications of using a methodology and its capabilities for structuring of thinking and action may only emerge when working in different situations, with different participants and under different conditions. The use of ETHICS may be a much easier task in a cooperative environment (e.g. in the banking sector) than would be the case in a regulated environment (e.g. in the military sector).

> Experience has shown that a consensus on a new system solution
> does not always emerge easily . . .
>
> (Mumford and Henshall, 1979)

The contribution or failings of a methodology may only be revealed when tested under different environmental conditions. In this context, learning is a never-ending activity. Just as the methodology creators have refined their methodologies from their learning, the methodology users too will have to revise the methodology based on their own learning experiences. We hope that this book has contributed to that learning and refining process.

CONCLUSION 2: METHODOLOGY PHILOSOPHY

All methodologies are underpinned by a set of philosophical paradigms. Because of this, they appeal to methodology users with similar beliefs. For instance, ETHICS generally appeals to those who subscribe to phenomenological paradigms and social values, SASS to those who generally view the world based on positivistic paradigms, and SSM to those who subscribe to hermeneutic/interpretative paradigms. When practised by those who share the same or similar philosophical paradigms, the learning phase of the methodology (i.e. to reach a competent level) becomes very much shorter. However, when those with different philosophical backgrounds and beliefs attempt to apply or consider methodologies, they may misinterpret, misunderstand or misrepresent the nature of the transformation which those methodologies intend to bring about in practice. See for example Newman's (1989) discussions about participation. This task is difficult enough for those who undertake theoretical debates, but it is even more so for those who have to apply methodologies in the 'action world'.

The philosophical paradigms embedded in methodologies demonstrate the philosophical beliefs of their creators. These paradigms are intended to help the methodology users extract information and make sense about the 'action world'. For example, methodologies based on positivistic paradigms help their users to focus attention on factual data, but ignore opinions. Methodologies based on phenomenological paradigms lead their users to consider that 'reality' does not exist independent of the perceiver, i.e. that 'reality' is the subjective interpretation of phenomena. Of course, what these philosophical paradigms do is lead those who internalize them to become conscious to aspects that match the paradigms and to ignore other rich and potentially useful information from the 'action world' that do not match the paradigms.

For example, would a scientist facing a loaded gun be interested in the velocity of the bullet? or would a phenomenologist, on noting a bank statement entry of £800 for a deposit of £1000, accept as legitimate the subjective interpretation of the bank manager?

There is a serious point here. Those who believe in scientific philosophy to give legitimacy to their actions would recognize and act on phenomenological paradigm-based information in the same way as those who believe in phenomenology would respond to human independent factual data (i.e. data that have shared meaning). The point we are making here is to explain that no one philosophy is capable of explaining away this complex thing called 'reality'. There are many accounts, events, instances and experiences of 'reality' that cannot be explained by *any one* philosophy. Each one provides a new insight and a new perspective. Methodology users who become alert to these philosophical assumptions embedded in a methodology and in their own thought processes are in a much better position to benefit from the use of that methodology than those who either believe in one philosophy or remain unconscious of the philosphical assumptions they make.

CONCLUSION 3: METHODOLOGY STEPS

The application of the NIMSAD framework in methodology evaluation clearly demonstrated that methodologies recognize some of the stages of the framework as being significant and others as being insignificant or irrelevant. For instance, in SASS, there is no explicit recognition of element 2 (the role of the investigator) or stage 1 of element 3 (the methods of investigation) as being relevant or significant to be included as a methodology step; consequently it does not offer any assistance in the structuring of the investigation.

The application of the framework also demonstrated that some methodologies had chosen to combine some stages. For instance, the logical and physical design stages (stages 6 and 7 of the framework) have been successfully combined in SSM under the conceptual model building step. In SASS, the differences between logical and physical design stages have been maintained (De Marco, 1979), but the conceptual clarity between the two forms of expression was not very clear. In ETHICS, the logical design of data was not given the same emphasis as was given to the physical design of human activities.

CONCLUSION 4: METHODOLOGY EMPHASIS

The use of the framework in methodology evaluation demonstrated that while methodologies in general contain many steps, they lay emphasis on some more than others. SASS in general focuses on the logical design aspects (stage 6 of element 3). For example, in De Marco (1979) and in Gane and Sarson (1979), there is very heavy emphasis on the definition of operational flows of formal data; they provide techniques for describing, designing and documenting these tasks (data flow diagrams, data dictionaries, etc.). In others, such as Yourdon and Constantine (1979), Page-Jones (1988) and Jackson (Sutcliffe, 1988; Ingevaldsson, 1990), the focus is on structuring the software design activities with the use of cohesion/coupling and time ordering techniques. However, collectively in structured system analysis and design approaches the emphasis is on the *solution design* stages of formal data.

When the framework is applied to the evaluation of ETHICS, we note that the emphasis is also placed on the systems design stage, but focused very much on the physical design aspects (stage 7 of element 3), i.e. the psychological, working practices and conditions of the human side of the system. Consequently, it offers structures and some guidelines within which to bring about involvement of the human actors. There is no support for structuring of the data aspects except to consider the physical characteristics of data handling through information technology. Here again, the emphasis of the methodology is on the *solution design* stages.

The evaluation of SSM using the framework leads to a different conclusion. The emphasis here is on the *problem formulation* stage. However, once this process clarifies what notional systems are to be taken further, the methodology loses interest in the subsequent implementation stages. Note that in SSM the design tasks are completed *before* conducting systemic analysis.

When mapped against the problem-solving phases of the framework, the methodology emphasis can be shown as in Table 11.1.

Table 11.1   Methodology emphasis table

	SASS	ETHICS	SSM
Problem formulation	No	No	Yes
Solution design	Yes	Yes	Yes
Design implementation	No	No	No

CONCLUSION 5: METHODOLOGY FOCUS

Using the extended version of Leavitt's (1972) model discussed in Chapter 3, methodology philosophy (conclusion 2), methodology steps (conclusion 3) and methodology emphasis (conclusion 4), new conclusions can be drawn as to the practice focus of the methodologies along the various dimensions of organizations.

None of the methodologies considered in our evaluation offered ways of improving efficiency in the situations, but they had all recognized its importance implicitly, as in the case of SASS, or explicitly, as in the case of ETHICS and SSM. Increasing efficiency *per se* of the existing information systems does not, however, necessarily lead to the improvement of organizational effectiveness; in fact, it may:

> ... very well contribute to the decline of organisational effectiveness. For example, as any accountant or business person may confirm, if one makes the 'supplier-payment' system as efficient as the 'order-processing' system, then that organisation may have little chance of survival in an environment that operates on credit-based transactions   (Jayaratna, 1988)

SASS attempts to re-examine and redesign existing data-related task activities before any consideration is given to automate the operations. For this reason, SASS can be defined as a *task-driven* methodology. Figure 11.1 illustrates the orientation of SASS on the organization.

However, concentration on the tasks and subsequent attempts to rationalize the related activities lead SASS to make assumptions about human behaviour (seek obedience or conformity from the users to designer-implemented

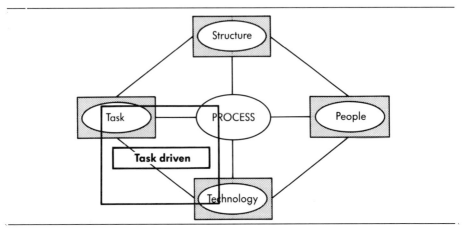

Figure 11.1   Task-driven domain

models) which seem reasonable only in highly deterministic, bureaucratic or authoritarian organizations. They have to rely heavily on clients, problem owners and user management to ensure that people operating the 'action systems' conform to the standards, procedures and interface requirements enforced by the design solutions.

ETHICS, by user participation, focuses attention on the 'people' side of organizations. Rather than attempt to optimize the technical aspects of the design solutions, it orients the design to meet the needs and aspirations of the human aspect. For this reason, methodologies of this type can be described as *process-driven* methodologies. Figure 11.2 illustrates this focus.

Both ETHICS and SASS rely on the clients or problem owners to define their requirements in a clear form before their design activities can begin. As the evaluation demonstrated, SASS relies on client requirements while ETHICS is clear in its acceptance of management-defined 'efficiency' objectives as a guide within which participants are encouraged to develop solutions to meet their job satisfaction needs.

However, where there are conflicting objectives, or no clear objectives, or uncertainty in terms of the client's 'desired state', the evaluation discussed how SASS or ETHICS cannot adequately address these ill-structured situations. The resolution of conflicts and the definition of 'desired states' and notional systems are very much the domain of people embedded in structures. SSM provides both the stages and the focus for addressing these issues, and

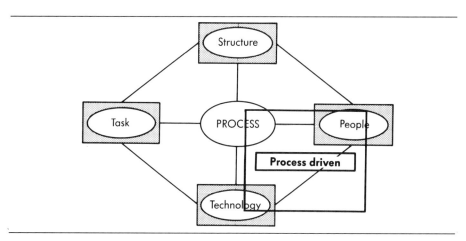

Figure 11.2   Process-driven domain

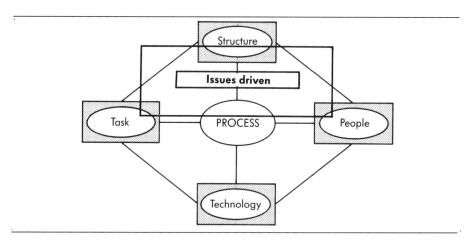

Figure 11.3   Issues-driven domain

hence can be considered as an *issues-driven* methodology. Figure 11.3 illustrates this domain of interest.

CONCLUSION 6: METHODOLOGY SUCCESS

Given the complexity of organizations, the evaluation of methodologies and complex industrial activities, it is difficult to conclude that methodologies can be considered successful in practice.

Methodologies are structuring mechanisms. Structures, by their very nature, are variety- and complexity-reducing mechanisms. This reduction of complexity is not taking place in the 'action world', but in the number and the dimensions of the elements that the methodology chooses to extract from the 'action world' for modelling and manipulation. On this basis, no one methodology can claim to be successful in practice. However, since methodologies focus their attention on some aspects of the 'action world', have general objectives in terms of what transformations they hope to bring about in practice, and offer ways of bringing about these transformations, they measure the dimensions along which they set out to address problems initially in order to establish their measures of success. SASS measures success by the degree of data-related activities that it helps to formalize and automate in practice; ETHICS measures its success by the degree of job satisfaction it brings for the participants; while SSM measures its success in terms of clarity, direction and desirable/feasible systems that it helps to derive in 'ill-structured' situations.

Success cannot be measured as such, since it is difficult to isolate the contribution of methodologies to the transformation of situations. As we have already discussed, the success of transformation depends mainly on the 'mental construct' of the methodology user, the nature of the 'problem situation', and the dynamic interactions of the methodology user and those in the 'problem situation'.

> Success in whatever shape, and to whatever extent, must ultimately depend on the willingness to identify and pursue the important questions, and in that pursuit willingly to place at risk all current reassurances of reality
>
> (D'Arcy and Jayaratna, 1985)

CONCLUSION 7: METHODOLOGY CONTEXT

Methodologies are used in three different contexts. This was one of the most important lessons we learned from our industrial activities.

THE CONTEXT OF CREATION

This is the context in which methodology creators abstract their experiences to form the methodology. The constructed methodologies reflect the 'mental constructs' of their creators. The steps of the methodology, its structure, chosen models, implied values and rationale give an indication as to how the creators perceive essential aspects of the 'action world'. For example, ETHICS reflects the concerns of its creator for the welfare of the people whose lives are affected by the designed systems (Mumford, 1983a). The context in which the methodology creators develop their methodologies influences what steps are

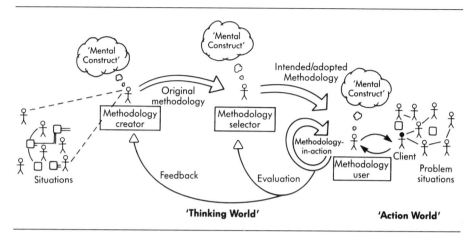

Figure 11.4   Methodology context

built into the methodology and what emergent properties are displayed by it. Figure 11.4 illustrates this context of the methodology creator.

THE CONTEXT OF INTERPRETATION

This is the context in which the methodology is interpreted by its users, who they try to interpret it through their own 'mental constructs'. However, unless the 'mental constructs' of the methodology users are congruent with the philosophy, values, beliefs and concerns of the methodology creators as implied in the methodology, its ultimate structuring may be very different from the structures and steps or the rationale of its creators. As Figure 11.4 illustrates, the context in which methodology users interpret the methodology may change its nature, form, structure and content. The context also includes the methodology users' perceptions and knowledge of the 'problem situation' characteristics. This is the *adopted/adapted* methodology.

THE CONTEXT OF ACTION

The structure, steps, models, values and philosophy of the methodology-in-action may very well be different from either those explicitly outlined in the methodology (creators' rationale) or those that were interpreted and changed by the methodology users in the context of their own 'mental constructs' (methodology users' rationale) before intervention. This is because a methodology has to match the dynamic nature of the situation and the interactions of the methodology users with those in the situation. However, this does not necessarily pose problems for the methodology users, especially if they consider the transformation to be a success (not conscious of shortcomings). Our interest, of course, is to engage in reflection-in-action (Schon, 1983) as a way of learning about these interventions. It is the lessons of abstraction which help us to develop our own expertise in the use of methodologies. As illustrated in Figure 11.4, the methodology-in-action may take a cyclical, iterative or other form of structure because of the dynamics of the situation. The 'real' evaluation loop from the 'action world' can be undertaken only by those methodology users who have first-hand information as to what actually happened in the particular situation. The use of the framework is to help the evaluation process of m1 before its use by the methodology users, to manage the transformation from m1 to m2 and to evaluate m3 during and after intervention. By doing this, we hope that the methodology users will (a) question the original methodology and its relevance to the situation (m1); (b) consider the changes from m1 to m2; (c) use a methodology by reflecting during intervention (from m2 to m3); and (d) become very conscious of undertaking the evaluation loop after intervention (m1, m2, m3, the situation and the 'mental construct').

Can m1 = m2 = m3?

The answer is yes, in scientific-based methodologies which attempt to disconnect the role or feelings of the methodology users, this is exactly what happens. However, if this is to be the case the original methodology m1 can only be at a general principles level (e.g. set theory, normalization principles) and must be in a language that can be understood and interpreted by the methodology users in the same way as that intended by the methodology creators. For example, the acceptance of mathematical rules by *all* in Figure 11.4 can make it much easier to establish m1 = m2 = m3. See what happens when m1 is of the type 'database methodology'. m2 will be almost identical to m1, but the test comes when m2 is used in the situation. The resulting m3 (its structure, steps and rationale) will be different in action, but considerable efforts will be made by the methodology users to conform to the principles of m2. In so doing the methodology users select those elements that match the features of m2 and report back, virtually ignoring m3 (the methodology-in-action) and disregarding all those data in the situation that could not be made to fit the features of m2. In this mapping, any data which are volatile, opinion-based and likely to change rapidly are not taken into account in the modelling process. Similarly, in software engineering methodologies, all subjective judgements of users are excluded from the software module construction unless they can be explicated and ranked using some criteria. This may be true of all methodologies.

Can m1 = m2 = m3 even where methodologies are of the interpretative kind?

The answer is that they should not be. Methodology users change the structure, steps and rationale in the context of their 'mental constructs' and the interactions with those in the situation, particularly the 'politics' of the situation. However, the evidence of case studies published in the literature ignores these changes; hence the reason for the SSM creators' (Checkland and Scholes, 1990) criticisms of others discussed in Chapter 10. In response to these criticisms, some SSM users have already begun to abandon the seven-stage version and to adopt the revised version and its application in modes 1 and 2. In the context of Figure 11.4, the feedback loop is reinforcing and positive. If they do, they are acting as if the methodology is independent of its users (i.e. m1 = m2 = m3), even though the methodology philosophy is of the interpretative kind.

No methodology is rich enough to capture or transform an 'action world'. Methodology users must become alert to the methodology changes (from m1 to m2 to m3) that occur when dealing with the complexities of the 'action world'.

CONCLUSION 8: THE 'CONTEXT' ENVIRONMENT OF METHODOLOGIES

The framework exclusively concentrated on setting the organizational context in which methodologies are applied in practice. While methodologies are concerned with the design of the *content*, the resulting systems have to contribute to and transform the *context* environment—see Figure 1.2. The 'action research' examples demonstrated the importance of this context environment. Therefore, it is concluded that methodology creators should explicitly consider what environmental conditions/settings are suitable for the application of their methodologies and what dimensions of the organization they aim to transform. By doing so, the creators can help their methodology users to question what type of situations they face and what, if any, changes they should undertake to adapt the methodology for that situation.

CONCLUSION 9: FRAMEWORK USE AS A METHODOLOGY

As Chapter 2 clarified, a framework is different from a methodology. The NIMSAD framework can be used for constructing a methodology only if methodology users consider the stages, structure and rationale of construction at a conscious level.

Consideration of the framework as a basis for a methodology cannot be undertaken in its current form for two reasons:

(1) In practice, stages 3, 4 and 5 of the problem-solving process of the framework tend to be carried out by clients/problem owners (mostly unconsciously), and the resulting notional system(s) tend to be offered at stage 1 thus altering the sequence of the stages. This change of structure does not affect the status of the framework, but removal of some of the stages will affect the nature of the framework. Therefore, the framework should not be considered as a methodology. (*Note that there is no reason why some of the stages of the problem solving process element of the framework cannot be selected and structured (with a rationale) to be used as a methodology in a given situation, in which case it is the methodology user who should take credit for its construction and subsequent success.*)

(2) A framework does not, cannot and should not offer any particular way of performing any one of the stages. If it were to do so, then it would lose its structural properties and could become a methodology. Since the NIMSAD framework demonstrates how various models, notions, techniques and methods can be employed for performing these stages without committing itself to any one, the framework cannot be turned into a methodology in its current form. (*There is no reason why a problem solver could not introduce ways of performing those stages and turn it into a methodology. In which case once again it is the methodology user who should take credit both for its construction and its successful use*).

CONCLUSION 10: FRAMEWORK ON PROBLEM FORMULATION

We consider that one of the biggest contributions the framework has made to problem solving is to *explicate* the process of problem formulation and to demonstrate the intellectual activity of deriving notional system(s). By so doing, we established how methodologies help to perform (or not) systemic analysis and the implications of taken-as-given requirement specifications. In the action research case studies 1, 2 and 4, the implications of these missing dimensions were explored. Calmes *et al.* (1991), in the French AFCET conference, used the framework to illustrate the missing dimension of systemic analysis and to show how the European OSSAD methodology addresses this very process.

Nielsen (1990) singles out the problem formulation phase (i.e. particularly stages 3, 4 and 5) for the only legitimate criticism of the framework. He points out that the separation of these stages is confusing, first because they cannot be found in any methodology, and secondly, because these stages are rarely carried out in that order in practice.

The first criticism is very valid. It also proves the point that many methodologies do not help to perform this stage. If this is the case, a potential methodology user must know about it. The role of this book is to alert a potential methodology user to these and other issues. The evaluation of methodologies in Chapters 8, 9 and 10 discussed how they address (or not) the activities of problem formulation.

As for Nielsen's second criticism, it should be pointed out that a framework (unlike a methodology) should not insist on a sequence of stages to be carried out in any order, only emphasize the need for having them. For example, SSM does not follow the sequence of stages presented in the framework construction, but the framework stages were used in Chapter 10 to demonstrate how SSM carries out systemic analysis. As regards practice, it is the very lack of conceptual clarity which has led some to comment that analysis contains elements of design and design contains elements of analysis. The conceptualization and abstraction process helps to establish the differences and to clarify the activities of systemic analysis and systemic design. In addition, the aim of the framework is not to show *how* the activities are to be carried out (this is the domain of methodologies) but to show *what* activities should be considered in a problem-solving situation. The order in which to perform the stages or to ignore the stages is the role of the methodology.

CONCLUSION 11: FRAMEWORK ON THE ROLE OF METHODOLOGY USERS

The framework, by focusing methodology users' attention on element 2 ('mental construct') helps to clarify the level of knowledge, skills and values necessary for the competent use of a methodology. Nielsen (1990), in his evaluation of 'approaches for evaluating methodologies' (i.e. frameworks), comments that NIMSAD is the only approach to call for critical reflection:

> When it comes to understanding a specific situation and deciding which methodology to use, NIMSAD is unusual. It

is unusual in the sense that it is not a framework which provides guide lines for performing (4) & (5) (*4 and 5 are conceptual model activities of Nielsen*) once and for all in a project e.g. when the project is established. On the contrary, it is a framework that is intended to guide the systems developer all the way through a project by providing opportunity 'at a conscious level of concern' to (re)evaluate and (re)select methodologies.

> ... By means of Schon's work on reflection-in-action I argued that the surveyed approaches, except Jayaratna's, have taken the stance of technical rationality in the sense that they are stable and general. I also argued that this stance is insufficient and that there is a need for appreciation approaches to take the stance of reflection-in-action in the sense of the dynamic and situational. (Nielsen, 1990)

The focus on the role of methodology users is critical because their 'mental constructs' dictate how a structure of a methodology is recognized and used for structuring their thinking and action. It is critical that the methodology users understand, appreciate and comprehend not only the nature, philosophy, models, emphasis and orientation of the methodology, but also gain an insight into their own 'mental constructs'. Success in practice depends not only on the methodology assistance, but rather on how its users structure their meaning of the situations and manage their interpersonal relationships with others.

CONCLUSION 12: FRAMEWORK AS AN INSTRUMENT OF LEARNING

The NIMSAD framework is not an *ideal* against which to consider the shortcomings of methodologies. The use of the framework in the evaluation of methodologies and of practice was not to establish that its stages are an 'ideal' (in the ontological sense) against which to approve or disapprove methodologies, but to use its elements and stages (in an epistemological sense) to generate questions about methodologies. These may be as to:
- whether they consider the stages explicitly
- why they consider the stages as being relevant to the situation
- how they combine or distinguish between the stages
- whether they ignore or assume these stages

- whether their own rationale for combining, ignoring or increasing stages can be considered relevant, sensible and persuasive.

For instance, in Chapters 8, 9 and 10 we observed how methodologies combine or interpret the logical and physical design stages. In SSM, the combination did not create any difficulty. In ETHICS, the combination weakened the logical design aspects, particularly the structuring of formal data. In SASS, the separation was useful, but its method of construction was difficult.

The use of the framework as an instrument of learning also helps to consider the implications of ignoring the role of critical self-reflection. It is only by considering the framework as an instrument for creating discussions and subjecting methodologies for critical examination that it could help in generating critical self-reflection as advocated by Schon (1983), Schein (1969) and Argyris (1982). In that sense, the success of the NIMSAD framework depends on the nature of the questions (see Chapter 7) it raises for methodologies and their use in practice for bringing about transformations. Achievements in practice depend very much on the skills and abilities of the methodology user, and not on any framework.

SUMMARY

Readers please note that the methodology evaluation in this book was conducted purely from the viewpoint of the author who took a deliberate attempt to evaluate methodologies from a conceptual perspective. The evaluation was based on the explanations provided by their creators on the rationale, structure, steps, etc. As invited in the Preface, readers must conduct their *own* evaluations and reach their *own* conclusions.

The NIMSAD framework elaborated within this book and used in methodology evaluation can help *only* to the extent that it raises a potential methodology evaluator's, selector's or user's thinking process. It in *no way* can contribute directly to the *pragmatic* success of the 'action world' intervention or successes of the methodology users; in fact, it may even cause considerable difficulties for the methodology users in their management of interpersonal and political relationships with their clients. It has absolutely *nothing* to contribute to the political process because it opens up communication channels, questions the rationale of action, and focuses attention away from a need to focus on individuals to a need to address critical issues.

The issues that were discussed in this book based on the NIMSAD framework are not intended to be easy for methodology users. Real understanding is a painful activity which should always create tension between our desire to satisfy practical needs and our desire to satisfy intellectual needs. It is for this reason that the methodology users' minds were focused on three elements other than the methodology itself, i.e. the 'problem situation', the 'mental constructs' of the problem solvers, and the evaluation. The more aware we as methodology users become of our own 'mental constructs', the better chance we have of understanding the 'mental constructs' of others. We must become alert to the fact that we may be using the methodology as a credible and legitimate instrument through which to satisfy our self-gains, to extend power and control over others, and to help achieve the career developments of our clients and ourselves. The role of the 'mental construct' of the NIMSAD framework is to focus our attention towards understanding not only the legitimacy of our own needs, but also those of others. We as methodology users must become consciously responsible for our actions. Every intervention in human affairs that does not create tension for us and our clients is either not a serious situation warranting the assistance of a methodology (help from explicit structuring) or it is a situation which will create tension, stress, anxieties and pain in others (victims) instead of in ourselves.

It is difficult to operate in an intellectual mode when others around you place political thoughts uppermost in their reasoning. However, by encouraging political thoughts to dictate our reasoning processes we not only avoid responsible human action but also self construct intellectual prisons from which we may have very little chance of escape. In pursuit of intellectual thoughts driven problem solving, the author wishes to leave the reader with an intellectual thought which might create political difficulties—'perhaps there are *no* problems in a problem situation except with those of us who consider them to be problems!'

On behalf of methodology creators, selectors, users beneficiaries and victims, the royalties resulting from this book are being donated to Amnesty International, Oxfam and other charities.

APPENDIX A

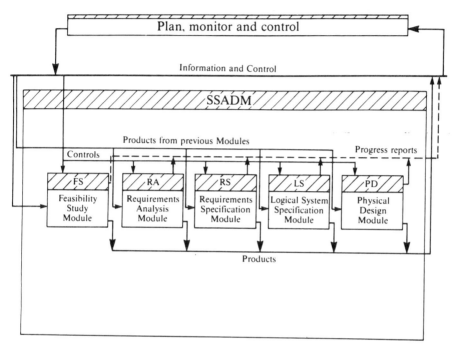

A methodology structure (SSADM)
(Adopted with permission from McGraw-Hill)

APPENDIX B

CRITERA FOR DETERMINING ILL-STRUCTURED SITUATIONS

Objectives:	are vague or
	are not agreed upon or
	are considered unrealistic or
	have not been formulated or set
Problems:	are not well understood and their causes not well appreciated
Attitudes:	are uncooperative and non-flexible
Boundary conditions:	are vague and not well defined
Communications:	are unreliable and ineffective
Relationships:	are difficult and highly political

(Adopted from Brian D'Arcy's lecture notes with permission)

APPENDIX C

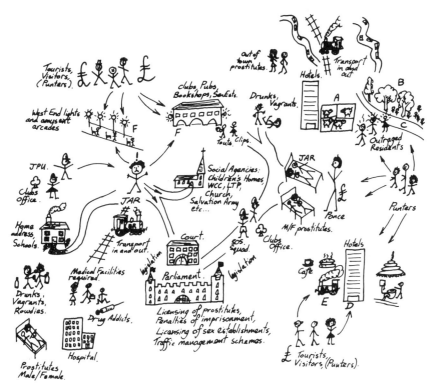

KEY	A	Shepherds Market Area	JPU	Juvenile Protection Unit
	B	Sussex Gardens Area		Clubs Office
	C	Bayswater Road Area	SOS	Street Offences Squad
	D	Piccadilly Circus Area	JAR	Juveniles at risk
	E	Victoria Station Area	WCC	Westminster City Council
	F	Soho Area	LTP	London Teenage Project

Rich Picture

(Adopted with permission from Plenum Press)

____ GLOSSARY OF TERMS ____

Action systems: are the operational version of our notional systems which are supposed to resolve the 'problem situation'.

Action world: is the situation in which methodologies are used for bringing about transformations (see also 'thinking world').

Computer technology: refers to the use of computers for exploration of its application potential. It emphasizes the exploration and experimentation of the computational power of the computers (see also information technology).

Diagnosis: is an expression of our understanding of a 'situation of concern'. This expression should describe both the logical and the physical aspects of the situation and, most importantly, the 'state' of the 'situation of concern'.

Educating and learning function: is an information function that helps to monitor and measure the effectiveness of the use of information and helps to increase this effectiveness by education and learning support.

Ethics: are standards by which we determine whether a given set of actions or behaviour is acceptable. Varies from context to context.

Event: is an outcome or a 'state' reached following or preceding a set of activities.

Experience: are sensations and emotions that we have gone through in our lives. They register knowledge and form models in our 'mental constructs' and help us to cope with the 'action world'.

Framework: is a meta-level model (a higher level abstraction) through which a range of concepts, models, techniques, methodologies can either be clarified and/or integrated. A framework is a static model.

Information management and control: is an information function that helps to manage systems development, processing and usability and educating and learning functions efficiency and effectively. Additionally it translates information strategies to realisable goals and informs about the capacities and potential abilities of the three functions.

Information processing and usability function: is an information function to ensure the most efficiently organized technical, manual, formal and informal means are employed for the acquisition, storage, processing, dissemination and presentation of information for supporting user decisions and actions on a continuing basis.

Information systems development: is an information function that is responsible for identifying, analysing, designing and implementing new information processing systems that are required for organizational survival and growth.

Information systems (Discipline): as a discipline includes subject knowledge and skills that are considered essential for understanding and on that basis improving or changing information systems functions and through them the context (organization). It is an *interdisciplinary* subject.

Information systems (Functions): within an organizational context refers to a formally organized set of activities that gathers, processes, stores and delivers useful information to organizational members. It has four other functions. Collectively it performs five information functions, namely processing and usability, educating and learning, systems development, management and control and strategy.

Information technology: refers to the use of computers in solving some specific user problem. In this sense it can serve as a means to an end although information technology can also generate new ends because of its active nature (see also computer technology).

Intellectual thoughts: intelligent thoughts that focus on the reasoning process. They help us to explore many possible ways of reasoning irrespective of the nature of conclusions (see also 'political thoughts').

Knowledge: is gained from understanding. It helps us to understand the context in which information can become meaningful.

Mental construct: is one's mental structure. It consists of a number of useful elements namely perceptual process, values, ethics, structuring process, reasoning ability, models, frameworks and roles. These interact to help make sense of situations, guide our actions etc.

Methodology: is an explicit way of structuring one's thinking and actions. Methodologies contain model(s) and reflect particular perspectives of 'reality' based on a set of philosophical paradigms. A methodology should tell us what steps to take, in what order and how to perform those steps but, most importantly, the reasons 'why' those steps should be taken, in that particular order.

Model: is a complete and coherent set of concepts which can underpin our understanding and actions. If we can externalize it then it gives us a chance to examine, understand and analyse their relevance and completeness. They also help us to design abstract or physical things.

Motives: are our innermost needs which we try to satisfy in the 'action world'. Often we are not aware of these ourselves or, if we are, we keep them secret.

Notional system: is a 'system' which we consider notionally as being relevant for resolving 'problems' in a situation. Its functions, when operational, are expected to overcome 'problems' and therefore transform the situation.

Perceptual process: is a mental filtering mechanism. It helps us to select information and other external events to which we should respond. Different people may interpret the same situation in different ways.

Political thoughts: intelligent thoughts that help us to set favourable conclusions first and then reason to justify those conclusions. They are concepts that help to focus on people (see also 'intellectual thoughts').

Prejudices: are persistent opinions and attitudes which we form from our experiences, values or through ignorance. Sometimes we form these as a way of coping with uncertainty.

Problem: is a mismatch between the perceived 'current state' of a situation and the perceived 'desired state' for that situation.

Problem situation: is a situation in which people perceive 'problems'. Quotation marks are to remind us that we should not assume that these are 'problems'.

Problem solver: is a person who undertakes the task of solving a 'problem' (see also 'problem').

Problem-solving process: can be considered as consisting of three major phases, namely:

- a problem formulation phase
- a solution design phase
- a design implementation phase.

It is through this process that we hope to solve 'problems'.

Prognosis: is the expression of our understanding of a 'desired state' for a particular 'situation of concern' including the design elements that will help to bring about the 'desired state'.

Prognosis outline: indicates a 'desired state' which we wish to reach.

Real world: is taken to consist of both the 'thinking world' and the 'action world' of an intended problem solver (see also 'action world' and 'thinking world').

Reasoning ability: is our ability to abstract 'essential' features from a given situation and engage in reasoning. It helps us to link reasoning with its conclusions and is essentially an ability to deal with concepts.

Roles: are explicit behavioural characteristics sets which can be attributed to a particular job or position. The incumbent is expected to follow these.

Situation of concern: is an expression used to show a part of a situation around which we have drawn a boundary. The content inside the boundary then becomes of interest to us.

Skills: are our ability to apply knowledge in practice. Skills reflect competence in the use of knowledge. These can be gained from continuous training and experiences.

Software engineering: is a series of steps undertaken to develop software to match the quality and needs of a software specification.

Stage: consists of a set of activities. For example, the problem solving process discussed in this book identifies eight stages which may be performed partially or fully by a methodology in any order.

Step: refers to sets of activities that are performed by a methodology. The order in which to undertake a series of steps show the methodology structure.

Structuring process: is a way of making sense of or bringing order to our thoughts and action. We expect methodologies to help us do this.

Systems: are powerful concepts which focus the mind of an observer or a problem solver on the integrative aspects of parts. Collectively the parts display emergent properties which are not found in the parts. Ontological use of this term makes the observer accept the boundary of a system without question. Epistemological use of the term makes the observer exercise a choice of where to draw the boundary and name that enclosure as a 'system'.

Systemic analysis: is the process of problem formulation using the epistemological notions of 'systems' (see also systemic design).

Systemic design: is the process of generating solutions using epistemological notions of 'systems' (see also systemic analysis).

Systems analysis: is the study of an existing system. The boundaries are taken as given (see also systems design).

Systems design: is the process of improving an 'existing' system. The boundaries of the 'system' are not in question (see also systems analysis).

Systems development cycle: outlines the steps which give rise to the birth (creation) of an 'action system' and terminates when it begins to perform (see also systems life cycle).

Systems life cycle: comes into being only when a 'system' that is developed by the systems development cycle becomes operational. It includes activity sets which enhance and help to adapt this 'system' to changes in the environment.

Thinking world: is the methodology user's conceptualization about the intended actions (see also 'action world' and 'real world').

Values: are beliefs that we consider to be 'good'. They are used as criteria for passing judgements about situations, the behaviour of others, and their action.

Weltanschauung: is one's world view. Unless we examine the perspectives we take when we look at 'reality' we remain ignorant of these views that give rise to the meanings we construct of that 'reality'.

BIBLIOGRAPHY

Ackoff, R. L. (1971) 'Towards a System of Systems Concepts', *Management Science*, vol. 17, no. 11.

Ackoff, R. L. (1976) 'Management Misinformation Systems', *Readings in Management Information Systems*, McGraw-Hill, USA.

Ackoff, R. L. and Emery, E. (1972) *On Purposeful Systems*, Tavistock Institute, London.

Ahituv, N. and Neumann, S. (1990) *Principles of Information Systems for Management*, Wm. C. Brown Publishers, USA.

Aktas, A. Z. (1987) *Structured Analysis and Design of Information Systems*, Prentice-Hall, New Jersey, USA.

Anderton, R. A. (1987) 'Information, Systems and the Construction of Meaning', *International Journal of Information Management*, Vol. 7.

Argyris, C. (1982) *Reasoning, Learning and Action*, Jossey-Bass, USA.

Argyris, C. and Schon, D. (1974) *Theory in Practice: Increasing Professional Effectiveness*, Jossey-Bass, USA.

Ashworth, C. and Goodland, M. (1990) *SSADM: A Practical Approach* McGraw-Hill, Maidenhead, UK.

Athiev N. and Neumann S. (1990) *Principles of Information Systems for Management*, Wm. C. Brown Publishers, USA.

Atkinson, C. and Checkland, P. (1988) 'Extending the Metaphor "System"', *Human Relations*, Vol. 41(10).

Avison, D. and Fitzgerald, G. (1988) *Information Systems Development*, Blackwell Scientific Publications, Oxford, UK.

Avison, D. E. and Wood-Harper, A. T. (1990) *Multiview*, Blackwell Scientific Publications, Oxford, UK.

Avison, D. E. and Wood-Harper, A. T. (1991) 'Information Systems Development Research: An Exploration of Ideas in Practice', *The Computer Journal*, vol. 34, no. 2.

Banathy, B. (1989) *Systems Design in Education: Perspectives, Approaches, Methods, Models and Systems*, Intersystems Publications, California, USA.

Banbury, J. (1987) 'Towards a Framework for Systems Analysis Practice', *Critical Issues in Information Systems Research*, Eds Boland, R. J. and Hirschheim, R., Wiley, Chichester, UK.

Beer, S. (1978) *Platform for Change*, Wiley, Chichester, UK.

Beer, S. (1979) *Heart of the Enterprise*, Wiley, Chichester, UK.

Beer, S. (1981) *Brain of the Firm*, Wiley, Chichester, UK.

Beer, S. (1988) *Diagnosing the System*, Wiley, Chichester, UK.

Benbasat, I. (1984) 'An Analysis of Research Methodologies', *The Information Systems Research Challenge*, Harvard Business School Press, Boston.

Berne, E. (1979) *Games People Play*, Penguin Books, UK.

Bjerkness, G. and Dahlbom, B. (1990) *Organizational Competence in Systems Development. A Scandinavian Contribution*, Chartwell Bratt Ltd, Sweden.

Boehm, B. W., Brown, J. R. and Lipow, M. (1977) 'Quantitative Evaluation of Software Quality', Software Phenomenology—working papers of the Software Lifecycle Management Workshop.

Boland, R. J. (1984) 'Phenomenology: A Preferred Approach to Research in Information Systems', *Research Methods in Information Systems*, Manchester Business School, UK.

Boland, R. J. (1990) 'Information Systems Use as a Hermeneutic Process', The Information Systems Research Arena of the 90s, eds Boland, R. J. and Hirschheim, R., IFIP WG 8.2 Conference Proceedings, Copenhagen.

Boland, R. J. and Hirschheim, R. (1987) *Critical Issues in Information Systems Research*, Wiley, UK.

Brandt, I. (1983) 'A Comparative Study of Information Systems Design Methodologies', *Information Systems Design Methodologies: A Feature Analysis*, North-Holland.

Bubenko, J. (1986) 'Information Systems Methodologies—A Research View', *Information Systems Design Methodologies: Improving the Practice*, North-Holland, also in SYSLAB report no. 14, February 1986.

Buckingham, R. A., Hirschheim, R., Land, F. F. and Tully, C. (1989) *Information Systems Education: Recommendations and Implementations*, Cambridge University Press, UK.

Burch, J. G., Strater, R. F. and Grudnitski, G. (1979) *Information Systems: Theory and Practice*, Wiley, New York, USA.

Burch, J. G. and Grudnitski, G. (1989) *Information Systems: Theory and Practice*, Wiley, New York, USA.

Burley, T. and O'Sullivan, G. (1990) *Operations Research*, Macmillan Education, UK.

Calmes, F., Charbonnel, G. and Dumas, P. (1991) 'Merise et Ossad: Deux Méthodologies à Comparer', Autour et à l'entour de Merise, AFCET, Sophia Antipolis, France, 17–19 April.

Chapin, N. (1981) 'Graphic Tools in the Design of Information Systems', *Systems Analysis and Design: A Foundation for the 1980s*, eds Cotterman, W., Couger, D., Enger, N. and Harold, F., North-Holland.

Checkland, P. B. (1981) *Systems Thinking, Systems Practice*, Wiley, Chichester, UK.

Checkland, P. B. (1988) 'Information Systems and Systems Thinking: Time to Unite?', *International Journal of Information Management*, vol. 8, no. 4, December.

Checkland, P.B. and Davies, L. (1986) 'The use of the term "Weltanschauung" in "Soft" Systems Methodology', *Journal of Applied Systems Analysis*, vol. 13.

Checkland, P. B. and Scholes, J. (1990) *Soft Systems Methodology in Action*, Wiley, Chichester, UK.

Churchman, C. W. (1968) *The Systems Approach*, Dell Publications, New York, USA.

Churchman, C. W. (1971) *The Design of Inquiring Systems*, New Basic Books, USA.

Churchman, C. W. (1982) *Thoughts and Wisdom*, Intersystems Publications, California, USA

Coad, P. and Yourdon, E. (1989) *Object-Oriented Analysis*, IEEE Transactions, New York, USA.

Computer Journal, The, Special Issue on Information Systems (1991), vol. 34, no. 2.

Cotterman, W., Cougar, J., Enger, N. and Harold, F. (1981) *Systems Analysis and Design: A Foundation for the 1980s*, Elsevier–North-Holland, USA.

Cutts, G. (1987) *SSADM*, Paradigm Press, London, UK.

Cyert, R. M. and March, J. G. (1969) 'A Behavioural Theory of Organizational Objectives', *Organizations: Systems, Control and Adaptation*, ed. Litterer, J., Wiley, New York, USA.

Dahlbom, B. and Mathiassen, L. (1993) *Computers in Context*, National Computing Centre—Blackwell Scientific, Massachusetts, USA.

D'arcy, B. (1991) Lecture notes, Sheffield Hallam University, UK.

D'Arcy, B. and Jayaratna, N. (1985) 'Systems Closure and Enquiry', *Systems Research*, vol. 12, no. 1.

Daniel, A. and Yates, D. (1969) *Basic Training for Systems Analysis*, Pitman Publishing, London, UK.

Date, C. J. (1990) *An Introduction to Database Systems*, Addison-Wesley, UK.

Davies, L. (1988) 'Understanding Organisational Culture', ed. Flood, R., *Systems Practice*, vol. 1, no. 1.

Davies, L. (1991) 'Researching the Organisational Culture Context of Information Systems Strategy: A Case Study of the British Army', *Information Systems Research*, North-Holland.

Davis, G. B. (1974) *Management Information Systems*, McGraw-Hill, Singapore.

Davis, G. B and Olson, M. (1985) *Management Information Systems*, Wiley, Singapore.

De Bono, E. (1980) *Lateral Thinking*, Pelican Books, UK.

De Marco, T. (1979) *Structured Analysis and Systems Specification*, Yourdon Press, New York, USA.

Dilthey, W. (1931) *Gesammelte Schriften*, Vol VIII, Weltanschauungslehre, B. G. Teubner, Stuttgart.

Downs, E., Clare, P. and Coe, I. (1988) *SSADM*, Prentice-Hall, UK.

Doyle, K. and Wood, B. (1991) 'Systems Thinking, Systems Practice: Dangerous Liaisons', *Systemist*, vol. 13(1).

Eden, C., Jones, S. and Sims, D. (1987) *Messing About in Problems*, Pergamon Press, UK.

Enger, N. L. (1981) 'Classical and Structured Systems Life Cycle Phases and Documentation', *Systems Analysis and Design: A Foundation for the 1980s*, eds Cotterman W., Couger, D., Enger, N. and Harold, F., Elsevier–North-Holland, New York, USA.

England, G. W. (1966) 'Personal Value Systems of American Managers', *Academy of Management Journal*, vol. 10, no. 1, March.

Eriksson, I. (1990); 'Simulation as a Learning Technique in Information Systems Development', *Organizational Competence in Information Systems Development*, eds Bjerknes, G., Dahlbom, B., Mathiassen, L., Stage, J., Thoresen, K., Vendelbo, P. and Aaen, I., Chartwell-Bratt, Sweden.

Espejo, R. and Watt, J. (1988) 'Information Management, Organizational and Managerial Effectiveness', *Journal of Operations Research*, vol. 39, no. 1.

Etzioni, A. (1985) *The Moral Dimension*, The Free Press, New York.

Farhoomand, A. F. (1987) 'Scientific Progress of Management Information Systems', *Data Base*, 19(2), Summer.

Fitzgerald, G. (1991) 'Validating New Information Systems Techniques: A Retrospective Analysis', *Information Systems Research: Contemporary Approaches and Emergent Traditions*, Elsevier Scientific Publications BV (North-Holland).

Fitzgerald, G., Stokes, N., and Woods, J. (1985) 'Feature Analysis of Contemporary Information Systems Methodologies', *The Computer Journal*, vol. 28, no. 3.

Flood, R. and Carson, E. R. (1988) *Dealing with Complexity*, Plenum Press.

Gadamer, H. G. (1976) *Philosophical Hermeneutics*, University of California Press, USA.

Galliers, R. D. (1985) 'In Search of a Paradigm for Information Systems Research', *Research Methods in Information Systems*, eds Mumford, E., Hirschheim, R., Fitzgerald, G. and Wood-Harper, T., Elsevier, Amsterdam.

Galliers, R. D. (1987) *Information Analysis: Selected Readings*, Addison-Wesley, UK.

Galliers, R. D. (1991) 'Strategic Information Systems Planning: Myths, Reality and Guidelines for Successful Implementation', *European Journal of Information Systems*, vol. 1, no. 1.

Galliers, R. D. and Land, F. F. (1987) 'Choosing Appropriate Information Systems Research Methodologies', *Communications of the ACM*, 30(11).

Galliers, R. D., Pattison, E. M. and Reponen, T. (1994) 'Strategic Information Systems Planning Workshops: Lessons from Three Cases', *International Journal of Information Management*, vol. 14, no. 1, February.

Gane, C. and Sarson, T. (1979) *Structured Systems Analysis: Tools and Techniques*, Prentice-Hall, New York, USA.

Guth, W. D. and Tagiuri, R. (1965) 'Personal Values for Corporate Strategy', *Harvard Business Review*, September–October.

Hamilton, S. and Ives, B. (1982) 'MIS Research Strategies', *Information and Management*, vol. 5.

Harrison, F. (1987) *The Managerial Decision Making*, Houghton Miffin, Boston, USA.

Hertzberg, F. (1968) 'One More Time: How Do You Motivate Employees?', *Harvard Business Review*, January–February.

Hicks, J. (1993) *Management Information Systems: A User Perspective*, West Publishing Company, St. Paul, USA.

Hirschheim, R. (1985) *Office Automation*, Wiley, Chichester, UK.

Hirschheim, R. and Klein, H. (1989) Four Paradigms of Information Systems Development, *Communications of the ACM*, vol. 32, no. 10.

Houdshel, G. and Walton, H. (1987) 'The Management Information and Decision Support (MIDS) System at Lockheed-Georgia', *MIS Quarterly*, March.

Howe, D. R. (1983) *Data Analysis for Data Base Design*, Edward Arnold.

Hult, M. and Lennung, S. (1980) 'Towards a Definition of Action Research: A Note and a Bibliography', *Journal of Management Studies*, vol. 17, no. 2.

Husserl, E. (1936) 'The Origin of Geometry', *Phenomenology and Sociology*, Penguin, Harmondsworth.

Ingevaldsson, L. (1990) *Software Engineering Fundamentals*, Chartwell Bratt, Sweden.

Jackson, M. C. (1982) 'The Nature of "Soft" Systems Thinking; The Work of Churchman, Ackoff and Checkland, *Journal of Applied Systems Analysis*, vol. 9.

Jayaratna, N. (1979) 'Systems Analysis: A Conceptual Approach to Complex Problem Solving!', *ASEAN Computer Yearbook 78/79*, Hong Kong Computer Society.

Jayaratna, N. (1986) 'Normative Information Model-based Information Systems Analysis and Design (NIMSAD): A Framework for Understanding and Evaluating Methodologies', *Journal of Applied Systems Analysis*, vol. 13.

Jayaratna, N. (1987) 'Design Enquiry', ISGSR Conference Proceedings, Budapest, July, ed. Peter Checkland, Hungary.

Jayaratna, N. (1988) 'Guide to Methodology Understanding and Information Systems Practice', *International Journal of Information Management*, vol. 8, no. 1.

Jayaratna, N. (1990) 'Systems Analysis: The Need for a Better Understanding', *International Journal of Information Management*, vol. 10, no. 3, September.

Jayaratna, N. (1991a) 'Systemic Analysis: Is it the Missing Link in the Systems Development Process', *Journal of Applied Systems Analysis*, vol. 18.

Jayaratna, N. (1991b) 'Learning from Theoretical Frames of References', *Information Systems Research: Contemporary Approaches and Emergent Traditions*, eds Nissen, H. E., Klein, H. and Hirschheim, R., Elsevier Science Publishers.

Jayaratna, N. and Thomson I. (1993a) 'Management Accounting: Can it Ever Become an Intellectual Discipline?', BAA Conference, Glasgow, UK.

Jayaratna, N. (1993b) 'Methodology Assistance in Practice—A Critical Evaluation', *Systemist*, vol. 15(1), February.

Jayaratna, N. (1993c) 'Plenary Address—Methodological Challenge for Information Systems', BCS Methodology Conference Proceedings, eds Jayaratna, N., Paton, G., Merali, Y. and Gregory, F., September.

Kanter, J. (1984) *Management Information Systems*, Prentice-Hall, New Jersey, USA.

Katz, D. and Khan, R. L. (1966) *Common Characteristics of Open Systems*, Wiley, UK.

Katz, F. E. and Rosenzweig, J. E. (1970) *Organization and Management : A Systems Approach*, McGraw-Hill, USA.

Kendall, K. and Kendall, J. (1992) *Systems Analysis and Design,* Prentice-Hall, New Jersey, USA.

Kendall, P. (1992) *Introduction to Systems Analysis and Design—A Structured Approach*, W.C. Brown Publishers, USA.

Kluback, W. and Weinbaum, M. (1957) *Dilthey's Philosophy of Existence: Introduction to Weltanschauungslehre*, Vision Press, London, UK.

Kolasa, B. (1969) *Introduction to Behavioural Science for Business*, Wiley, USA.

Kolb, D., Rubin, I. and Osland, J. (1991) *Organisational Behaviour, An Experimental Approach*, Prentice-Hall, New Jersey, USA.

Koontz, H. and Bradspies, R. (1969) 'Managing Through Feedforward Control', *Emerging Concepts in Management*, eds Wortman, M. and Luthans, F., Macmillan, New York, USA.

Korth, H. and Silberschatz, A. (1986) *Database Systems Concepts*, McGraw-Hill, USA.

Land, F. (1987) 'From Software Engineering to Information Systems Engineering', UNICOM Seminar on Participation in Systems Design, London, April.

Land, F. and Hirschheim, R. (1983) 'Participative Systems Design: Rationale, Tools and Techniques', *Journal of Applied Systems Analysis*, vol. 10.

Leavitt, H. (1972) 'The Volatile Organization: Everything Triggers Everything Else', *Managerial Psychology*, The University of Chicago Press, USA.

Leavitt, H. and Whistler, T. (1958) 'Management in the 1980s', *Harvard Business Review*, 36, November–December.

Lewin, K. (1958) 'Group Decisions and Social Change', *Readings in Social Psychology*, Henry Holt, New York, USA.

Lucas, H. C. Jr. (1985) *The Analysis, Design and Implementation of Information Systems*, McGraw-Hill, New York, USA.

Lucas, H. C. Jr. (1987) *Information Systems Concepts for Management*, McGraw-Hill, New York, USA.

Lundberg, M. (1993) *Handling Change Processes, A Systems Approach*, Chartwell-Bratt, Sweden.

Maddison, (1984) *Information Systems Methodologies*, Wiley, UK.

Martin, J. (1976) *Principles of Data Base Design Management*, Prentice-Hall, New Jersey, USA.

Martin, J. (1985) *Systems Design from Provably Correct Constructs*, Prentice-Hall, New Jersey, USA.

Martin, J. and McClure, C. (1988) *Structured Techniques—The Basis for CASE*, Prentice-Hall, New Jersey, USA.

Maslow, A. (1943) 'A Theory of Human Motivation', *Psychological Reviews*, no. 50.

Mathiassen, L. and Nielson, P. (1990) 'Surfacing Organizational Competence', 'Simulation as a Learning Technique in Information Systems Development', *Organisational Competence in Information Systems Development*, Chartwell-Bratt, Sweden.

Maturana, H. and Varela, F. (1980) *Autopoiesis and Cognition*, Reidel, Dordrecht.

McFadden, F. and Hoffer, J. (1991) *Database Management*, Benjamin/Cummings Publishing Company, California, USA.

McFarlan, W. (1984) 'Information Technology Changes the Way you Compete', *Harvard Business Review*, 62, May–June.

McMenamin, S. and Palmer, J. (1984) *Essential Systems Analysis*, Yourdon Press/Prentice-Hall, USA.

Miles, R. K. (1988) 'Combining "Soft" and "Hard" Systems Practice: Grafting or Embedding', *Journal of Applied Systems Analysis*, vol. 15.

Miller, G. (1956) 'The Magical Number Seven, Plus or Minus Two: Some Limits on Our Capability for Processing Information', *The Psychological Review*, 63(2), March.

Miller, J. (1978) *Living Systems Theory*, McGraw-Hill, USA.

Mingers, J. (1992)'Questions and Suggestions in using "Soft" Systems Methodology', *Systemist*, vol 14(2), May.

Mingers, J. (1993) 'SSM and Information Systems', *Systemist*, vol 14(3), August.

Morgan, G. (1986) *Images of Organisation*, Sage Publications, California, USA.

Morton, M. S. (1984) 'The State of the Art of Research', *Information Systems Research Challenge*, Harvard Business School Press, Boston, USA.

Mumford, E. (1981) 'Participative Systems Design: Structure and Method', *Systems, Objectives, Solutions*, North-Holland.

Mumford, E. (1983a) *Designing Participatively*, Manchester Business School, Manchester.

Mumford, E. (1983b) *Designing Human Systems*, Manchester Business School, Manchester.

Mumford, E. and Henshall, D. (1979) *A Participative Approach to Computer Systems Design*, Associated Business Press.

Murdick, R. (1975) *Introduction to Management Information Systems*, Prentice-Hall, New Jersey, USA.

Murdick, R. and Ross, J. (1977) *Information Systems for Modern Management*, Prentice-Hall, New Jersey, USA.

Nielsen, P. (1990) 'Approaches to Appreciate Information Systems Methodologies', *Scandinavian Journal of Information Systems*, vol. 2, Denmark.

Newman, M. (1989) 'Some Fallacies in Information Systems Development', *International Journal of Information Management*, vol. 9, no. 2.

Nissen, H-E. (1987) 'Information Systems Development for Responsible Human Action', *Systems Development for Human Progress*, eds Klein, H. and Kumar, K., North-Holland, Amsterdam.

Nissen, H-E. (1992) 'Let's Not Devise Another Philogiston Theory', *Information Systems Concepts*, eds Falkenberg, Roland and El-Sayed, Elsevier Science Publishers, Amsterdam.

Nissen, H-E., Klien, H. and Hirschheim, R. (1990) 'The Information Systems Research Arena of the 90s', IFIP WG 8.2 Conference Proceedings, Copenhagen, December.

Nissen, H-E. and Sandstrom, G. (1988) *Quality of Work versus Quality of Information Systems*, University of Lund, Sweden.

Nunamaker, J. F. and Bonsynski, B. (1981) 'Formal and Automated

Techniques of Systems Analysis and Design', *Systems Analysis and Design: A Foundation for the 1980s*, eds Cotterman, W., Couger, D, Enger, N. and Harold, F., Elsevier–North-Holland, New York, USA.

Oliga, J. (1988) 'Methodological Foundations of Systems Methodologies', *Systems Practice*, vol. 1, no. 1.

Olle, W., Sol, H. G. and Tully, C. (1983) *Information Systems Design Methodologies: A Feature Analysis*, North-Holland, Amsterdam.

Olle, W., Sol, H. G. and Verrijn-Stuart, A. (1982) *Information Systems Design Methodologies: A Comparative Review*, North-Holland, Amsterdam.

Olle, W., *et al.* (1991) *Information Systems Methodologies*, Addison-Wesley, UK.

Page-Jones, M. (1980) *The Practical Guide to Structured Systems Design*, Prentice-Hall, New Jersey, USA.

Palvia, P. and Nosek, J. T. (1989) 'A Comprehensive Assessment of Systems Life Cycle Techniques and Methodologies', Proceedings of the DSI Conference, New Orleans, USA.

Passos, J. (1976)— see Checkland P. and Scholes J. (1990).

Patching, D. (1987) 'Soft Systems Methodology and Information Technology', *Management Services*, August.

Peters, L. (1988) *Advanced Structured Systems Analysis and Design*, Prentice-Hall, New Jersey, USA.

Pettigrew, A. (1984) 'Contextualist Research: A Natural Way To Link Theory and Practice', *IS Research—A Doubtful Science*, Manchester Business School, Manchester.

Porter, M and Millar, V. (1985) 'How Information Gives you Competitive Advantage', *Harvard Business Review*, 63, July–August.

Pressman, R. S. (1982) *Software Engineering: A Practitioner's Approach*, McGraw-Hill, Auckland.

Quang, P. T. and Chartier-Kastler, (1991) *Merise in Practice*, Macmillan Education, UK.

Rhodes, W. (1987) 'Table-Driven Package Saves Security Pacific Millions of Dollars', *Infosystems*, vol. 34, June.

Rodriguez-Ulloa, R. (1988) 'The Problem Solving System: Another Problem Content System', *Systems Practice*, vol. 1, no. 3.

Ross, D. (1977) 'Structured Analysis: A Language for Communicating Ideas', *Software Engineering*, vol. 2, no. 1.

Ryan, B. (1973)—see Checkland, P. and Scholes, J. (1990).

Sandstrom, G. (1985) *Towards Transparent Databases*, Chartwell-Bratt, Sweden.

Schein, E. (1969) *Process Consultation: Its Role in Organisation Development*, Addison-Wesley, UK.

Schoderbek, P., Schoderbek, C. and Keflas A. (1990) *Management Systems: Conceptual Considerations*, Richard Irwin, Boston, USA.

Schon, D. (1983) *The Reflective Practitioner—How Professionals Think in Action*, Basic Books, USA.

Senn, J. (1984) *Analysis and Design of Information Systems*, McGraw-Hill, USA.

Shackel, B. (1969) 'Man-Computer Interaction: The Contributions of Human Sciences', *Ergonomics*, vol. 12.

Shackel, B. (1990) 'Human Factors and Usability', *Human Computer Interaction*, eds Preece, J. and Kelle, L., Prentice-Hall, UK.

Simon, H. A. (1978) 'Rationality as Process and Product of Thought', *American Economic Review*, vol. 68.

Sol, H. C. (1983) 'A Feature Analysis of Information Systems Design Methodologies: Methodological Considerations', in Olle, W. *et al.*, North-Holland, Amsterdam.

Sprague, Jr. and McNurlin, B. (1986) *Information Systems Management in Practice*, Prentice-Hall, London, UK.

Stage, J. (1990) 'Analyzing Organisations in System Development', *Organizational Competence in Systems Development*, eds Bjerknes, G., Dahltom, B., Mathiassen, L., Nurminen, M., Stage, J., Thorssen, K., Vendelbo, P. and Aaen, I., Chartwell-Bratt, Sweden.

Stamper, R. (1988) 'Analysing the Cultural Impact of a System', *International Journal of Information Management*, vol. 8, no. 3.

Stone, E. (1981) *Research Methods in Organisation Behavior*, IL: Scott-Foresman, Chicago, USA.

Susman, G. I. (1987) 'Action Research: A Sociological Systems Perspective', *Beyond Method*, Sage Publications.

Susman, G. I. and Evered, R. (1978) 'An Assessment of the Scientific Merits of Action Research', *Administrative Science Quarterly*, vol. 23.

Sutcliffe, A. (1988) *Jackson Systems Development*, Prentice-Hall, New Jersey, USA.

Swanson, B. (1988) *Information Systems Implementation*, Irwin, USA.
US General Accounting Office, FMGSD–80–4, USA.

Van Gigch, J. P. (1978), *Applied General Systems Theory*, Harper and Row, New York, USA.

Vickers, G. (Sir) (1980) 'Education in Systems Thinking', *Journal of Applied Systems Analysis*, vol. 7.

Vickers, G. (Sir) (1983) *Human Systems are Different*, Harper and Row, London.

Vogel, D. R. and Wetherbe, J. C. (1984) 'MIS Research: A Profile of Leading Journals and Universities', *Data Base*, vol. 16, no. 3, Fall.

Wainright, M., De Hayes, D., Hoffer, J. and Perkins, W. (1991) *Managing Information Technology*, Macmillan Publishing Company, UK.

Ward, J., Griffiths, P. and Whitmore, P. (1990) *Strategic Planning For Information Systems*, Wiley, Chichester, UK.

Weick, K. E. (1984) 'Theoretical Assumptions and Research Methodology Selection', *The Information Systems Research Challenge*, Harvard Business School Press, Boston.

Williams, Jr., R. M. (1967) 'Individual and Group Values', *Annuals of American Academy of Political and Social Science*, USA.

Wilson, B. (1990) *Systems Concepts, Theory, Methodologies and Applications*, Wiley, UK.

Winograd, T. and Flores, F. (1987) *Understanding Computers and Cognition*, Addison-Wesley, UK.

Wood-Harper, A. T. (1989) *Information Systems Definition*, Phd Thesis, University of East Anglia.

Wood-Harper, A. T. and Fitzgerald, G. (1982) 'A Taxonomy of Approaches to Systems Analysis', *The Computer Journal*, vol. 25, no. 1.

Wood-Harper, A. T., Antill, L. and Avison, D. E. (1985) *Information Systems Definition: The Multiview Approach*, Blackwell Scientific Publications, UK.

Wynekoop, J. and Conger, S. (1991) 'A Review of Computer Aided Software Engineering Research Methods', *Informations Systems Research*, Elsevier Scientific Publications BV (North-Holland), Amsterdam.

Yourdon, E. (1989) *Modern Structured Analysis*, Prentice-Hall, New Jersey, USA.

Yourdon, E. and Constantine, E. (1979) *Structured Design*, Prentice-Hall, New Jersey, USA.

Zelkowitz, M. V. (1978) 'Perspectives on Software Engineering', *ACM Computer Surveys*, vol. 10, no. 2.

INDEX

Abstract skills, 204
Action world, 50, 51, 52, 62, 63, 64, 65, 67,
    84, 85, 102, 109, 111, 113, 114, 115,
    116, 122, 125, 134, 180, 190, 192,
    215, 222, 223, 228, 230, 231, 233
Action systems, 104, 110, 111, 112, 127, 154,
    157, 216
Action research, 45, 54, 60, 64, 66, 74, 77, 81,
    82, 86, 111, 143, 175, 178, 179, 221,
    231
Adapted/adopted methodology, 115, 229
Aspirations, 155
Attitudes, 99, 104
Authority, 121, 139, 188

Behaviour, 98
Beliefs, 42, 65, 104, 119, 179
Beneficiaries, 58, 68, 189, 206
Boundary of concern, 78, 121
Boundary, 75, 77, 78, 91, 94, 96, 121, 124,
    127, 136, 137, 138, 146, 149, 154,
    159, 165, 169, 183, 184, 191, 211

CATWOE, 179, 182, 195, 196, 198, 200, 201,
    217
Challenge, 71, 72, 73, 86
Clients, 50, 51, 58, 62, 68, 81, 84, 86, 88, 90,
    102, 103, 111, 112, 121, 123, 133,
    137, 143, 154, 178, 181, 202, 212
Coherence, 37, 97
Communication, 161
Competence, 113, 116, 134, 135, 156, 157
Complexity, 66, 116, 162, 179, 180, 209, 227
Computer technology, 6, 14
Computer science, 3, 4
Concepts, 51, 52, 64, 114, 124
Conceptual model, 97, 100, 135, 136, 138,
    140, 200, 206
Conceptual/logical design, 75, 98, 102, 126,
    146, 168, 199
Concerns, 110, 117, 178, 185
Conclusions, 70, 71
Conflict, 72, 127, 155, 156, 158, 170, 174, 178, 181
Conscious, 115, 119
Consensus, 160, 162, 171, 179
Constitutive rules, 183, 210, 211, 212
Constraints, 112, 170
Consultancy, 64, 74

Consultation, 161
Consultative, 160
Control, 70
Creative, 96, 97
Critical, 58, 69, 96, 117, 124, 125, 189, 201
Cultural analysis, 185
Current state, 83, 84, 86, 88, 91, 124, 167,
    204

Data flow diagram, 80, 83, 139, 146, 207,
    224
Decomposition, 141
Democracy, 161
Design implementation, 74, 93, 104, 107,
    225
Desired situation, 84
Desired state, 84, 85, 86, 88, 91, 92, 96, 110,
    112, 113, 123, 124, 144, 145, 165,
    166, 167, 190, 202, 203, 204, 226
Destinies, 153, 158, 162, 170
Determination, 161, 162
Diagnosis model, 82, 91, 96, 99, 139, 141,
    146, 162
Diagnosis, 74, 79, 80, 84, 88, 91, 93, 94, 95,
    103, 104, 122, 128, 142, 152, 162,
    185, 192, 203
Disasters, 109

Educating and learning function, 8, 11, 13, 17,
    27, 29
Effective, 120, 135, 142, 148, 151
Effectiveness, 58, 104, 108, 109, 111, 112, 113,
    115, 132, 152, 211, 225
Efficiency, 152, 172, 173, 199, 211, 225
Efficient, 109, 112
Embedding, 207
Emotional, 134, 155, 157, 186, 190, 204
Empowerment, 153
Enquiry, 90, 91, 92
Environment, 98, 100, 105, 120, 128, 134, 135,
    148, 159, 179, 180, 195, 221, 231
Epistemological, 40, 41, 49, 75, 91, 94, 115,
    116, 120, 178, 181, 182, 183, 184,
    190, 191, 193, 194, 195, 205, 207,
    218
ETHICS, 15, 42, 81, 151, 174, 224, 225, 226,
    228, 250, 252
Ethics, 66, 73, 109, 110, 119, 136, 157, 158,

Ethics *continued*
 170, 171, 180, 182, 183, 189, 193,
 204, 211
Evaluation, 16, 48, 49, 53, 57, 73, 75, 79, 107,
 108, 109, 111, 112, 113, 128, 138,
 149, 154, 159, 165, 173, 175, 215,
 217, 221, 223
Examination, 85, 86, 89, 92, 114, 116, 137,
 174
Expectation, 89, 110, 144, 162, 165
Experience, 67, 68, 97, 115, 120, 121, 125,
 126, 127, 135, 143, 155, 165, 201,
 210
Expression, 81, 83, 84, 139, 141

Facilities, 105
Failure, 71, 95, 109, 161
Formal systems model, 181, 196, 197, 198
Framework, 16, 42, 44, 45, 47, 49, 61, 69, 74,
 77, 78, 89, 93, 106, 107, 108, 116,
 117, 121, 124, 128, 136, 142, 150,
 162, 163, 174, 179, 183, 189, 199,
 202, 205, 210, 214, 217, 218, 221,
 223, 231, 232, 233, 235
Functional, 215
Functions, 104, 106, 143
Future analysis, 171

Grafting, 207

Hermeneutic paradigms, 175, 176
Human activity systems, 177, 178, 184

Ideal, 141, 142, 155, 190, 210
Ill-structured, 66, 89, 110, 118, 179, 180, 182,
 190, 203, 226
Implementation, 102, 103, 106, 117, 127, 149,
 151, 173, 204, 206
Information, 5, 7, 8, 11, 23, 58, 59, 60, 63, 67,
 77, 78, 79, 82, 96, 97, 99, 103, 104,
 121, 143, 172, 184
Information processing and usability function,
 8, 11, 14, 17, 27, 29, 32, 43, 102
Information processing systems, 16, 35, 42, 43,
 57, 58, 132, 138, 142, 148, 150, 207
Information systems, 3, 4, 8, 11, 15, 17, 20,
 21, 23, 24, 27, 30, 31, 35, 57, 87, 97,
 102, 108, 109
Information systems development function,
 8, 13, 16, 17, 24, 27, 29, 32, 43, 102
Information technology, 6, 7, 14, 15, 19, 21,
 22, 23, 24, 156, 157, 172
Innovation, 126
Instrument, 190
Intellectual, 66, 68, 70, 71, 72, 86, 109, 117,
 145, 182, 184, 185, 203, 209
Intended methodology, 115, 116, 212

Interdisciplinary, 8, 21, 27
Interpersonal, 58, 63, 66, 68, 86, 89, 108, 119,
 120, 127, 135, 139, 156, 157, 160,
 171, 174, 185, 190, 204
Intervention, 62, 108, 109, 110, 111, 113, 157,
 158, 189, 215, 235
Investigation, 91, 122, 137, 138, 141, 159,
 160, 184, 193
Involvement, 161, 162, 164, 206
Issue-based systems, 190, 191, 192, 207

Knowledge, 63, 67, 68, 80, 85, 97, 113, 114,
 120, 126, 134, 135, 139, 154, 155, 159,
 172, 187, 201

Learning, 108, 113, 118, 181, 182, 205, 208,
 215, 223, 246, 258
Lessons, 108, 113, 115, 173, 215

Management and control function, 8, 17, 27,
 34
Manipulate, 70, 71
Mental construct, 64, 65, 70, 73, 75, 76, 77,
 78, 79, 84, 88, 89, 96, 113, 115, 116,
 117, 134, 138, 143, 145, 150, 154,
 156, 158, 159, 162, 178, 179, 180,
 181, 183, 189, 203, 209, 228, 229,
 230, 255
Methodology, 16, 19, 24, 34, 35, 36, 37, 38,
 39, 40, 42, 44, 45, 46, 48, 49, 51, 53,
 59, 63, 64, 66, 68, 74, 76, 77, 78, 79,
 84, 85, 87, 90, 91, 95, 97, 107, 110,
 114, 126, 146, 149, 151, 164, 216, 221
Methodology context, 216, 228, 229,
 221
Methodology creator, 134, 222, 229
Methodology-in-action, 115, 116, 209, 210,
 212, 213, 242, 254
Methodology user, 71, 79, 92, 107, 109, 111,
 113, 119, 120, 122, 123, 126, 128,
 132, 134, 138, 143, 146, 154, 155,
 158, 165, 173, 174, 178, 179, 181,
 183, 184, 185, 188, 189, 191, 209,
 212, 213, 216, 221, 222, 228, 229
Models, 51, 52, 59, 64, 69, 77, 81, 82, 84,
 85, 88, 89, 93, 94, 97, 100, 102, 103,
 105, 110, 112, 114, 116, 121, 123,
 126, 135, 154, 157, 158, 159, 171,
 184
Moral, 73, 110, 136, 157, 180, 182, 193, 204
Motives, 66, 70, 85, 89, 139, 154, 184, 218

Needs, 85, 112, 119, 120, 151, 152, 154, 155,
 158, 170, 171, 173, 215, 218
NIMSAD, 44, 45, 46, 47, 48, 49, 53, 57, 61,
 73, 78, 106, 108, 116, 117, 125, 128,
 142, 146, 150, 158, 162, 167, 168,

NIMSAD *continued*
    174, 183, 189, 199, 202, 205, 210,
    217, 218, 221, 223, 231
Norms, 178, 182, 185
Notional system, 74, 88, 89, 90, 91, 92, 93,
    95, 96, 105, 110, 112, 123, 124, 125,
    126, 127, 128, 144, 163, 166, 167,
    189, 190, 194, 202, 205, 207

Ontological, 40, 75, 94, 120, 137, 157, 159, 183,
    184, 207
Organization, 59, 61, 62, 63, 66, 69, 87, 88,
    109, 111, 115, 132, 148, 151, 152,
    155, 189, 193, 226
Original methodology, 115, 212, 213, 230
Outline shape, 83, 84

Participation, 153, 154, 156, 158, 160, 161, 162,
    222
Participative, 162
Perceptual process, 65
Phenomenological, 151, 159, 207, 222, 223
Philosophy, 36, 37, 38, 42, 48, 114, 118, 120,
    122, 134, 181, 192, 208, 215, 223, 225
Physical design, 75, 100, 102, 128, 172, 201
Political, 66, 68, 70, 71, 72, 73, 86, 89, 110,
    113, 115, 118, 119, 120, 124, 125,
    128, 133, 144, 145, 146, 150, 156,
    158, 161, 171, 174, 180, 182, 184,
    185, 189, 190, 204, 211, 213, 214,
    215, 218
Political system, 187
Power, 71, 72, 73, 115, 121, 125, 134, 135,
    153, 158, 162, 169, 171, 179, 187,
    188, 189, 193
Prejudices, 66, 139, 154, 184
Primary task system, 190, 191, 192, 193, 194
Problem content, 178
Problem context, 185
Problem solving, 37, 73, 75, 79, 81, 116, 186,
    224
Problem solver, 49, 50, 51, 52, 53, 57, 58, 59,
    61, 62, 63, 64, 67, 68, 69, 73, 75, 77,
    84, 85, 86, 88, 89, 90, 97, 103, 107,
    113, 128, 134, 154, 178, 181, 216,
    221
Problem solving process, 49, 53, 57, 73, 74,
    83, 91, 92, 93, 95, 102, 103, 104, 107,
    108, 112, 114, 117, 128, 175, 204,
    210, 216, 217, 221
Problem perceivers, 58
Problem formulation, 74, 75, 82, 90, 91, 92,
    94, 95, 96, 102, 107, 112, 113, 121,
    124, 144, 145, 150, 204, 225
Problem owners, 58, 81, 84, 85, 89, 102, 103,
    110, 117, 178, 181, 183, 185, 190,
    204, 226

Problem situation, 49, 53, 57, 61, 63, 66, 67,
    72, 73, 75, 79, 107, 108, 110, 111,
    112, 114, 116, 117, 128, 131, 148,
    151, 175, 179, 199, 205, 216, 217,
    221
Problems, 13, 31, 48, 50, 51, 58, 63, 65, 73,
    74, 75, 78, 84, 85, 87, 88, 91, 95, 107,
    108, 111, 112, 123, 124, 128, 136,
    139, 141, 144, 146, 149, 154, 155,
    159, 162, 166, 168, 174, 184, 203
Prognosis, 74, 84, 88, 89, 103, 192, 203
Prognosis model, 99, 101, 102
Prognosis outline, 84, 85, 86, 87, 90, 91, 123,
    128, 144, 165, 190, 201
Purpose, 109, 110, 166

Questions, 109, 113, 114, 115, 116, 117, 128,
    144, 165, 167, 189

Rational, 44, 86, 92, 107, 110, 116, 117, 124,
    144, 145, 211, 229, 231
Rationalizing, 71
Real world, 50, 180
Reality, 65, 85, 90, 118, 151, 165, 176, 178,
    222
Reason, 70, 71, 86, 89, 91, 108, 113, 127, 133,
    170
Reasoning ability, 67
Reasoning process, 68, 72, 73, 109, 125
Reflection-in-action, 78, 230
Relevance, 86, 88, 91, 95, 96, 97, 105, 108,
    110, 112, 113, 116, 122, 126, 143,
    152, 167, 177, 190, 191, 193, 202,
    203, 217
Relevant, 137, 138, 155, 178, 183, 189, 192
Representative, 160, 162
Resources, 99, 105, 110, 111, 112, 118, 153
Responsible human action, 66
Rich picture, 79, 81, 82, 183, 185, 186, 187,
    203, 217
Rigorous, 58, 146, 151, 163
Rigour, 148, 177
Roles, 69, 86, 87, 95, 96, 99, 104, 121, 125,
    133, 143, 154, 155, 157, 159, 161,
    166, 172, 176, 178, 179, 181, 182,
    185
Root definition, 182, 190, 191, 194, 199, 200,
    201, 202, 211, 217

SASS, 131–149, 224, 225, 226, 228
Scientific, 90, 120, 132, 223, 230
Situation of concern, 74, 76, 78, 79, 81, 82,
    83, 84, 89, 91, 92, 94, 103, 104, 105,
    111, 116, 117, 121, 123, 128, 136,
    137, 142, 159, 183, 185, 187, 189
Skills, 66, 68, 84, 85, 89, 99, 110, 113, 120,
    124, 125, 126, 127, 134, 135, 138,

Skills *continued*
    154, 156, 171, 172, 174, 182, 184,
    187, 201, 218
Social system, 187
Software life cycle, 33
Solution design, 74, 93, 94, 95, 96, 102, 107,
    225
Specification, 91, 124, 125
SSM, 16, 36, 40, 81, 82, 95, 115, 168, 175–
    218, 224, 225, 226, 228, 231
Stakeholders, 103, 104, 118, 126, 177, 189
State, 31, 79, 83, 84, 85, 87, 94, 112, 123, 142,
    143, 144, 165, 176, 187, 189, 203
Strategy and planning function, 8, 27
Structure, 38, 41, 42, 49, 66, 75, 87, 99, 106,
    110, 114, 115, 116, 122, 135, 148,
    151, 160, 170, 175, 188, 199, 208,
    212, 229, 231
Structured analysis, 131
Structured methodology, 41, 82, 83, 99, 119,
    138, 139, 154, 156, 196, 207
Structuring, 47, 68, 76
System, 40, 48, 60, 67, 74, 75, 90, 91, 94, 95,
    127, 148, 159, 177, 182, 196, 211
System design, 90, 97, 127, 171, 182
Systemic analysis, 90, 91, 92, 94, 95, 96, 107,
    136, 146, 174, 199, 201, 203, 224
Systemic design, 90, 94, 95, 96, 107, 127, 133,
    136
Systems analysis, 90, 91, 93, 224
Systems development cycle, 30, 31, 32, 42
Systems development, 34, 35, 66, 90, 104,
    105, 111, 132, 135, 138, 155, 181,
    183
Systems life cycle, 30, 32, 42

Systems specification, 88, 93, 98

Target document, 131, 149
Task, 96
Technical, 156, 157, 160, 180, 211, 215
Techniques, 52, 66, 84, 110, 114, 134, 135,
    136, 138, 143, 146, 147, 150, 159,
    160, 164, 172, 184, 187
Thinking process, 73
Thinking world, 51, 102
Thought process, 67, 68, 70, 71, 72, 73,
    102
Tools, 132, 134, 147, 186
Transformation, 52, 53, 61, 68, 91, 109, 111,
    117, 135, 165, 174, 178, 180, 182,
    195, 196, 200, 201, 210, 218, 223,
    228

Unique, 189, 190, 203, 204, 211

Validity, 153
Values, 42, 65, 66, 69, 72, 119, 136, 153, 154,
    156, 157, 178, 179, 182, 185, 209,
    222, 229
Variances, 169, 173
Viability, 153
Victims, 58, 68, 188, 189, 193, 206

Weakness, 71, 73, 95, 97, 145, 160,
    169
Well-structured, 181, 211
Weltanschaung, 41, 42, 178, 179, 182,
    185, 186, 189, 190, 193, 195, 210,
    211
World image, 176, 178, 179, 184